REMEMBERING THE KANJI

I

a complete course on
how not to forget the meaning and writing of
Japanese characters

James W. Heisig

Published by JAPAN PUBLICATIONS TRADING CO., LTD.,
1-2-1, Sarugaku-cho, Chiyoda-ku, Tokyo, 101 Japan

Distributors:

UNITED STATES: *Kodansha International/USA, Ltd. through Farrar, Straus & Giroux, 19 Union Square West, New York 10003.*
CANADA: *Fitzhenry & Whiteside Ltd., 195 Allstate Parkway, Markham, Ontario L3R 4T8.*
BRITISH ISLES: *Premier Book Marketing Ltd., 1 Gower Street, London WC1E 6HA.*
EUROPEAN CONTINENT: *European Book Service PBD, Strijkviertel 63, 3454 PK De Meern, The Netherlands.*
AUSTRALIA AND NEW ZEALAND: *Bookwise International, 54 Crittenden Road, Findon, South Australia 5023.*
THE FAR EAST AND JAPAN: *Japan Publications Trading Co., Ltd., 1-2-1, Sarugaku-cho, Chiyoda-ku, Tokyo, 101 Japan*

First edition: 1977
Second edition: 1985
Third edition, First printing: July 1986
           Seventh printing: February 1990

ISBN 0-87040-739-2
ISBN (JAPAN) 4-88996-002-3

Printed in Japan

CONTENTS

PREFACE

For some years now I have been tempted at regular intervals to prepare a new edition of this book, first issued in 1977 under the title *Adventures in Kanji-Land*. What prevented me on each occasion was the hope that someone better qualified than I would take up the task of revision and republication, or perhaps take up the basic concept behind the method and produce something similar. That hope, along with the demands of my own work in totally unrelated fields, led me to let the final two copies of the first edition lie buried in a bottom drawer for this past seven years, only occasionally to be taken out and dusted off by a curious visitor asking to make a photocopy. That I have chosen at last to undertake a revision myself is due as much to the encouragement of many who used the book in its original form as to the endless chorus of frustrated young students of Japanese languishing on the wrong side of the "kanji curtain." I say this because I am as convinced as ever that there is no good reason for that curtain to become an impenetrable wall for the student of Japanese.

But there are reasons, nonetheless. While I have not undertaken any systematic research on methods of kanji instruction, I should like to offer some impressions of why this happens, based on talks with numerous students and teachers of the language from several of the countries of Asia, Europe, and the Americas.

Virtually all of them would agree with me, I think, that learning to write the kanji with native proficiency is the greatest single obstacle to the foreigner approaching Japanese—indeed so great as to be *presumed* insurmountable. After all, if even well-educated Japanese study the characters formally for nine years, use them daily, and yet frequently have trouble remembering how to reproduce them, much more than English-speaking people have with the infamous spelling of their mother tongue, is it not unrealistic to expect that even with the best of intentions and study methods those not raised with the kanji from their youth should manage the feat? Such an attitude may never actually be spoken openly by a teacher standing before a class, but as long as the teacher believes it, it readily becomes a self-fulfilling prophecy. This attitude is then transmitted to the student by placing greater emphasis on the supposedly simpler and more reasonable skills of learning to speak and read the language. In fact, as this book seeks to demonstrate, nothing could be further from the truth.

There are other factors as well. For one thing, Japanese teachers tend to draw on their own experience when they teach others how to write. Having begun as small children in whom the powers of abstraction are relatively undeveloped and for whom constant repetition is the only workable method, they are not likely ever to have considered reorganizing their pedagogy to take advantage of the older student's facility with generalized principles. For another, the reading and writing of the characters is taught simultaneously on the grounds that one is useless without the other. The immediate problem with this approach is that it begs the basic question of why they could not better be taught one *after* the other, concentrating on what is for the foreigner the simpler task, writing, and later turning to reading.

The obvious victim of the conventional methods is the student, but on a subtler level the reconfirmation of unquestioned biases also victimizes the Japanese teachers themselves, the most devoted of whom are prematurely denied the dream of fully internationalizing their language.

Most of these impressions, let it be said, only developed after I had myself learned the kanji and published the first edition of this book. At the time I was convinced, as I wrote in the pages of the Introduction, that proficiency in writing the kanji could be attained in four to six weeks if one were to make a full-time job of it. Of course, the claim raised more eyebrows than hopes among teachers with far more experience than I. Still, my own experience with studying the kanji and the relatively small number of students I have directed in the methods of this book, bears that estimate out, and I do not hesitate to repeat it here.

A word about how the book came to be written. I began my study of the kanji one month after coming to Japan with absolutely no previous knowledge of the language. Because travels through Asia had delayed my arrival by several weeks, I took up residence at a language school in Kamakura and began studying on my own without enrolling in the course already in progress. A certain impatience with my own ignorance compared to everyone around me, coupled with the freedom to devote myself exclusively to language studies, helped me during those first four weeks to make my way through a basic introductory grammar. This provided a general idea of how the language was constructed but, of course, almost no facility in using any of it.

Through conversations with the teachers and other students, I quickly picked up the impression that I had best begin learning the kanji as soon as possible, since this was sure to be the greatest chore of all. Having no idea at all how the kanji "worked" in the language, yet having found my own pace, I decided—against the advice of nearly everyone around me—to continue to study on my own rather than join one of the beginners' classes.

The first few days I spent pouring over whatever I could find on the history and etymology of the Japanese characters, and examining the wide variety of systems on the market for studying them. It was during those days that the basic idea underlying the method of this book came to me. The following weeks I devoted myself day and night to experimenting with the idea, which worked well enough to encourage me to carry on with it. Before the month was out I had learned the meaning and writing of some 1,900 characters and had satisfied myself that I would retain what I had memorized. It was not long before I became aware that something extraordinary had taken place.

For myself, the method I was following seemed so simple, even childish, that it was almost an embarrassment to talk about it. And it had happened as such a matter of course that I was quite unprepared for the reaction it caused. On the one hand, some at the school accused me of having a short-term photographic memory that would fade with time. On the other hand, there were those who pressed me to write up my "methods" for their benefit. But it seemed to me that there was too much left to learn of the language for me to get distracted by either side. Within a week, however, I was persuaded at least to let my notes circulate. Since most everything was either in my head or jotted illegibly in note books and on flash-cards, I decided to give an hour each day to writing everything up systematically. One hour soon became two, then three, and in no time at all I had laid everything else aside to complete the task. By the end of that third month I brought a camera-ready copy to Nanzan University in Nagoya for printing. During the two months it took to complete the printing I added an Introduction. Through the kind help of Mrs. Iwamoto Keiko of Tuttle Publishing Company, most of the 500 copies were distributed in Tokyo bookstores, where they sold out within a few months.

Meantime, I was busy trying to devise another method for simplifying the study of the reading of the characters, which was later completed as a companion volume to the first. These notes were never published but only photocopied for limited distribution. But of that, another time.

After the month I spent studying how to write the kanji, I did not return to any formal review of what I had learned. When I would meet a new character, I would learn it as I had the others, but I have never felt the need to retrace my steps or repeat any of the work. Admittedly, the fact that I now use the kanji daily in my teaching, research, and writing is a distinct advantage not available to one outside a Japanese university. But I remain convinced that whatever facility I have I owe to the procedures outlined in this book.

Perhaps only one who has seen the method through to the end can appreciate both how truly uncomplicated and obvious it is, and how accessible to any average student willing to invest the time and effort. For while the method is *simple* and does eliminate a great deal of wasted effort, the task is still not an *easy* one. It requires as much stamina, concentration, and imagination as one can bring to it. Of that, too, I am convinced.

Nagoya, Japan   James W. Heisig
10 May 1985

INTRODUCTION

The aim of this book is to provide the student of Japanese with a simple method for correlating the writing and the meaning of Japanese characters in such a way as to make them both easy to remember. It is intended not only for the beginner, but also for the more advanced student looking for some relief to the constant frustration of forgetting how to write the kanji and some way to systematize what he or she already knows. By showing how to break down the complexities of the Japanese writing system into its basic elements and suggesting ways to reconstruct meanings from those elements, the method offers a new perspective from which to learn the kanji.

There are, of course, many things that the pages of this book will *not* do for you. You will read nothing about how kanji combine to form compounds. Nor is anything said about the various ways to pronounce the characters. Furthermore, all questions of grammatical usage have been omitted. These are all matters that need specialized treatment in their own right. Meantime, remembering the meaning and the writing of the kanji—perhaps the single most difficult barrier to learning Japanese—can be greatly simplified if the two are isolated and studied apart from everything else.

What makes forgetting the kanji so natural is their *lack of connection with normal patterns of visual memory*. We are used to hills and roads, to the faces of people and the skylines of cities, to flowers, animals, and the phenomena of nature. And while only a fraction of what we see is readily recalled, we are confident that, given proper attention, anything we choose to remember, we can. That confidence is lacking in the world of the kanji. The closest approximation to the kind of memory patterns required by the kanji is to be seen in the various alphabets and number-systems we know. The difference is that while these symbols are very few and often sound-related, the kanji number in the thousands and have no consistent phonetic value. Nonetheless, traditional methods for learning the characters have been the same as those for learning alphabets: drill the shapes one by one, again and again, year after year. Whatever ascetical value there is in such an exercise, the more efficient way would be to relate the characters to something other than their sounds in the first place, and so to break ties with the visual memory we rely on for learning our alphabets.

The origins of the Japanese writing system can be traced back to ancient China and the 18th century before the Christian era. In the form in which we find Chinese writing codified some 1000 years later, it was made up largely of pictographic, detailed glyphs. These were further transformed and stylized down through the centuries, so that by the time the Japanese were introduced to the kanji by Buddhist monks from Korea and started experimenting with ways to adapt the Chinese writing system to their own language (about the 4th to 7th century of our era), they were already dealing with far more ideographic and abstract forms. The Japanese made their own contributions and changes in time, as was to be expected. And like every modern Oriental culture that uses the kanji, they continue to do so, though now more in matters of usage than form.

So fascinating is this story that many have encouraged the study of etymology as a way to remember the kanji. Unfortunately, the student quickly learns the many disadvantages of such an approach. As charming as it is to see the ancient drawing of a woman etched behind its respective kanji, or to discover the rudimentary form of a hand or a tree or a house, when the character itself is removed, the clear visual memory of the familiar object is precious little help for recalling how to write it. Proper etymological studies are most helpful *after* one has learned the general-use kanji. Before that time, they only add to one's memory problems. We need a still more radical departure from visual memory.

Let me paint the impasse in another, more graphic way. Picture yourself holding a kaleidoscope up to the light as still as possible, trying to fix in memory the particular pattern which the play of light and mirrors and colored stones has created. Chances are you have such an untrained memory for such things that it will take some time; but let us suppose that you succeed after ten or fifteen minutes. You close your eyes, trace the pattern in your head, and then check your image against the original pattern until you are sure you have it remembered. Then someone passes by and jars your elbow. The pattern is lost, and in its place a new jumble appears. Immediately your memory begins to scramble. You set the kaleidoscope aside, sit down, and try to draw what you had just memorized, but to no avail. There is simply nothing left in memory to grab hold of. The kanji are like that. One can sit at one's desk and drill a half dozen characters for an hour or two, only to discover on the morrow that when something similar is seen, the former memory is erased or hopelessly confused by the new information.

Now the odd thing is not that this occurs, but rather that instead of openly admitting one's distrust of purely visual memory, one accuses oneself of a poor memory or lack of discipline and keeps on following the same routine. Thus, by displacing the blame on an improper use of visual memory, one overlooks the possibility of another form of memory which could handle the task with relative ease: *imaginative memory.*

By imaginative memory I mean the faculty to recall images created purely in the mind, with no actual or remembered visual stimuli behind them. When we recall our dreams we are using imaginative memory. The fact that we sometimes conflate what happened in waking life with what merely occurred in a dream is an indication of how powerful those imaginative stimuli can be. While dreams may be broken up into familiar component parts, the composite whole is fantastical and yet capable of exerting the same force on perceptual memory as an external stimulus. It is possible to use imagination in this way also in a waking state and harness its powers for assisting a visual memory admittedly ill-adapted for remembering the kanji.

In other words, if we could discover a limited number of basic elements in the characters and make a sort of alphabet out of them, assigning to each its own image, fusing them together to form other images, and so building up complex tableaus in imagination, the impasse created by purely visual memory might be overcome. Such an imaginative alphabet would be every bit as rigorous as a phonetic one in restricting each basic element to one basic value; but its grammar would lack many of the controls of ordinary language and logic. It would be like a kind of dream-world where anything at all might happen, and happen differently in each mind. Visual memory would be used minimally, to build up the alphabet. After that, one would be set loose to roam freely inside the magic lantern of imaginative patterns according to one's own preferences.

In fact, most students of the Japanese writing system do something similar from time to time, devising their own mnemonic aids but never developing an organized approach to their use. At the same time, most of them would be embarrassed at the academic silliness of their own secret devices, feeling somehow that there is no way to sophsticate the ridiculous ways their mind works. Yet if it *does* work, then some such irreverence for scholarship and tradition seems very much in place.Indeed, shifting the attention from why one *forgets* certain kanji to why one *remembers* others should offer motivation enough to undertake a more thoroughgoing attempt to systematize imaginative memory.

The basic alphabet of the imaginative world hidden in the kanji we may call, following traditional terminology, *primitive elements* or simply *primitives*. These are not to be confused with the so-called "radicals" which form the basis of etymological studies of sound and meaning, and now are used for the lexical ordering of the characters. In fact, most of the radicals are themselves primitives, but the number of primitives is not restricted to the traditional list of radicals.

The primitives, then, are the fundamental strokes and combinations of strokes from which all the characters are built up. Calligraphically speaking, there are only nine possible kinds of strokes in theory, seventeen in practice. A few of these will be given *primitive meanings,* that is, they will serve as fundamental images. Simple combinations will yield new primitive meanings in turn, and so on as complex characters are built up. If these primitives are presented in orderly fashion, the taxonomy of the most complex characters is greatly simplified and no attempt need be made to memorize the primitive alphabet apart from actually using them.

The number of primitives, as we are understanding the term, is a moot question. Traditional etymology counts some 224 of them. We shall draw upon these freely, and also ground our primitive meanings in traditional etymological meanings, without making any particular note of the fact as we proceed. We shall also be departing from etymology to avoid the confusion caused by the great number of similar meanings for differently shaped primitives. Wherever possible, then, the generic meaning of the primitives will be preserved, although there are cases in which we shall have to specify that meaning in a different way, or depart from it altogether, so as to root imaginative memory in familiar visual memories. Should the student later turn to etymological studies, the procedure we have followed will become more transparent, and should not cause any obstacles to the learning of etymologies.

The list of elements which we have singled out as primitives proper (Index II) is restricted to the following four classes: basic elements which are not kanji, kanji which appear as basic elements in other kanji with great frequency, kanji which change their meaning when they function as parts of other kanji, and kanji which change their shape when forming parts of other kanji. Any kanji which keeps both its form and its meaning and appears as part of another kanji *functions* as a primitive, whether or not it occurs with enough frequency to draw attention to it as such.

The roughly 2,000 characters chosen for study in these pages (given in the order of presentation in Index I and arranged according to the number of strokes in Index III) include the basic 1850 general-use kanji established as standard by the Japanese Ministry of Education in 1946,[1] roughly another 60 used chiefly in proper names, and a handful of characters that are convenient

---

1. In 1981 an additional 95 characters were added to this list. They have been incorporated in this Second Edition.

for use as primitive elements. Each kanji is assigned a *key-word* which represents its basic meaning, or one of its basic meanings. The key-words have been selected on the basis of how a given kanji is used in compounds and on the meaning it has on its own. There is no repetition in key-words though many are nearly synonymous. In these cases, it is important to focus on the particular flavor which that word enjoys in English, so as to evoke connotations distinct from similar key-words. To be sure, many of the characters carry a side range of connotations not present in their English equivalents, and vice-versa; many even carry several ideas not able to be captured in a single English word. By simplifying the meanings through the use of key-words, however, one becomes familiar with a kanji and at least one of its principal meanings. The others can be added later with relative ease, in much the same way as one enriches one's understanding of one's native tongue by learning the full range of feelings and meanings embraced by words already known.

Once we have the primitive meanings and the key-word relevant to a particular kanji (cataloged in Index IV), the task is to create a composite ideogram. Here is where fantasy and memory come into play. The aim is to shock the mind's eye, to disgust it, to enchant it, to tease it, or to entertain it in any way possible so as to brand it with an image intimately associated with the key-word. That image in turn, inasmuch as it is composed of primitive meanings, will dictate precisely how the kanji is to be penned—stroke for stroke, jot for jot. Many characters, perhaps the majority of them, can be so remembered on a first encounter, provided sufficient time is taken to fix the image. Others will need to be reviewed by focusing on the association of key-word and primitive elements. In this way, mere drill of visual memory is all but entirely eliminated.

Since the goal is not simply to remember a certain number of kanji, but also to learn *how* to remember them (and others not included in this book), the course has been divided into three parts. Part One provides the full associative story for each character. By directing the reader's attention, at least for the length of time it takes to read the explanation and relate it to the written form of the kanji, most of the work is done for the student even as a feeling for the method is acquired. In Part Two, only the skeletal plots of the stories are presented, and the individual must work out his or her own details by drawing on personal memory and fantasy. Part Three, comprising the major portion of the course, provides only the key-word and the primitive meanings, leaving the remainder of the process to the student.

It will soon become apparent that the most critical factor is the *order of learning the kanji*. The method is simplicity itself. Once more basic characters have been learned, their use as primitive elements for other kanji can save a great deal of effort and enable one to review known characters at the same time as one is learning new ones. Hence to approach this course haphazardly, jumping ahead to the later lessons before studying the earlier ones, will entail a considerable loss of efficiency. If one's goal is to learn to write the entire list of general-use characters, then it seems best to learn them in the order best suited to memory, not in order of frequency or according to the order in which they are taught to Japanese children. Should the individual decide to pursue some other course, however, the indices should provide all the basic information for finding the appropriate frame and the primitives referred to in that frame.

It may surprise the reader casually leafing through these pages not to find a single drawing or pictographic representation. This is fully consistent with what was said earlier about placing the stress on imaginative memory. For one thing, pictographs are an unreliable way to remember all but very few kanji; and even in these cases, the pictograph should be *discovered* by the student by toying with the forms, pen in hand, rather than *given* in one of its historical graphic forms. For another, the presentation of an image actually inhibits imagination and restricts it to the biases of the artist. This is as true for the illustrations in a child's collection of fairy tales as it is for the various phenomena we shall encounter in the course of this book. The more original work the individual does with an image, the easier will it be to remember a kanji.

Before setting out on the course plotted in the following pages, attention should be drawn to a few final points. In the first place, one must we warned about setting out too quickly. It should not be assumed that because the first characters are so elementary, they can be skipped over hastily. The method presented here needs to be learned step by step, lest one find oneself forced later to retreat to the first stages and start over. 20 or 25 characters per day would not be excessive for someone who has only a couple of hours to give to study. If one were to study them full-time, there is no reason why the entire course could not be completed successfully in four to six weeks. By the time Part One has been traversed, the student should have discovered a rate of progress suitable to the time available.

Second, the repeated advice given to study the characters with pad and pencil should be taken seriously. While simply remembering the characters does not, one will discover, demand that they be written, there is really no better way to improve the aesthetic appearance of one's writing and acquire a "natural feel" for the flow of the kanji than by writing them. The method will spare one the toil of writing the *same* character over and over in order to learn it, but it will not supply the fluency at writing that comes only with constant practice. If pen and paper are inconvenient, one can always make do with the palm of the hand, as the Japanese do. It provides a convenient square space for jotting on with one's index finger when riding in a bus or walking down the street.

Third, the kanji are best reviewed by beginning with the key-word, progressing to the respective story, and then writing the character itself. Once one has been able to perform these steps, reversing the order follows as a matter of course. More will be said about this later in the book.

In the fourth place, it is important to note that the best order for *learning* the kanji is by no means the best order for *remembering* them. They need to be recalled when and where they are met, not in the sequence in which they are presented here. For that purpose, recommendations are given in Lesson 5 for designing flash-cards for random review.

Finally, it seems worthwhile to give some brief thought to any ambitions one might have about "mastering" the Japanese writing system. The idea arises from, or at least is supported by a certain bias about learning that comes from over-exposure to schooling: the notion that language is a cluster of skills that can be rationally divided, systematically learned, and certified by testing. The kanji, together with the wider structure of Japanese—and indeed of *any* language for that matter—resolutely refuse to be mastered in this fashion. The rational order brought to the kanji in this book is only intended as an aid to get you close enough to the characters to befriend them, let them surprise you, inspire you, enlighten you, resist you, and seduce you. But they cannot be mastered without a full understanding of their long and complex history and an insight into the secret of their unpredictable vitality—all of which is far too much for a single mind to bring to the tip of a single pen.

That having been said, the goal of this book is still to attain native proficiency in writing the Japanese characters and associating their meanings with their forms. If the logical systematization and the playful irreverences contained in the pages that follow can help spare even a few of those who pick it up the grave error of deciding to pursue their study of the Japanese language without aspiring to such proficiency, the efforts that went into it will more than have received their reward.

Kamakura, Japan   James W. Heisig
10 February 1977

Part One:

——————

STORIES

LESSON 1

Let us begin with a group of 15 kanji, all of which you probably knew before you ever opened this book. Each kanji has been provided with a single *key-word* to represent its basic meaning. Some of these characters will also serve later as *primitives* with a meaning different from the meaning they have as kanji. Although it is not necessary at this stage to memorize the special primitive meaning of those characters, a special remark preceded by a star [*] has been appended for future reference.

The *number of strokes* is given in square brackets at the end of each explanation, followed by the stroke-by-stroke *order of writing*. It cannot be stressed enough how important it is to learn to write each kanji in its proper order. As easy as these first characters may seem, therefore, study them all with a pad and pencil to get into the habit from the very start.

Finally, note that each key-word has been carefully chosen and should not be tampered with in any way if you want to avoid confusion later on.

1. one ——

In Chinese characters, the number **one** is laid on its side, unlike the Roman numeral I, which stands upright. As you would expect, it is written from left to right. [1]

——

* As a primitive element, the key-word meaning is discarded, and the single horizontal stroke takes on the meaning of *floor* or *ceiling,* depending on its position: if it stands above another primitive element, it means *ceiling;* if below, *floor.*

2. two ——

Like the Roman numeral II which reduplicates the numeral I, the kanji for **two** is a simple reduplication of the horizontal stroke that means *one.* The order of writing goes from above to below, with the first stroke slightly shorter. [2]

— —

3. three
三

And like the Roman numeral III which triples the numeral I, the kanji for **three** simply triples the single horizontal stroke. In writing it, think of *"1 + 2 = 3"* in order to keep the middle stroke shorter. [3]

一   二   三

4. four
四

Actually this character is composed of two primitive elements, *mouth* 口 and *human legs* 儿 which we shall be meeting in the coming lessons. Presuming that you already knew the numbers 1 to 10 before you ever opened this book, we shall pass over this kanji's "story" until later.

Note how the second stroke is written left-to-right and then top-to-bottom. This is consistent with what we have already seen in the first three numbers and enables us to state a general principle that you might keep in the back of your head when writing more complicated characters later on: WRITE NORTH TO SOUTH, WEST TO EAST, NORTHWEST TO SOUTHEAST. [5]

丨   冂   冋   四   四

5. five
五

As with *four,* we shall postpone learning the primitive elements in this charater. Note how the general principle we learned in the last frame applies here when you are writing the kanji for **five**. [4]

一   丁   五   五

6. six
六

The primitive elements here are *tophat* and *animal legs* 八 . But here again, we shall pass them by for the time being. [4]

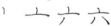

7. seven

Note how the first stroke "cuts" through the second. This distinguishes **seven** from the primitive for *spoon* 匕 , in which the horizontal stroke stops short. [2]

* As a primitive, this form takes on the meaning of *diced,* i.e. "cut" into little pieces, consistent both with the way the character is written and with its association with the kanji for *cut* 切 to be learned in a later lesson (Frame 85).

8. eight

Just as the Arabic numeral "8" is composed of a small circle followed by a larger one, so the kanji for **eight** is composed of a short line followed by a longer line, slanting towards it but not touching it. And just as the lazy "8" ∞ is the mathematical symbol for "infinity," so the expanse opened up below these two strokes is associated by the Japanese with the sense of "all-encompassing." [2]

9. nine

If you take care to remember the stroke order of this kanji, you will not have trouble later keeping it distinct from the kanji for *power* 力 (Frame 858). [2]

* As a primitive, we shall use this kanji to mean *baseball team* or simply *baseball*. The meaning, of course, is derived from the *nine* players who make up a team.

10. ten

Turn this character 45° either way and you have the X used for the Roman numeral ten. [2]

一 十

* As a primitive, this character sometimes keeps its meaning of *ten* and sometimes is used for needle, a meaning derived from the kanji for *needle* 針 (Frame 274). Since the kanji itself is never used as a primitive, there is no need to worry about confusing the primitive with the kanji. In fact, we shall be following this procedure regularly.

11. mouth   口

Like several of the first characters we shall learn, the kanji for **mouth** is a clear pictograph. Since there are no circular shapes among the kanji, the square must be used to depict the circle. [3]

* As a primitive, this form also means *mouth*. Any of the range of possible images that the word suggests—an opening or entrance to a cave, a river, a bottle, as well as the largest hole in one's head—can be used for the primitive meaning.

12. day   日

This is intended to be a pictograph of the sun. Recalling what we said in the previous frame about round forms, it is easy to see the circle and the big smile which characterize our simplest drawings of the sun—like those yellow badges with the words "Have a nice **day!**" [4]

丨 冂 冃 日

* As a primitive, this means either *sun* or *day* or a *tongue wagging in the mouth*. This latter meaning, incidentally, derives from an old character outside the standard list meaning something like "sayeth" and written almost exactly the same, except that the stroke in the middle does not touch the right side.

13. month   月

This character is actually a picture of the moon, with the two horizontal lines representing the left eye and mouth of the mythical "man in the moon." (Actually, the Japanese see a hare in the moon, but it is a little far-fetched to find one in the kanji.) And one **month**, of course, is but a turn of the moon. [4]

> * As a primitive element, this character can take on the sense of either *moon, flesh,* or *part of the body.* Why this is so will be explained in a later chapter.

---

14. rice field

Another pictograph, this kanji looks like a bird's-eye view of a **rice field** divided into four plots. Be careful when writing this character to get the order of the strokes correct. You will find that it fits in perfectly with the principle indicated in Frame 4. [5]

> * When used as a primitive element, the meaning of *rice field* is most common, but now and again it will take the meaning of *brains,* from the fact that it looks a bit like that tangle of grey matter nestled under our skulls.

---

15. eye

Once again, if we round out the corners and curve the middle strokes upwards and downwards respectively, we get something resembling an **eye**. [5]

> * As a primitive, the character keeps its sense of *eye,* more specifically, an *eyeball.* In the middle of a complex kanji, the primitive will sometimes be turned on its side like this ▭ .

Although only 9 of the 15 kanji treated in this lesson are formally listed as primitives—the elements that join together to make up other kanji—some of the others may also take on that function from time to time, only not with enough frequency to merit learning them as separate primitive elements and attaching special meanings to them. In other words, whenever one of the kanji already learned is used in anther kanji, it will retain its key-word meaning unless we have assigned a special primitive meaning to it.

LESSON 2

In this lesson, we learn what a "primitive element" is by using the first 15 kanji as pieces that can be fitted together to form new kanji, 18 of them to be exact. Whenever the primitive meaning differs from the key-word meaning, you may want to go back to the original frame to refresh your memory. From now on, though, you should learn *both* the key-word and the primitive meaning of new kanji as they appear. An INDEX OF PRIMITIVE ELEMENTS has been added at the end of the book.

16. old

古

The primitive elements that compose this character are *ten* and *mouth*, but you may find it easier to remember it as a pictograph of a tombstone with a cross on top. Just think back to one of those grave-yards you have visited, or better still, used to play in as a child, with **old** inscriptions on the tombstones.

This departure from the primitive elements in favor of a pic-tograph will take place now and then at these early stages, and almost never after that. So you need not worry about cluttering up your memory with too many character "drawings." [5]

一 十 古 古 古

* Used as a primitive element, this kanji keeps its key-word sense of *old*, but care should be taken to make that abstract notion as graphic as possible.

17. I

吾

There are actually a number of kanji for the word **I**, but the others tend to be more specific than this one. The key-word here should be taken in the general psychological sense of the "perceiving subject." Now the one place in our bodies that all 5 senses are concentrated is in the head, which has no less than *five mouths:* 2 nostrils, 2 ears, and 1 mouth. Hence, *five mouths* = **I**. [7]

一 丁 五 五 五 吾 吾

18. risk

Remember when you were young and your mother told you never to look directly into the *sun* for fear you might burn your *eyes*? Probably you were foolish enough to **risk** a quick glance once or twice; but just as probably, you passed that bit of folk wisdom on to someone else as you grew older. Here, too, the kanji that has a *sun above and an eye* right below looking up at it has the meaning of **risk**. (See Frame 12.) [9]

19. companion 朋

The first **companion** that God made, as the Bible story goes, was Eve. Upon seeing her Adam exclaimed *"flesh of my flesh!"* And that is precisely what this character says, in so many strokes. [8]

20. bright 明

Among nature's **bright** lights, there are two that the biblical myth has God set in the sky, the *sun* to rule over the day and the *moon* to rule the night. Each of them has come to represent one of the common connotations of this key-word: the sun, the **bright** light and the moon the **bright** intuition of the poet and the seer. (See Frame 13.) [8]

21. chant 唱

This one is easy! You have one *mouth* making no noise (the choir master) and two *mouths with wagging tongues* (the minimum number for a chorus). So think of the key-word, **chant**, as monastery singing and the kanji is yours forever. (See Frame 12.) [11]

) 冂 口 口ˡ 口冂 口冃 口阝 口뮤 唱 唱 唱

22. sparkle

What else can the word **sparkle** suggest if not a diamond? And if you've ever held a diamond up to the *sun,* you will have noticed how every facet of it becomes like a miniature *sun.* This kanji is a picture of a tiny *sun* in three places (that is, "everywhere"), to give the sense of something that **sparkles** on all sides. Just like a diamond. In writing the primitive element three times, note how the rule for writing given in frame Frame 4 holds true not only for each individual element but also for the character as a whole. [12]

23. goods

As with the character for *sparkle,* the triplication of a single element in this character indicates "everywhere" or "heaps of." When we think of **goods** in modern industrial society, we think of something that has been mass-produced—that is produced for the "masses" of open *mouths* waiting like fledglings in a nest to "consume" whatever comes their way. [9]

24. spine

This character is more like a picture of two of the bones in the **spine** linked by a single stroke. [7]

25. prosperous

What we mentioned in the previous two frames about 3 of something meaning "everywhere" or "heaps of" was not meant to be taken lightly. In this kanji we see *two suns,* one atop the other, which is easily confused in memory with the *three suns* of *sparkle* if we are not careful. Focus on the number this way: since we speak of **prosperous** times as *sun*ny, what could be more **prosperous** than a sky with *two* *suns* in it? Just be sure to SEE them there. [8]

丶　冂　冋　日　尸　呂　呂　昌

---

26. early   早

This kanji is actually a picture of the first flower of the day, which we shall, in defiance of botanical science, call the *sun*-flower, since it begins with the element for *sun* held up on a stem with leaves, the pictographic representation of the final two strokes. This time, however, we shall ignore the pictographic meaning and imagine *sun*-flowers with *needles* for stems, which can be plucked and used to darn your socks.

The sense of **early** is easily remembered if one thinks of the *sun*-flower as the **early**-riser in the garden because the *sun,* showing favoritism towards its namesake, shines on it before all the others. (See Frame 10.) [6]

丶　冂　冋　日　旦　早

* As a primitive element, this kanji takes the meaning of *sun-flower,* which was used to make the abstract word *early* more graphic.

---

27. rising sun   旭

This character is a sort of nickname for the Japanese flag with its well-known emblem, the **rising sun.** If you can picture two seams running around that great red *sun* and imagine it sitting on a *baseball* bat for a flagpole, you have a slightly irreverent but not altogether inaccurate picture of how the sport has caught on in the Land of the **Rising Sun.** [6]

丿　九　九　旭　旭　旭

---

28. generation   世

We generally consider one **generation** as a period of thirty (or *ten* plus *ten* plus ten) years. If you look at this kanji in its final form—not in its stroke-order—you will see three *tens.* When writing it think of the lower horizontal lines as "addition" lines written under numbers to add them up. Thus: *ten, ten* "plus" *ten* "plus" yields thirty. Actually, it's a lot easier doing it with a pencil than reading it in a book. [5]

29. stomach 胃

You will need to refer back to Frames 13 and 14 here for the special meaning of the two primitive elements that make up this character: *flesh (part of the body)* and *brain*. What the kanji says, if you look at it, is that the *part of the body* that keep's the *brain* in working order is the **stomach**. To keep the elements in proper order, when you write this kanji, think of the *brain* as being "held up" by the *flesh*. [9]

30. nightbreak 旦

While we normally refer to the start of the day as "day break," Japanese commonly refers to the "opening up of night" into day. Hence the choice of this rather odd key-word, **nightbreak**. The single stroke represents the *floor* (have a peek again at Frame 1) of the horizon over which the *sun* is poking its head. [5]

31. gall bladder 胆

The pieces in this character should be immediately visible: on the left, the element for *part of the body,* and on the right the character for *nightbreak* which we have just met. What all of this has to do with **gall bladder** is not immediately clear. But if we give a slight twist to the traditional biblical advice about not letting the sun set on your anger (which ancient medicine associated with the choler or bile that the **gall bladder** is supposed to filter out) and change it to "not letting the *night break* on your anger, the work is done. And the improvement is not a bad piece of advice in its own right, since anger, like so many other things, can be stilled by letting the sun set on it and then "sleeping on it." [9]

32. span

"Sunrise, sunset, sunrise, sunset..." goes the chant of the Fiddler on the Roof. You can almost see the journey of the *sun* as it moves from one horizon (the *floor*) to its noon-day heights in the sky overhead (*ceiling*) and then disappears over the other horizon, day after day, marking off the **span** of our lives. [6]

Let us end this chapter with two final pictographic characters which happen to be among the easiest to recognize for their form but among the most difficult to remember how to write. We introduce them here to run an early test on whether or not you have been paying close attention to the stroke-order of the characters your have been learning.

33. concave

You couldn't have asked for a better key-word for this kanji! Just have a look at it: a perfect image of a **concave** lens (remembering, of course, that the kanji square off rounded things), complete with its own little "cave." Now all you have to do is learn to write it. [5]

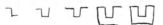

34. convex

Maybe this helps you see how the Japanese have no trouble keeping **convex** distinct from *concave*. Note the odd feeling of the **third** stroke. If it doesn't feel all that strange now, by the time you are done with this book it will. This is the only time you will ever have to write this shape in Japanese. [5]

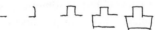

LESSON 3

After Lesson 2, you should now have some idea of how an apparently complex and difficult kanji can be broken down into simple elements that make remembering it a great deal easier. After completing this lesson you should have a clearer idea of how the course is laid out. We merely add a couple of primitive elements to the kanji we already know and see how many new kanji we can form—in this case 18 in all—and when we run out, add more primitive. And so on, until there are no kanji left.

In Lesson 3 you will also be introduced to primitive elements which are NOT themselves kanji but only used to construct other kanji. These are marked with a star [*] instead of a number. As long as you have no trouble remembering these elements as they appear, there is no need to make a special effort to study them. The sheer frequency with which most of them show up should make it automatic.

---

* walking stick |

This primitive element is a picture of just what it is: a cane or **walking stick**. It carries with it the connotations of lameness and whatever else one associates with a cane. Rarely—but very rarely—it will be laid on its side. Whenever this occurs, it will ALWAYS be driven through the middle of some other primitive element. In this way it will not get confused with the primitive meanings of *one*. [1]

|

---

* a drop of   ╯

The meaning of this primitive is obvious from the first moment you look at it, though just what it will be **a drop of** will differ from case to case. The important thing is not to think of it as something insignificant like a "drop in the bucket" but as something so important that it can change the whole picture—like a **drop of** arsenic in your mother-in-law's coffee.

In general, it is written from to right to left, but there are times when it can be written left to right. At other times it can be stretched out a bit. (In cases where you have trouble remembering this, it may help to think of it as an **eye-dropper dripping drops of** something or other.) Examples will follow in this lesson. [1]

35. olden times

A *walking stick* is needed for *days* of **olden times,** since *days,* too, get old—at least insofar as we refer to them as the "good old days." The main thing here is to think of "good old days" when you hear the keyword **olden times.** The rest will take care of itself. [5]

36. oneself

You can think of this kanji as a stylized pictograph of the nose, that little *drop* that Mother Nature set between your *eyes.* The Japanese refer to themselves by pointing a finger at their nose—giving us an easy way to remember the kanji for **oneself.** [6]

* The same meaning of *oneself* can be kept when this kanji is used as a primitive element, but you will generally find it better to give it the meaning of *nose,* both because it accords with the story above and because it is the first part of the kanji for *nose* (Frame 678).

37. white

The color **white** is a mixture of all the primary colors, both for pigments and for light, as we see when a prism breaks up the rays of the *sun.* Hence, a single *drop of sun* spells **white.** [5]

* As a primitive, this character can either retain its meaning of *white* or take the more graphic meaning of a *white bird or dove.* This latter stems from the fact that it appears at the top of the kanji for *bird* which we shall get to later (Frame 1941).

38. hundred

The Japanese refer to a person's 99th birthday as a *"white* year" because *white* is the kanji you are left with if you subtract *one* from a **hundred**. [6]

39. in

The elements here are a *walking stick* and a *mouth*. Remember the trouble your mother had getting medicine oil **in** your *mouth*? Chances are it crossed her mind more than once to grab something handy, like your grandfather's *walking stick*, to pry open your jaws while she performed her duty. Keep the image of getting something **in** from the outside, and the otherwise abstract sense of this key-word should be a lot easier than trying to spoon castor oil **into** a baby's *mouth*. [4]

40. thousand

This kanji is almost too simple to pull apart, but for the sake of practice, have a look at the *drop* above and the *ten* below. Now put the elements together by thinking of squeezing two more zeros out of an *eye-dropper* alongside of the number *ten* to make it a **thousand**. [3]

41. tongue

The primitive for *mouth* and the character for *thousand* naturally form the idea of **tongue** if one thinks of a *thousand mouths* able to speak the same language, or as we say, "sharing a common **tongue.**" Especially if you take the image literally: a single **tongue** being passed around from *mouth* to *mouth*. [6]

42. measuring box 升

This is the character for the little wooden box that the Japanese use for measuring things, as well as for drinking saké out of. Simply imagine the outside as spiked with a *thousand* sharp *needles,* and the quaint little **measuring box** becomes a drinker's nightmare!

Be very careful when you write this character not to confuse it with the writing of *thousand.* The reason for the difference gives us a chance to clarify another general principle of writing that supersedes the one we mentioned in Frame 4: WHEN A SINGLE STROKE RUNS VERTICALLY THROUGH THE MIDDLE OF A CHARACTER IT IS WRITTEN LAST. The principle applies to *thousand;* it does not apply to **measuring box.** [4]

43. rise up 昇

The picture here is made up of the two primitive elements: a *sun* and a *measuring box.* Just as the *sun* can be seen **rising up** in the morning from—where else?—the land of the rising sun, this kanji has the *sun* rising up out of a Japanese *measuring box*, which we can then call the *"measuring box* of the **rising-up** *sun."* [8]

44. round 丸

We speak of **"round** numbers," or **"rounding** a number off," meaning to add an **insignificant** amount to bring it to the nearest 10. For instance, if you add just a wee bit, the tiniest *drop,* to *nine*, you end up with a **round** number. [3]

* As a primitive, this element takes the meaning of a *fat man,* which is easy to remember if you think of a grotesquely *fat man* whose paunch so covers the plate that he always gets on base by being hit by the pitch. Hence a *round baseball player* becomes a *fat man.*

45. measurement   寸

This kanji actually stood for a small **measurement** used prior to the
metric system, a bit over an inch in length, and from there acquired
the sense of **measurement**. In the old system, it was one-*tenth* of a
shaku (which we shall meet in frame Frame 1070). The picture,
appropriately, represents one *drop of* a *ten* (with a hook!). [3]

   * As a primitive, we shall use this to mean *glue* or *glued to*. There is
   no need to devise a story to remember this, since the primitive
   will appear so often you would have to struggle hard NOT to
   remember it.

46. specialty   専

Ten . . . rice-fields . . . glue. That is how one would read the primitive
elements of this kanji from top to bottom. Now if we make a simple
sentence out of these elements, we get: *"Ten rice-fields glued together."*

   A **specialty,** of course, refers to one's special *"field"* of endeavor
or competence. In fact, few people remain content with a single
specialty and usually extend themselves in other *fields* as well. This is
how it is that the picture of *ten fields glued* together comes to
represent a **specialty.** [9]

47. Dr.   博

At the left we have the *needle*; at the right, the kanji for *specialty,*
plus an extra *drop* at the top. Think of a **Dr.** who is a *specialist* with a
needle (an acupuncturist) and let the *drop* at the top represent the
period at the end of Dr..

   In principle we are trying to avoid this kind of device, which
plays on abstract grammatical conventions; but I think you will
agree, after you have had occasion to use the right side of this kanji
in forming other kanji, that the exception is merited in this case. [12]

> * The primitive form of this kanji eliminates the *needle* on the left, and gets the meaning of an *acupuncturist.*

We have already seen one example of how to form primitives from other primitives, when we formed the *nightbreak* out of *sun* and *floor* (Frame 30). Let us take two more examples of this procedure right away, so that later we can do so without having to draw any particular attention to the fact.

---

* divining rod

This is a picture of a **divining rod**, composed of *a drop* and *a cane,* but easy enough to remember as a pictograph. Alternately, you can think of it as a **magic wand**. In either case, it is used to suggest images of magic or fortune-telling.

Normally it is written in the stroke order given here, though at times the order is reversed. This has simply to be learned when it is met; there are no rules for it. [2]

* Although it falls outside of the list of general-use kanji, this element is actually a kanji in its own right, having virtually the same meaning as the kanji in the next frame.

---

48. fortune-telling

This is one of those kanji which is a real joy of simplicity: a *divining rod* with a *mouth*—or in the more ordinary phrase, **fortune-telling**.

Note how conveniently the movement from top to bottom (the movement in which the kanji are written) is also the order of the elements which make up our story and key-word, first *divine,* then *mouth*. This will not always be possible, but where it is, memory has almost no work at all to do. [5]

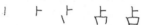

---

49. above

The two directions, **above** and below, are usually pointed at with the finger. But the characters do not cooperate with that custom, so we have to choose something else, easily remembered. The primitives show a *magic wand* standing **above** a *floor*—"magically," you might say. Anyway, go right on to the next frame, since the two belong together and are best remembered as a unit, just as the words **above** and *below* suggest one another. [3]

50. below

Here we see our famous miraculous *magic wand* hanging, all on its own, **below** the *ceiling*, as you probably already guessed would happen. In addition to giving us two new kanji, the two shapes given in this and the previous frame also serve to fix the use of the primitives for *ceiling* and *floor*, by drawing our attention successively to the line standing above and below the primitive element to which it is related. [3]

51. eminent

The word **eminent** suggests a famous or well-known person. So all you need to do—given the primitives of a *magic wand* and a *sunflower*—is to think of the world's most **eminent** magician as one who uses a *sunflower* for a *magic wand* (like a flower-child who goes around turning the world into peace and love). [8]

* mist

Here is our second example of a primitive composed of other primitives but not itself a kanji. At the bottom is the primitive (also a kanji) for *early* or *sunflower*. At the top, a *needle*. Conveniently, **mist** falls *early* in the morning, like little *needles* of rain, to assure that the *sunflower* blooms *early* as we have learned it should. [8]

52. morning   朝

On the right we see the *moon* fading off into the first light of
morning, and to the left, the *mist* that falls to give Nature a shower to
prepare it for the coming heat. If you can think of the *moon*
tilting over to spill *mist* on your garden, you should have no trouble
remembering which of all the elements in this story are to serve as
primitives for constructing the character. [12]

LESSON 4

At the risk of going a little bit too fast, we are now going to introduce five
new primitive elements, all of which are very easy to remember either
because of their frequency or because of their shape. But remember: there
is no reason to study the primitive by themselves. They are being presented systematically to make their learning automatic.

*   animal legs   ハ

Like the four that follow it, this primitive is not a kanji in its own
right, though it is said to be derived from 八 , the character we
learned earlier for *eight*. It ALWAYS comes at the bottom of the
primitive to which it is related. It can mean the **legs** of any kind of
animal: anything from a grizzly's paws to an octopus' tentacles to the
spindleshanks of a spider. (The one animal not allowed is our friend
homo sapiens, whose legs figure in the next frame.) Even where the
term **legs** will apply metaphorically to the **legs** of pieces of furniture,
it is best to keep the association with **animal legs**. (At the point, go
back and review Frame 6.) [2]

丿   丿丶

* human legs 丿乚

Notice how these legs are somewhat shapelier and more highly evolved than those of the so-called "lower animals." The one on the left, drawn first, is straight; while the one on the right bends gracefully and ends with a hook. Though they are not likely to suggest the **legs** of any **human** you know, they do have something of the look of someone out for a stroll, especially if you compare them to *animal legs*.

If you had any trouble with the kanji for the number *four,* now would be the time to return to it. [2]

丿 丿乚

* wind 几

This primitive gets its name from the full kanji for the **wind** (Frame 524). It is called an "enclosure" because other elements are often drawn in the middle of it, though it can also be compressed together like this 几 so that there is no room for anything in it. The main thing to remember when writing this element is that the second stroke bends OUTWARDS, like a gust of **wind** blown from above. In addition to the basic meaning of **wind**, we shall also have occasion to use the image of a **weather-vane**. The derivation is obvious. [2]

* bound up 勹

Like *wind,* the element meaning **bound up** is also an enclosure which can wrap itself around other elements, and can also be compressed. When it does not actually enclose anything—usually because there is not enough room—and is set on top, the little hook at the end is dropped off, like this: ⌒ . The sense of **bound up** is that of being "tied and gagged" or wrapped up tightly. If you have trouble remembering when the hook is present and when not, you might think of it as a **chain** when it encloses something and as a **rope** when it does not. [2]

丿 勹

* horns   ＼＇

This primitive element ALWAYS appears at the top of the element to which it is related, and is always attached to the first horizontal line to come under it: the **horns** can never be left hanging in the air. To avoid it, an extra horizontal stroke (like a *one*) is even sometimes added. The final kanji of this Lesson gives an example.

  The meaning of this element is wide enough to embrace bulls, rams, billy goats, and moose, but not musical instruments. As with other elements with such "open" meanings, it is best to settle on one that you find most vivid and stick with that image consistently. [2]

                          ＼   ＼／

53. only   只

When we run across abstract key-words like this one, the best way to get an image is to recall some common but suggestive phrase in which the word appears. For instance, we think the expression "it's the **only** one of its kind." Then we imagine a barker at a side-show advertising some strange pac-man like creature he has inside his tent, with only a gigantic *mouth* and two wee *animal legs*. [5]

                    ＼   ⊓   ⊐   尸   只

54. shellfish   貝

To remember the primitive elements that make up **this kanji**, an *eye* and *animal legs,* you might be tempted to think of it as a pictograph of a **shellfish** with its ridged shell at the top and two little *legs* sticking out of the bottom. But that might not help you recall later just how many ridges to put on the shell. Better to imagine a freakish shellfish with a single, gigantic *eye* roaming the beaches on its slender little *legs,* scaring the wits out of the sunbathers. [7]

  * When used as a primitive, the meaning of *oyster* and *clam* will
    often come in handy.

55. upright

Now take the last primitive, the *shellfish,* and set a *magic wand* over it, and you have the kanji for **upright.** After all, the *clam* and the *oyster* are incapable of walking **upright.** It would take a magician with his *wand* to pull off such a feat—which is precisely what we have in this kanji. [9]

56. employee

How do we get a *mouth* over a *shellfish* to mean an **employee?** Simple. Just remember the advice new **employees** get about keeping their *mouths* shut and doing their job, and then make that more graphic by picturing an office building full of white-collar workers scurrying around with *clams* pinched to their *mouths.* [10]

57. see

The elements which compose the character for **see** are the *eye* firmly fixed to a pair of *human legs.* Surely, somewhere in your experience, there is a vivid image just waiting to be dragged up to help you remember this character. . . [7]

58. newborn babe

The top part of the kanji in this frame, you will remember, is the character for *olden times,* those days so old they needed a walking stick to get around. Western mythical imagination has old "Father Time" leaning on his sickle with a **newborn babe** crawling around his *legs,* the idea being that the circle of birth-and-death goes on.

Incidentally, this is the only time that the kanji for *olden times* will appear as a primitive element in another kanji, so try to make the most of it. [7]

```
丿   儿   冂   旧   旧   旧   児
```

---

59. beginning

"In the **beginning** . . ." starts that marvelous shelf of books we call the Bible. It talks about how all things were made, and tells us that when the Creator came to humanity he made *two* of them, man and woman. While we presume he made *two* of every other animal as well, we are not told as much. Hence *two* and a pair of *human legs* come to mean **beginning.** [4]

---

60. page 頁

What we have to do here is turn a *shellfish* into a *page* of a book. The *one* at the top tells us that we only get a rather short book, in fact only *one* **page**. Imagine a title printed on the shell of an *oyster,* let us say "Pearl of Wisdom," and then open the quaint book to its *one* and only page, on which you find a single, radiant *drop of* wisdom, one of the masterpiece poems of nature. [9]

* As a primitive, this kanji takes the unrelated meaning of a *head* (preferably one detached from its body), derived from the character for *head* (Frame 1441).

---

61. stubborn 頑

This character refers to the block-*headed* persistent **stubborness** of one who sticks to an idea or a plan just the way it was at the *beginning,* without letting anything that comes up along the way alter things in the least.

Even if that explanation makes "sense," it doesn't make for good learning because the word "beginning" is too abstract. So let us recall the image we used two frames ago—Adam and Eve in their Eden—and try again: The root of all **stubbornness** goes back to the *beginning,* with two brothers, each **stubbornly** defending his own way of life and asking their God to bless it favorably. Abel stuck to agriculture, Cain to animal-raising. Picture these two with their giant, swelled *heads,* each vying for the favors of heaven, a **stubborn** grimace on their faces. No wonder something unfortunate happened! [13]

一 二 テ 元 元 元 秊 秊 秒 秒 頑 頑 頑

62. mediocre   凡

While we refer to something insignificant as a "*drop* in the bucket," the kanji for **mediocre** suggests the image of a "*drop* in the *wind.*" [3]

63. defeat   負

Above we have the condensed form for *bound up*, below the familiar *shellfish.* Now imagine two *oysters* engaged in *shell*-to-*shell* combat, the one who is **defeated** being *bound* and gagged with seaweed, the victor towering triumphantly over it. The *bound shellfish* thus becomes the symbol for **defeat.** [9]

／ ⺈ 𠂉 ⺈ 角 角 角 負 負

64. ten thousand   万

Japanese counts higher numbers in units of **ten thousand**, unlike the West, which advances according to units of one thousand. (Thus, for instance, 40,000 would be read "four **ten-thousands**" by a Japanese.) Recalling that the comma is used in larger numbers to *bind up* a numerical unit, the elements for *one* and *bound up* naturally come to form **ten thousand**.

   The order of strokes here needs special attention, both because it falls outside the general principles we have learned already, and because it involves writing the element for *bound up* in an order opposite to the one we learned. If it is any consolation, this exception is consistent every time these three strokes come together. [3]

65. phrase   句

Combining the two primitives *bound up* and *mouth*, it is easy to see how this character can get the meaning of a **phrase**. After all, a **phrase** is nothing more than a number of words *bound up* tightly and neatly so that they will fit in your *mouth*. [5]

／　勹　勹　句　句

66. texture   肌

Ever notice how the **texture** of your face and hands is affected by the *wind*? A day's skiing or sailing makes them rough and dry, and in need of a good soft cream to soothe the burn. So whenever a *part of the body* gets exposed to the *wind,* its **texture** is affected. (If it is any help, the Latin word hiding inside of **texture** means how something is "to the touch.") [6]

丿　刀　月　月　肌　肌

67. decameron   旬

There simply is not a good phrase in English for the block of ten days which this character represents. So we resurrect the classical phrase, **decameron**, whose connotations Boccaccio has done much to enrich for us. Actually, it refers to a journey of ten *days* taken by a band of people—that is, a group of people *bound together* for the *days* of the **decameron**. [6]

／　勹　勹　句　旬　旬

68. ladle   勺

If you want to *bind up drops of* anything—water, soup, lemonade—you use something to scoop these *drops* up with, which is what we call a **ladle**. See the *drop* inside the **ladle**? [3]

／　勹　勺

69. bull's eye

The elements *white bird* and *ladle* easily suggest the image of a **bull's eye** if you imagine a rusty old *ladle* with a **bull's eye** painted on it in the form of a tiny *white bird,* who lets out a little "peep" every time you hit the target. [8]

／　亻　竹　竹　白　白　的　的

70. neck

首

Reading this kanji from the top down, we have: *horns . . . nose.* Together they bring to mind the picture of a moose-head hanging on the den wall, with its great *horns* and long *nose.* Now while we would speak of cutting off a moose's "head" to hang on the wall, the Japanese speak of cutting off its **neck.** It's all a matter of how you look at it. Anyway, if you can allow the word *neck* to conjure up the image of a moose with a very l-o-n-g *neck* hanging over the fireplace, whose **horns** you use for a coatrack and whose *nose* has spickets left and right for scotch and water, you should have no trouble with the character.

Here we get a good look at what we mentioned when we first introduced the element for *horns:* that they can never be left floating free and require an extra horizontal stroke to prevent that from happening, as is the case here. [9]

LESSON 5

That is about all we can do with the pieces we have accumulated so far, but as we add each new primitive element to those we already know, the number of kanji we will be able to form will increase by leaps and bounds.

If we were to step outside of the standard list, there are actually any number of other kanji that we could learn at this time. Just to give you an idea of some of the possibilities (though you should not bother to learn them now), here are are a few, with their meanings: 唄 (*pop song*), 泪 (*teardrops*), 吋 (*inch*), 肘 (*elbow*), 叱 (*scolding*).

While many of the stories you have learned in the previous lessons are actually more complex than the majority you will learn in the later chapters, they are the first stories you have learned, and for that reason are not likely to cause you much difficulty. By now, however, you may be wondering just how to go about reviewing what you have learned. Obviously it won't do simply to flip through the pages you have already studied, because the order already gives them away. The best method is to design for yourself a set of flash-cards that you can add to as you go through the book.

If you have not already started doing this on your own, you might try it this way: Buy heavy paper (about twice the thickness of normal index cards), unlined and with a semi-glossy finish. Cut it into cards of about 9 cm. long and 6 cm. wide. On one side, make a large ball-pen drawing of one kanji in the top two-thirds of the card. (Writing done with fountain pens and felt-tip pens tends to smear with the sweat that comes from holding them in your hands for a long time.) On the bottom right-hand corner, put the number of the frame in which the kanji appeared. On the back side, in the upper left-hand corner, write the key-word meaning of the character. Then draw a line across the middle of the card and another line about 2 cm. below it. The space between these two lines can be used for any notes you may need later to remind you of the primitive elements or stories you used to remember the character. Only fill this in when you need to, but make a card for every kanji as soon as you have learned it.

50

BELOW

—————————————

puɐ𝗠 BEˈ⅃O𝗪 ⅼᴉ
ɔᴉƃɐɯ ɥʇᴉ𝗔 ɹooⅼɟ

The rest of the space on the card you will not need now, but later, when you come to learn the readings of the characters, you might use the space above the double-lines. The bottom half of the card, on both sides, can be left free for inserting kanji compounds (front side) and their readings and meanings (back side).

A final note about reviewing. You have probably gotten into the habit of writing the character several times when memorizing it, whether you need to or not; and then writing it MORE times for kanji that you have trouble remembering. There is really no need to write the kanji more than once, unless you have trouble with the stroke-order and want to get a better "feel" for it. If a kanji causes you trouble, spend time clarifying the imagery of its story. Simply rewriting the character will reinforce any latent suspicions you still have that the "tried and true method" of learning by repeating is the only reliable one—which is the very bias we are trying to uproot. Also, when you review, REVIEW ONLY FROM THE KEY-WORD TO THE KANJI, NOT THE OTHER WAY AROUND. The reasons for this, along with further notes on reviewing, will come later.

We are now ready to return to work, adding a few new primitives one by one, and seeing what new characters they allow us to form. We shall cover 24 new kanji in this lesson.

---

71. fishguts   乙

The kanji shown here actually represents the "second" position in the old Chinese zodiac, which the Japanese still use as an alternate way of enumeration, much the same way that English will revert to Roman numerals. Among its many other meanings are "pure," "tasteful," "quaint," and—get this—"**fish guts.**" Since it is a pictograph of a fishhook, let us take this latter as the key-word meaning. [1]

乙

* We will keep *fishhook* as the primitive meaning. Its shape will rarely be quite the same as that of the kanji. When it appears at the bottom of another primitive, it is straightened out, almost as if the weight of the upper element had bent it out of shape. And when it appears to the right of another element, the short horizontal line that gets the shape started is omitted and it is stretched out and narrowed, all for reasons of space and aesthetics. Examples of these alterations (which are consistent) follow.

---

72. riot   乱

In a **riot,** manners are laid aside and tempers get short, even in so courtesy-conscious a land as Japan. This kanji show what happens to a **rioting** *tongue:* it gets "barbed" like a *fishhook,* and sets to attacking the opposition, to *hook* them as it were. [7]

´　二　千　千　舌　舌　乱

73. straightaway   直

Begin with the top two primitives, *ten* and *eyes*. Together they
represent a laboratory full of scientists hovering over a single item,
like *ten* sets of *eyes* scrutinizing every detail. Now what falls under
their gaze, the next element, is the *fishhook*, being examined for its
qualities to hook the fish **straightaway** and without delay—which is
what its designer had in mind in straightening it out in the first
place. [8]

一　ナ　广　方　方　有　有　直　直

* tool   六

Although this primitive is not very common, it is useful to know, as
the following examples will show. Conveniently, it is always drawn
at the very bottom of any kanji in which it figures. The first stroke,
the horizontal one, is detached from anything above it, but is
necessary to distinguish **tool** from *animal legs*. The sense of the
element is a carpenter's **tool**, which comes from its pictogaphic
representation of a small table with legs (make them *animal legs* if
you need a more graphic image), so that any element laying on top of
it will come to be viewed as a **tool** in the hands of a carpenter. [3]

一　宀　六

74. tool   具

Here is the full kanji on which the last frame is based. If you can
think of a table full of carpenter's **tools** of all sorts, each equipped
with its own *eye* so that it can keep a watch over what it is doing, you
won't have trouble later keeping the primitive and the kanji apart. [8]

75. true   真

Here again we meet the composite element, *ten eyes*, combined with
tool. Recalling what we had to say earlier (Frame 73), if one can think

of the key-word in the sense in which we speak of a precision tool as "true," it should not be hard to imagine ten eyes examining and testing it thoroughly to ascertain whether it actually is or not. [10]

一　十　广　疒　有　首　自　直　直　真

---

* by one's side   　　　　广

This primitive has the look of *ten,* except that the left stroke is bent down toward the left. It indicates where your hands (your *ten* fingers) fall when you let them droop: **by your side.**

The stroke order of this character can be reversed; but whichever stroke is written last, that stroke should be drawn longer than the other. The difference is slight, and all but unnoticeable in printed characters, but should be learned all the same. [2]

一　广

---

76. craft   　　　　工

The pictograph of an "I" beam, like the kind used in heavy construction work, gives us the character for **craft** in general. [3]

一　丁　工

* As a primitive element, the key-word retains the meaning of *craft* and also takes on the related meaning of *artificial.*

---

77. left   　　　　左

By combining the primitive and the kanji of the last two frames and reading the results, we get: *by one's side . . . craft.* Conveniently, the **left** has traditionally been considered the "sinister" *side,* where dark and occult *crafts* are cultivated. Note how the second stroke droops over to the **left** and is longer than the first. [5]

一　ナ　ナ　ナ　左

---

78. right   　　　　右

When thinking of the key-word **right,** in order to avoid confusion with the previous frame, take advantage of the double-meaning here, too. Imagine a little *mouth* hanging down *by your side*—like a little voice of conscience—telling you the **right** thing to do. Here the second stroke should reach out to the **right** and be drawn slightly longer than the first. [5]

ノ 一 ナ 右 右

79. possess   有

The picture here is of someone with a slab of *meat* dangling *by the side*, perhaps from a belt or rope tied around the waist. Think of it as an evil spirit in **possession** of one's soul, who can be exorcized only by allowing fresh *meat* to hang *by one's side* until it begins to putrify and stink so bad that the demon departs. Take careful note of the stroke order. [6]

ノ 一 ナ 右 有 有

80. bribe   賄

To the left we have the primitive for a *shellfish,* and to the right the kanji we just learned for *possess.* Keep the connotation of the last frame for the word *possess,* and now expand your image of *shells* to include the ancient value they had as *money* (a usage that will come in very helpful later on). Now one who is *possessed* by *shells* is likely to abandon any higher principles to acquire more and more wealth. These are the easiest ones to **bribe** with a few extra *shells.* [13]

丨 冂 冂 冃 目 貝 貝 貯 貯 賄 賄
賄

81. tribute   貢

A **tribute** has a kind of double-meaning in English: honor paid freely and *money* collected by coercion. Simply because a ruler bestows a noble name on a deed is hardly any consolation to the masses who must depart from their hard-earned *money.* Little wonder that this ancient *craft* of getting *money* by calling it a **tribute** has given way to a name closer to how it feels to those who pay it: a tax. [10]

一 亠 二 干 万 石 青 青 音 頁 頁

82. paragraph   項

To the right we see a *head* and to the left an element that means *craft*.
When we think of a **paragraph**, we immediately think of a *heading*
device to break a text into parts. (Think of the elaborate *heads* often
seen at the start of medieval manuscripts and the task becomes
easiser still.) Just where and how to do it belongs to the writer's *craft*.
Hence, we define **paragraphing** as the *"heading craft"* to remember
this character. [12]

一 T I I⁻ I⁻ 圩 圹 项 项 项 项 项 项

83. sword   刀

Although this character no longer looks very much like a **sword**, it
does have some resemblance to the handle of the **sword**. As it turns
out, this is to our advantage, in that it helps us keep distinct two
primitive elements based on this character. [2]

丁 刀

 * In the form of the kanji, this primitive means a *dagger*. When it
   appears to the right of another element, it is commonly stretched
   out like this リ and takes the sense of a great and flashing *sabre,*
   a meaning it gets from a character we shall learn later (Frame
   1671).

84. blade   刃

Think of using a *dagger* as a razor **blade,** and it shouldn't be hard to
imagine cutting yourself. See the little *drop of* blood clinging to the
blade? [3]

丁 刀 刃

85. cut   切

To the right we see the *dagger* and next to it the number *seven* whose primitive meaning we decided would be *diced* (Frame 7). It is hard to think of **cutting** anything with a knife without imagining one of those skillful Japanese chefs. Only let us say that he has had too much to drink at a party, grabs a *dagger* encased on the mantlepiece and starts *dicing* up everything in sight, starting with the hors d'oeuvres and going on to the furniture and the carpets . . . [4]

一　十　切　切

86. seduce   召

A *sword* or *dagger* posed over a *mouth* is how the character for "beckoning" is written. The related but less tame key-word **seduce** was chosen because it seemed to fit better with the, how shall we put it, Freudian implications of the kanji. (Observe if you will that it is not sure whether the long slender object is **seducing** the small round one or vice-versa.) [5]

フ　フ　フ　召　召

* The primitive meaning remains the same: *seduce*.

87. shining   昭

Let the key-word suggest **shining** one's shoes, the purpose of which is to *seduce* the *sun* down on them for all to see. [9]

丨　冂　冃　日　日⁷　日⁷　日⁷　昭　昭

88. rule   則

The character depicts a *clam* alongside a great and flashing *sabre*. Think of digging for *clams* in an area where there are gaming **rules** governing how large a find has to be before you can keep it. So you take your trusty *sabre,* which you have carefully notched like a yardstick, crack open a *clam* and then measure the poor little beastie to see if it is as long as the **rules** say it has to be. [9]

丨　冂　冃　冃　目　貝　貝　則　則

* wealth

In service of the following frame, we may introduce here a somewhat
rare primitive meaning **wealth**. It takes its meaning from the
common image of the over-**wealthy** as over-fed. More specifically,
the kanji shows us *one* single *mouth* devouring all the harvest of the
fields, presumably while those who labor in them go hungry. Think
of the phrase exactly as it is written when you draw the character,
and the disposition of the elements is easy. [9]

89. vice-

The key-word **vice-** has the sense of someone second-in-command.
The great and flashing *sabre* to the right (its usual location, so you
need not worry about where to put it from now on) and the *wealth* on
the left combine to create an image of dividing one's property to give
a share to one's **vice-***wealth*holder. [11]

90. separate

In the Old East, the samurai and his *sabre* were never **separated**.
They were constant companions, like the cowboy of the Old West and
his six-shooter. This character depicts what must have been the
height of **separation**-anxiety for a samurai: to be *tied up with a rope*
and unable to get at his *sabre* leaning only a few feet away from him.
Look at that *mouth* bellowing out for shame and sorrow!

Note the order in which the element for *tied up* is written—just as it
had been with the character for *ten thousand*. [7]

91. street

The picture here is of a **street**-sign on a long pole: Hollywood and
Vine, if you please, or any **street** that immediately conjures up the

image of a **street**-sign to you. [2]

* Used as a primitive, we change the meaning of the key-word and take the shape to signify a *nail* or a *spike*. Should it happen, on reviewing, that you find the pictographs get jumbled, then think of jerking a *street*-sign out of the ground and using it as a *nail* to repair your garage roof.

---

92. village   町

Street-signs standing at the corner of the *rice-fields* depict the **village-limits**. (Remember what was said earlier: when used as a primitive, a kanji may either take its primitive meaning or revert to the original meaning of its key-word.) [7]

---

93. can   可

Remember the story about the "Little Engine that **Could**" when you hear this key-word, and the rest is simple. See the determined little locomotive huffing and puffing up the mountain, spitting railroad *spikes* out of its *mouth* as it chews up the line to the top. [5]

---

94. place on the head   頂

The key-word is actually a formal metaphor meaning "humble acceptance." Reading off the two primitive elements in the order of their writing, we have: *nail . . . head.* As in "hitting the *nail* on the *head*. Now one presumes that most people can handle metaphors, but if you were to run into a dimwit working in a hardware store who only knew the literal meaning of things, and were to ask him, in your best Japanese, to **place on your head** *a nail*, he might conceivably miss the point and cause you considerable torment. [11]

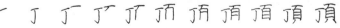

LESSON 6

The last group of primitives took us pretty far, and probably forced you to pay more attention to the workings of imagination. In this lesson we shall concentrate on primitives that have to do with people.

As you were reminded in Frame 92, even those kanji that are given special meanings as primitives may also retain their key-word meaning when used as primitives. This is done not only because it is convenient for making stories, but also because it helps to reinforce the original meaning of the character.

95. child 子

This kanji is a pictograph of a **child** wrapped up in one of those handy cocoons that Japanese mothers fix to their backs to carry around young **children** who cannot get around by themselves. The first stroke is like a wee head popping out for air; the second shows the body and legs all wrapped up; and the final stroke shows the arms sticking out to cling to the mother's neck. [3]

  * As a primitive, the meaning of *child* is retained, though you might imagine them a little older, able to run around and get in more mischief.

96. cavity 孔

Probably the one thing most *children* fear more than anything else is the dentist's chair. Once a *child* has seen a dentist holding the x-rays up to the light and heard that ominous word **cavity**, even though it is not likely to know that the word means "hole" until it is much older, it will not be long before those two syllables get associated with the drill and that row of shiny *hooks* the dentist uses to torture people who are too small to fight back. [4]

ㄱ 孑 孑 孔

97. complete

了

Learn this character by returning to Frame 95 and the image given there. The only difference is that the "arms" have been left off (actually, only tucked inside). Thus a *child* with its arms wrapped up into the back-sack is the picture of a job successfully **completed**. [2]

98. woman

女

You have probably seen somewhere the form of a squatting **woman** drawn behind this character, with two legs at the bottom, two arms (the horizontal line) and the head poking out the top. A little far fetched, until you draw the character and feel the grace and flow of the three simple strokes. Remembering the kanji is easy; learning to write it beautifully is another thing. [3]

* The primitive meaning is the same: *woman.*

99. fond

好

The phrase, to be **fond** of someone has a natural gentleness about it, and lends a sense of tenderness to the sense of touching by giving us the related term "to **fond**le." The character likens it to a woman **fond**ling her *child.* [6]

100. likeness

如

Pardon me if I revert to the venerable old Dr. Freud again, but his eye for symbolism is often helpful to appreciate things which more earthy imaginations once accepted more freely but which we have learned to cover over with a veneer of etiquette. For instance, the fact that things like the *mouth* of a cave served as natural ritual substitutes for the opening through which a *woman* gives birth.

Hence, in order to be reborn as an adult, one may have to pass through something that bears a **likeness** to the *mouth* of the womb. [6]

101. mama   母

Look closely at this kanji and you will find the outline of the kanji for *woman* in it, though it has been expanded to make space for the two breasts that make her a **mamma**. The association of this sound to a baby nursing at its mother's breast has afforded some scholars of comparative linguistics a way to explain the presence of the same word across a wide range of language-groups. [5]

* As a primitive we shall add the meaning of *breasts* in accord with the explanation given above. Take careful note of the fact that the form is altered slightly when this kanji serves as a primitive, the final two dots joined together to form a longer stroke. An example follows in the next frame.

102. pierce   貫

If one is asked to think of associations for the word **pierce**, among the first to come to mind is that of **piercing** one's ears to old earrings, a quite primitive form of self-mutilation that has survived into the 20th century. The kanji here is read, top to bottom: *mother . . . oyster.* All you need to do is imagine **piercing** an ear so that it can hold a *mother*-of-pearl you have just wrested from an *oyster.* [11]

103. elder brother   兄

By now kanji like this one should "look like" something to you even though it is more of an "ideogram" than a "pictograph." The large *mouth* on top and the *human legs* below almost jump off the page as a caricature of **elder brother**, the one with the big *mouth* (or if you prefer a kinder image, the one who "has the say" among all the children). [5]

一 冂 口 尸 兄

* As a primitive this character will take the meaning of *teenager,* in accord with the familiar image of the big *mouth* and the gangling, clumsy *legs.*

104. overcome 克

In this frame we get a chance to use the kanji we just learned in its primitive meaning of *teenager.* The *needle* on top indicates one of the major problems confronting the *teenager* growing up in today's world: drugs. Many of them will fall under the shadow of the *needle* at some time during those tender years, but only when a whole generation rises up and decides that "We Shall **Overcome**" the plague, will the *needle* cease to hang over their heads, as it does in this character. [7]

LESSON 7

In this lesson we turn to primitive elements having to do with quantity. We will also introduce a form known as a "cliff," a sort of overhead "enclosure" that comes in a variety of shapes. But let us begin slowly and not get ahead of ourselves, for it is only after you have mastered the simple forms that the apparently impenetrable complexities of later primitives will dissolve. The primitives we give here will immediately suggest others, based on what we have already learned. Hence the somewhat haphazard order among the frames of this lesson.

105. little 小

The sense of **little** which this character represents is not the same as "a little bit." That meaning comes in the next frame. Here **little** means "small" or "tiny." The image is actually of three *little drops,* the first of which (the one in the middle) is written larger so that the kanji has some shape to it. The point of writing it three times is to rub the point in: **little, little,** nothing but **little.** [3]

* The primitive of the same shape keeps the same meaning. Drawn above a horizontal line, its form is slightly altered, the last two strokes turning inwards, like this ᵛ .

106. few

First we need to look at the fourth stroke, the *drop* at the bottom which has been extended into a longer diagonal stroke. This happens because a single, isolated drop will NEVER appear beneath its relative primitive in its normal size, for fear it would drop off and get lost. As for the meaning, let the tiny *drop* indicate a further belittling of what is already *little*—thus making it a **few** of something *little*. [4]

107. large

Here we have a simple pictograph of a person, taking up the space of an entire character and giving it the sense of **large.** It shouldn't be hard to locate the two legs and outstretched arms. [3]

* As a primitive, we need a different meaning, since the element representing the human person will come up later. Hence, this shape will become a *large dog* or, if you prefer, a *St. Bernard dog.* In Frame 238 we will explain why this choice was made.

* cliff

This primitive means precisely what it looks like: a steep **cliff.** You can almost see someone standing at the top looking down into the abyss below. [2]

⼀ ⼚

108. many

"**Many** *moons* ago," begins much of Amerindian folklore—a colorful way of saying "Once upon a time" and a great deal of help for remembering this kanji. Here we have two *moons* (three of them would take us back to the beginning of time, which is further than we want to go), lacking the final stroke because they are partially hidden behind the clouds of time. [6]

109. evening

Just as the word **evening** adds a touch of formality or romanticism to the ordinary word "night," so the kanji for **evening** takes the ordinary looking *moon* in the night sky and has a cloud pass over it (as we saw in the last frame). [3]

* The primitive keeps the same meaning and connotation as the kanji.

110. eventide

In the next lesson we will meet the character for morning-*tide* and the element for *drops of water*. But let's get ahead of ourselves this once to learn an uncommon but simple kanji. Playing on the key-word, we can see the *drops of water* inching their way ashore in the *evening*. [6]

111. outside

On the left, the primitive for *evening;* and on the right, that for the *magic wand*. Now as every magician worth his abracadabra knows, bringing your *magic wand* out into the *evening* air makes your magic much more powerful than if you were to stay indoors. Hence, *evening* and *magic wand* takes you naturally **outside**. [5]

ノ ク タ タ| 外

112. name   名

Perhaps you have heard of the custom, still preserved in certain African tribes, of a father creeping into the tent or hut of his new-born child on the night of the child's birth, to whisper into its ear the **name** he has chosen for it, before making his choice public. It is an impressive **naming** custom and fits in tidily with the way this character is constructed: *evening . . . mouth*. At *evening* time, a *mouth* pronounces the **name** that will accompany one throughout life. [6]

ノ ク タ 夕 名 名

113. stone   石

With a *mouth* under a *cliff,* what else could we have here but the entrance to a secret cavern, before which a great **stone** has been rolled so that none may enter. Perhaps it is the hiding place where Ali Babba and his band of thieves have stored their treasures, in which case that magic word known to every school child who ever delighted over the tales of the Arabian Nights should be enough to push the **stone** aside. But take care—the *cliff* is steep, and one slip will send you tumbling down into the ravine below. [5]

    This is the one and only time that the second stroke in *cliff* will reach over to the middle of the horizontal stroke. If you think of the edge jutting outwards (in keeping with the story above), the problem should be taken care of.

一 厂 厂 石 石

* The *stone* is a quite common primitive element, for which we need not restrict ourselves to great boulders but can use *stones* of any size or shape.

114. resemblance

The word **resemblance** should suggest, among other things, a son's **resemblance** to his father. A "chip off the old block" is the way we often put it, but the character is more simple. It speaks of a *small* bit of *flesh.* [7]

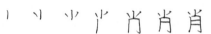

* When used as a primitive, the sense of *resemblance* is replaced with that of *spark* or *candle.* (If you want an explanation: the kanji for moon also carries a secondary sense of fire, which we omitted because we are keeping that meaning for other primitives.)

---

115. nitrate

The word **nitrate** should immediately suggest a beaker of **nitric** acid which, as every high-school chemistry student knows, can eat its way through some pretty tough substances. Here we imagine pouring it over a *rock* and watching the *sparks* fly as it bores a hole through the *rock.* [12]

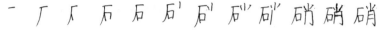

---

116. smash

We begin with the two elements on the right, *baseball* and *needle.* Since they will be coming together from time to time, let us give the two of them the sense of a game of cricket in which a *needle* is laid across the wicket. Then imagine using a *rock* for a ball. A **smash** hit would probably splinter the bat in all directions, and a **smashing** pitch would do the same with the *needle* wicket. [9]

---

117. sand

Good **sand** for beaches has *few* or no *stones* in it. That means that all of us whose feet have been spoiled by too much time in shoes don't have to watch our step as we cavort about. [9]

---

118. plane

Long before the invention of the carpenter's **plane**, people used knives and machetes (or here, *swords*) to smoothe out their woodwork. If you have ever seen the process, you will have been amazed at the speed and agilty with which the adept can **plane** a hunk of wood into shape. Indeed, you can almost see the *sparks* fly from their *swords*. [9]

---

119. ray   光

There are really only 2 primitives here, *small* and *human legs*. The 4th stroke that separates them is added for reasons of aesthetics. (If that doesn't make sense, trying write the kanji without it and see how ugly the results look, even to your beginner's eye.) Now if you have wondered what those little particles of "dust" are that dance around in the light-**rays** that come through the window and fall on your desk, try imagining them as *small* and disembodied *human legs,* and you should have no trouble with this character. [6]

| 丨 | 丶丨 | 丷 | 业 | 屮 | 光 |

---

120. plump   太

"**Plump**" is one of those delightful English words that sound like their meaning. No sooner do you hear it than you think of a round and ample-bodied woman falling into a sofa like a *large drop* of oil plopping into a fishbowl—kerrrr-**plump**! [4]

一 ナ 大 太

---

121. utensil   器

The picture in this kanji may not be a pleasant one. It shows a large and fluffy **St. Bernard dog** stretched out on a table all stuffed and stewed and garnished with vegetables, its paws in the air and an apple in its mouth. At each corner of the table sits an eager but empty *mouth,* waiting for the **utensils** to arrive so the feast can begin. [15]

哭 器 器

122. stinking 臭

This character is a bit friendlier to the animal world. Our friend the *St. Bernard* is alive and well, his *nose* in the air sniffing suspiciously after something **stinking** somewhere or other. [9]

123. exquisite 妙

The primitive for *woman* is on the left (there and at the bottom of another primitive is where you will always find her), and to the right the element for few. When we refer to a *woman* as looking **exquisite**, we have it in mind to pay her a compliment for being of a kind we meet but *few* and far between. To be pedantic about it, the Latin word at the root of the word exquisite carries this sense of "seeking out" the rare from the ordinary. [7]

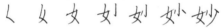

124. focus 省

When we think of **"focusing on"** something, we usually take it in a metaphorical sense, though the literal sense is not far behind. It means to block out what is non-essential in order to fix our *eye* on a *few* important matters. The kanji suggests picking up a *few* things and holding them before one's *eye* in order to **focus** on them better. [9]

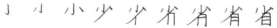

125. thick 厚

When we refer to someone as **thick**-skinned or **thick**-headed, we are usually quick to add—even if only under our breath—something about their upbringing, since we cherish the belief that by nature people are basically tender and sensitive. The Japanese character for **thick** depicts a *child* abandoned out on the wild *cliffs,* exposed to the heat of the *sun,* and thus doomed to develop a head and skin as thick as the parent who left it there. [9]

一 厂 厂 厂 戶 戶 厚 厚 厚

126. strange

The elements we are given to work with here are *St. Bernard dog* and *can*. Since the latter is too abstract, let us return to its elements: a *mouth* with *nails*. Now all we need do is create a fictitous "Strange But True" column in the Sunday funnies, featuring a *St. Bernard* whose *mouth* has been *nailed* shut because he was hitting the brandy keg around his neck too hard. [8]

一 ナ 大 太 产 奇 奇 奇

LESSON 8

Four basic elements, it was once believed, make up the things of our universe: earth, wind, fire, and water. We have already met the element for wind, and now we shall introduce the others, one by one, in a somewhat lengthy lesson. Fortunately for our imaginations, these suggestive and concrete primitives play a large role in the construction of the kanji, and will help us create some vivid pictures to untangle some of the complex jumbles of strokes that follow.

127. stream   川

We have taken the image of a river **stream** over into English to describe things that fall down in straight lines, or ripple along in lines. All of this is more than evident in the kanji given here, a pictograph of a **stream**. [3]

丿 丿丨 丿丨丨

> * As a primitive, this character adds to the meaning of *stream* the more vivid image of a *flood*. Note, however, that there are certain small changes in the writing of the element, depending on where

it appears relative to other elements:
    on the left, it is written 川
    on the top, it is written   巛
    on the bottom, it is written   川

---

128. state   州

Here we see *drops of* land (little islets) rising up out of a *stream,*
creating a kind of sandbar or natural breakwater. Ever wonder how
the **state-line** is drawn between **states** separated by a river? If there
were little *drops of* land as in this kanji, there'd be nothing to it. [6]

丶 丿 丬 州 州 州

---

129. obey   順

In primitive language, this character would read *stream . . . head*. And
that turns out to be convenient for remembering its meaning of obey.
Either one **obeys** the person who is *head* of an organization or else
obeys by following the *stream* of opinion ("current" practice, we call
it). Both these senses come together in this kanji. [12].

丿 刂 川 川 川 川 順 順 順 順 順 順

---

130. water   水

This character, which looks a bit like a snowflake, is actually a pictograph of **water**—not any particular body of water or movement of
water, but simply the generic name for **water**. Should you have any
difficulty remembering it, simply think of a *walking cane* being
dropped vertically into the *water,* sending *droplets* out in all four
directions. Then all you need to learn is how to write it in proper
order. [4]

* As a primitive, this character can keep its form, or it can be represented by three dots written to the left of another primitive, like
this: 冫 . This latter is more normal, as we shall see later in this
lesson.

131. icicle

The primitive for *water* in its full form tells us that we have something to do with *water* here. The extra dot to the left added as a second stroke changes the picture from a splash caused by a cane dropped into water to form an **icicle**. If you hold an **icicle** up to the light, you can usually see little crystallizations of five-pointed stars inside of it, which is the shape we have in this kanji. [5]

132. eternity

This kanji also uses the full form of *water,* though its meaning seems to have nothing at all to do with *water.* Remember what William Blake said about seeing "infinity in a grain of sand and **eternity** in an, hour"? Well, reading this character from top to bottom, we see "**eternity** in a *drop of water.*" [5]

133. spring

Call to mind the image of a fresh, bubbling **spring** of *water,* and you will probably notice how the top of the **spring** you are thinking of, the part where the "bubbling" goes on, is all *white.* Happily, the *white* is just where it should be, at the top, and the *water* is at the bottom. [9]

* We will keep this image of a *spring* when using this kanji as a primitive, but would only draw attention to the fact that its form is slightly abbreviated: the two small *drops* at the bottom replace the fuller lines that appear in the kanji for *water,* giving us 泉.

134. meadow

Though the kanji is broad enough to embrace both meanings, the **meadow** you should imagine here is not a flatland plain but a mountain **meadow** in the Austrian Alps (perhaps the opening scene of "The Sound of Music" will help). Simply think of little *springs* bubbling up across the **meadow** to form a sort of path that leads you right to the brink of a precipitous *cliff.* Now if you can see someone skipping along merrily, dodging in and out of the *springs,* and then falling headlong over the *cliff,* you have a grizzly story that should help fix this kanji in memory. [10]

135. petition   願

A *meadow* and a *head* is all we are given to work with in the kanji for **petition.** Since the key-word already suggests something like a formal request made of some higher power, let us imagine a gigantic Wizard-of-Oz *head* located in the middle of the flowery *meadow* we used in the last frame. Then just picture people kneeling hopefully before it **petitioning** for whatever it is they want. (The scarecrow wanted brains, the lion, courage, and the tin man a heart. What about you?) [19]

136. swim   泳

The primitive to the left, you will recall from Frame 130, represents *water.* To the right, we see the kanji for *eternity.* Knowing how much children like **swimming,** what could be a better image of *eternal* bliss than an endless expense of *water* to **swim** in without a care in the world? [8]

`   ヽ    ヽ   ジ  ジ  汀  汋  泳  泳`

137. marsh   沼

Unlike the meadow with its cliffs, the **marsh**-lands are low and near a source of *water* that feeds them until they are soggy through and through. Why certain land becomes **marshy** is probably due to the fact that it felt thirsty, and so tried its best to *seduce* the *water* over to its side. But, like most inordinate *seductions,* the last state of the victim is worse than the first. Hence the slushy **marsh.** [8]

`   ` シ ゛ シ 氵 沼 沼 沼 沼 沼

---

138. open sea   沖

This kanji could hardly be simpler. The key-word **open sea** readily suggests being out *in the middle of* a great body of *water.* Thinking of it in this way should avoid confusion with the kanji for "open" which we will meet later on. [7]

`   ` ゛ シ 氵 氵 氵 沖 沖

---

139. creek   江

Unlike the river, the ocean, the lake, and the pond, the **creek** is often no more then a dribble of *water* trickling down a small gulley. While the geological history of the larger bodies of *water* is hard to surmise sometimes, all of us know from our childhood how **creeks** are made, and probably even dug one or two in our time. All you need to do is find a mainstream of *water* somewhere and dig a little path into dry land. The **creek** is thus a lesson in *water-craft,* as this kanji would agree. [6]

`   ` ゛ シ 氵 汀 江 江

---

140. soup   汁

To make **soup,** one begins with *water* and then starts adding things to it, often leftovers from the icebox. This is how the thick **soup** or stew called "seven-in-one" is made. This kanji does it three better, giving us a *ten*-ingredient soup. [5]

`   ` ゛ シ 氵 汁

---

141. tide   潮

Before we get to explaining this character, take a look at it and see if you can figure out the primitive elements on your own ... On the left is the *water*—that much is easy. On the right we have only one primitive, the kanji for *morning* learned back in Frame 52. See how an apparently complex kanji falls apart neatly into manageable pieces?

To get the meaning of the key-word **tide**, just think of it in connection with the character for *eventide* which we learned back in Frame 110. Here we have the *morning*-**tide**, its complement.

By the way, if you missed the question about the number of primitives, it is probably because you forgot what we said earlier about kanji becoming primitives, independently of the pieces that make them up. As a rule, look for the largest kanji you can write and proceed from there to primitives stranded and on their own. [15]

` ＼ ⟩ ⟩ 氵 氵 沽 泸 浐 渖 渖 潮

潮 潮 潮

---

142. source   源

With the advice of the last frame in mind, it is easy to see *water* and *meadow* in this character for **source**. Both in its etymology (it has a common parent with the word "surge") and in popular usage, **source** suggests the place *water* comes from. In this kanji, it is under the *meadow,* where we just saw it breaking the surface in those bubbly little springs. [13]

` ＼ ⟩ 氵 汇 沉 沪 沪 沪 源

源 源

---

143. lively   活

When we speak of a **lively** personality or a **lively** party, we immediately think of a lot of chatter. This kanji depicts the idea of **lively** by having *tongues* babble and splash around like flowing *water*. [9]

` ＼ ⟩ 氵 汗 汗 浐 活 活

---

144. extinguish   消

Among the many things *water* is useful for is *extinguishing* fires.

First of all, take the *water* at the left as the *drops of water* that are used to depict *water* in general. In the best of all possible worlds, the the most efficient way to **extinguish** a fire would be to see that each *drop of water* hits one *spark* of the conflagration. An unthinkable bit of utopian fire-fighting, you say to yourself, but helpful for assigning this key-word its primitives. [10]

丶　一　氵　氵'　氵'′　氵″　沪　沪　消　消

---

145. but of course   況

This key-word is a connector used to link contrasting phrases and sentences together with much the same flavor as the English phrase, **but of course.** Just picture yourself ready to go off on your first date as a *teenager,* and having your mother grill you about your manners and ask you embarrassing questions about your hygiene. "Did you have a good shower?" "**But of course** . . ." you reply, annoyed. So *water* and *teenager* combine to give us **but of course.** [8]

丶　一　氵　氵'　沪　沪　沪　況

---

146. river   河

The character in this frame represents a step up from the *stream* we met in Frame 127; it is a full-sized **river.** The *water* to the left tells us what we are dealing with, and the *can* at the right tells us that our "little engine that *could"* has now gone amphibious and is chugging down the Mighty Mississip' like a regular riverboat. [8]

丶　一　氵　氵一　沪　沪　沪　河

---

147. overnight   泊

When you stop at an inn for an **overnight** rest, all you expect is a bit of *water* for a wash and a set of clean *white* sheets to wrap your weary bones in. [8]

丶　一　氵　氵′　氵′　泊　泊　泊

148. lake

Water . . . old . . . flesh. You have heard of legends of people being abandoned in the mountains when they had become too old to work. Well, here is a legend about people being set adrift in the *waters* of a stormy **lake** because their *flesh* had gotten too *old* to bear the burdens of life. [12]

` ⺀ ⺭ 汁 汁 沽 沽 湖 湖 湖 湖

149. fathom

Connoting to measure the depth of *water,* the key-word **fathom** begins with the *water* primitive. To its right, we set the compound-primitive for *rule* (Frame 88) which we learned in the sense of a "ruler" or "measure." Hence, when we *rule water* we **fathom** it. What could be simpler? But be careful; its simplicity is deceptive. Be sure to picture yourself **fathoming** a body of *water* several hundred feet deep by using a *ruler* of gargantuan proportions. [12]

` ⺀ ⺭ 氵 氿 沮 泪 泪 泪 測 測 測

150. soil

土

I don't like it any more than you do, but this kanji is not the pictograph it is trumped up to be: a mound of **soil** piled on the ground. All I can recommend is that you memorize it as it is. Anyway, it will be occurring with such frequency that you have almost no chance of forgetting it, even if you try. [3]

* As a primitive, the sense of *soil* is extended to that of *ground* because of its connection with the kanji for the same (Frame 515). From there it also takes the added meanings of *dirt* and *land.*

151. spit

We have here a rather small *mouth* (it is always compressed when set on the left) next to a much larger piece of *dirt.* It is not hard to

imagine what you might do if you got a *mouth* full of *dirt*. As least I
know what I would do: **spit** it out as fast and far as I could! [6]

｜　口　口　口　吐　吐

---

152. pressure

圧

One of the things that causes the erosion of *soil* is the excessive
pressure of the top*soil* on the lower *soil*. This can be caused by any
number of things from heavy rainfall to heavy buldings to the
absence of sufficient deep-rooted vegetation to hold the layers
together. Here we see a steep *cliff* without a tree in sight. The slight-
est **pressure** on it will cause a landslide, which you can almost see
happening in this character. [5]

一　厂　厂　厈　圧

---

153. cape

埼

The **cape** pictured here is a jut of *land* like **Cape** Cod. The *soil* on the
left tells us we have to do with *land,* and the *strange* on the right tells
us it is a **cape** where unusual things go on. Put a haunted house on it,
an eerie sky overhead, and a howling wind rustling through the trees,
and you have yourself a picture of **Cape** *Strange.* [11]

一　十　土　圤　圹　圿　圹　埣　埼　埼　埼

---

154. hedge

垣

The **hedge** depicted in this frame is the miraculous **hedge** of briar
roses that completely *spanned* the castle *grounds* in which Sleeping
Beauty lay for a hundred years, so that none but her predestined
beloved could find their way through it. [9]

一　十　土　圹　圹　圻　垣　垣　垣

---

155. square jewel

圭

Now I am going to do something unusual. The character in this frame
is going to get one meaning and the primitive another, with no

relation at all between the two. In time, I hope you will see how helpful this is.

The kanji key-word, **square jewel**, depicts a mammoth precious stone, several feet high, made by piling up large heaps of *soil* on top of one another. Not something you would want to present your beloved on your wedding day, but a good image for remembering this rare character, used chiefly in personal names nowadays. [6]

> * As a primitive, we shall use this character to mean *ivy*, that creepy vegetation that covers the surface of the *ground* to form a sort of "second" *ground* that can get somewhat tricky to walk on without tripping.

156. seal   封

Think of the key-word, **seal**, as referring to a letter you have written and are preparing to close. Instead of using the traditional wax-**seal**, you *glue* a sprig of *ivy* on the outside. In this way the elements *ivy* and *glue* give you a curious and memorable way to **seal** your secret letters. [9]

157. horizon   涯

After seeing a constant **horizon** of *water, water* everywhere for months at sea, could there be anything more delightful to the eyes than to look astern and see the *ivy*-clad *cliffs* of land on a new **horizon**? Of course, you'd need the eyes of a stellar telescope to recognize that the vegetation was in fact *ivy*, but the phrase "*ivy*-clad *cliffs*" has such a nice ring to it that we won't worry about such details. [11]

158. Buddhist temple   寺

You have heard of people "attaching" themselves to a particular sect? Here is your chance to take that metaphor literally and imagine some

fellow walking into a **Buddhist temple** with a fervent resolve to
attach himself to the place. Since there is plenty of unused *land*
around the precincts, he simply picks out a suitable patch, brushes
the soles of his feet with *glue* and so joins the **Buddhist temple** as a
"permanent member." [6]

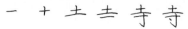

159. time   時

"What is **time**?" asked St. Augustine in his memoirs. "Ask me not, and I
know. Ask me, and I cannot tell you." Here we have the kanji's
answer to that perennial riddle. Time is a *sun* rising over a *Buddhist
temple.* That sounds almost like a Zen kōan whose repetition might
yield some deep secret to the initiated. At any rate, imagining a monk
seated in meditation pondering it might help us remember the
character. [10]

160. level   均

The "level" this key-word refers to is not the carpenter's tool but
rather the even surface of a thing. It pictures *soil* being scooped up
into a *ladle* and then made *level* (apparently because one is measuring
soil). The excess *drops of soil* are brushed off the top, which accounts
for the added *drop* at the *ladle's* edge. [7]

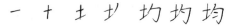

161. fire   火

Just as sitting before a **fire** enlivens the imagination and lets you see
almost anything you want to in the flames, this kanji is so simple it
lets you see almost any sort of **fire** you want to see. It no longer makes
a good pictograph, but I invite you to take a pencil and paper and
play with the form—first writing it as shown below and then adding
lines here and there—to see what you can come up with. Everything
from matchbooks to cigarette lighters to volcanic eruptions to the
destruction of Sodom and Gomorrah have been found here. No doubt
you, too, will find something interesting to bend your memory

around these four simple strokes. [4]

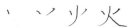

> * To avoid confusion with other characters and primitives, it is best
> to keep to the meaning of a *fireplace* (or *hearth*) or a raging
> *conflagration* like a forest-fire or a towering inferno for this
> kanji. To complicate matters only slightly, there is another primi-
> tive element for *fire* based on this one. It is written ,,,, and refers
> to a *cooking-fire* or an *oven-fire*.

162. inflammation

A *fire* belongs IN the *hearth,* not OVER it. When the *fire* spreads to the
rest of the house, we have an **inflamed** house. And as with any
inflammation—including those that attack our bodies—the danger is
always that it might spread if not checked. This is the sense behind
the reduplication of the kanji for *fire*. [8]

163. anxiety

The existential condition of **anxiety** that arises from the inevitable
frustration of our worldly passions is contained in this character.
The *head* is set *aflame,* causing deep torment of spirit (and a whopper
of a headache). [13]

164. thin

The primitives in this kanji read: *water . . . inflammation*. Taking
inflammation in its medical sense, the first *water*-related *inflammation*
that pops into mind is dehydration, the principal symptom of which
is that it makes one shrivel up and look very, very **thin**. If that is
hard to remember, try thinking it backwards: a very **thin** chap passes
by and you imagine him suffering from (being *inflamed* with)
dehydration (hence the element for *water*). [11]

丶 丶 氵 氵 氵 氵 氵 氵 氵 氵 淡

165. lamp 灯

Since it is very hard to read by the *fireplace* without going blind from the flickering of the flames or burning up from the heat, our ancestors invented a way to *nail* down a bit of that *fire,* just enough to light up their evening newspapers and no more. Voilà! The **lamp.** [6]

丶 丶 丷 火 灯 灯

166. farm 畑

Looking at the primitives, a *fireplace* and a *rice-field,* we find the essential ingredients for a **farm**: a warm *hearth* to sit by at night, and a well-plowed *field* to grow one's crops in by day. [9]

丶 丷 丷 火 㷧 灯 畑 畑 畑

167. disaster 災

Of all of nature's **disasters,** this kanji picks out two of the worst: *floods* and *fires.* To recall the disposition of the elements, think of nature's solution to nature's own problem: a great *flood* pouring down over a great forest-*fire.* [7]

〈 《 巛 巛 災 災 災

168. ashes 灰

The kanji for **ashes** naturally includes the primitive for *fire,* or more specifically, a *fireplace.* Now what do you do with that bucket of **ashes** you have just cleaned out of the *fireplace*? You walk to the edge of a *cliff* and tip it upside down, watching as they are swept away in the wind like a swarm of grey mosquitos. Thus the *fire,* once it has turned to **ashes,** ends up at the bottom of the *cliff.* [6]

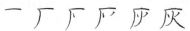

169. spot

If you look into the flickering of a *fire* for a long time and then turn aside, you will see **spots** before your eyes. Although nobody ever thought of such a thing before—as least as far as I know they didn't—imagine using those **spots** as a technique for *fortune-telling*. The witch sits before her cauldron-*fire* and watches the **spots** that show up when she turns to look at you, and from that *tells your fortune*. [9]

170. illuminate

Although the range of possible meanings which the kanji for **illuminate** can have is about as rich as the connotations of the English word, we focus on one sense: to make something *shine*. If you glaze a pot and put it into the *oven* to *fire* it, you in fact **illuminate** it. Hence the kanji for **illuminate** compares the kanji for *shining* with the primitive element for the *oven's fire*. [13]

171. fish

The composition of this kanji shows three elements, which we list in the order of their writing: *bound up . . . rice-field . . . cooking-fire*. We can join them together by thinking of a three-part story: first a **fish** is caught and *bound up* on a line with its unfortunate school-mates; when the fisherman gets home, he cuts off the head and tosses it, with the entrails, out into the *rice-fields* for fertilizer; and the rest he sets in a skillet over a *cooking-fire* for his supper. [11]

172. fishing

To the story we have just made about *fish*, this kanji for the profession of **fishing** adds yet another element BEFORE the others:

namely the *water,* where the fish was happily at home before being caught, disemboweled, and eaten. [14]

丶 丶 氵 氵 氵 氵 泮 渔 渔 渔 渔 渔
渔 渔

LESSON 9

Although the study of the four basic elements undertaken in the last lesson brought us a lot of new characters—46 in all—we have but scratched the surface as far as water, earth, wind, and fire are concerned. Perhaps by now it is clear why I said that we are lucky that they appear so frequently. The range of images they suggest is almost endless.

At any rate, let us carry on with new "roof" and "enclosure" primitives. But first, a primitive-kanji that we might have included in the last group but omitted so as not to get distracted from the four elements.

173. ri   里

That's right—a **ri.** Don't bother looking it up in your English dictionary; it's a Japanese word for measuring distances. One **ri** is about 4 kilometers or 2-1/2 miles. The kanji depicts how the measure came to be used. Atop we see the *rice field,* and below the element for *land.* Those four sections you see in the *rice field* (and which we made mention of when first we introduced the character in Frame 14) are actually measurements of *land,* much the same as farm-sections in the United States have given us the notion of a "country mile." The *land* division based on the size of a *rice field* is called a **ri.** [7]

  * To get a more concrete primitive meaning for this kanji, we shall refer to it as a *computer,* a meaning deriving from the kanji for *logic* which we will meet in Lesson 12.

174. black   黒

Like most things electrical, a *computer,* too, can overheat. Just ima-gine *flames* pouring out of it and charring the keyboard, the monitor, and your desk a dark, sooty **black** color. [11]

丶　冂　冃　日　日　甲　甲　里　里　黒　黒　黒

175. black ink   墨

Besides meaning **black ink,** this kanji also appears in the word for an inked string which is **pulled taut and then snapped to mark a surface,** much the same as one might use a chalked **string**. Here it is used to mark off the *dirt* with lines for a football game. [14]

丶　冂　冃　日　日　甲　甲　里　里　黒　黒　黒

墨　墨

176. carp   鯉

These are the same **carp** you see in Japan's famous **carp**-streamers. Only here we find a small home *computer* or two strung on the line by a father anxious for his son not only to have the courage and determination of a **carp** swimming upstream but also the efficiency and memory of a *computer*. Ugh. [18]

丿　勹　勹　角　角　角　角　魚　魚　魚　魚

鯉　鯉　鯉　鯉　鯉　鯉

177. quantity   量

Think of **quantity** as having to do with measuring time and distance, and the rest is simple: you have a **quantity** of time in the new day that begins with *nightbreak*, and a **quantity** of distance in the rural *ri*. [12]

丶　冂　冃　日　日　旦　昌　昌　昌　昌　量　量

178. rin

No doubt you will find it in your heart to forgive me for forcing yet another Japanese word on you in this frame when you hear that this is the last time it will happen for the rest of the book. One **rin** is equal to about 1/1000 of a yen—or rather was worth that much when it still made economic sense to mint them. While inflation took its toll on this kanji as a monetary unit, it survived with the not at all surprising sense of something "very, very tiny."

The kanji shows a *cliff* with a *computer* under it, apparently because it has been pushed over into the abyss by someone fed up with the thing. The total worth of one home *computer* that has fallen over rock and bramble for several hundred feet: about one **rin**! [9]

一 厂 厓 厓 戻 戻 厔 厙 厘

179. bury 埋

When we speak of **burying** something (or someone, for that matter), we usually mean putting them under*ground*. Only here, we are **burying** our beloved *computer* which has served us so well these past years. Behind us a choir chants the "Dies irae, dies illa" and there is much wailing and grief among the bystanders as they pass by to shovel a little *dirt* into what will be its final resting place. R.I.P. [10]

一 十 土 圠 圹 圹 坥 坥 埋 埋

Before going any further, we might pause a moment to look at precisely WHERE the primitive elements were placed in the kanji of the last frame: the *ground* to the left and the *computer* to the right. Neither of these are absolutely fixed positions. The kanji for *spit* (Frame 151), for instance, puts *ground* on the right, and that for *plains* (Frame 1596) will put the *computer* on the left. While there is no reason to bother memorizing any "rules," a quick glance through a few generalized principles may help. Use them if they help; if not, simply adjust the story for a problem character in such a way as to help you remember the position of the elements relative to one another. In any case, here are the principles:

1. Many kanji used regularly as primitives have a "strong" position or two from which it is able to give a basic "flavor" to the character. For example, *ground* at the left (or bottom) usually

indicates something to do with earth, soil, land, and the like; *fire* at the bottom in the form of the four dots, or at the left in its compressed kanji form, usually tells us we have to do with heat, passion, and the like; a *mouth* at the left commonly signifies something to do with eating, coughing, spitting, snoring, screaming, and so forth. Where these elements appear elsewhere in the kanji, they do not have the same overall impact on its meaning as a rule.

2. Some primitive elements ALWAYS have the same position in a kanji. We saw this earlier in the case of the primitive meaning *head* (Frame 60) and that for the long *sword* (Frame 83), as well as in the three drops of *water* (Frame 130).

3. Enclosures like *cliffs* (see Frame 125) and *bound up* (Frame 63) are always set above whatever it is they enclose. Others, as we shall see later, "wrap up" a kanji from the bottom.

4. All things being equal, the element with the fewer strokes (usually the more common element) has first rights to the "strong" position at the left or bottom. (Note that the left and bottom cannot BOTH be the dominant position in the same character. Either one or the other of them will dominate, usually the left.) The characters for *nitrate* (Frame 115) and *chant* (Frame 21) illustrate the point.

---

* hood   冂

In addition to the basic meaning of **hood**, this shape can be used for a **glass cover**, such as that used to serve "pheasant under glass." Note its difference from the element for *wind:* the second stroke is hooked INWARDS here. To help remember this detail, think of the wind as blowing "out" and a **glass canopy** as keeping something "in." Among the related images suggested by this primitive are: a monk's **cowl**, a riding **hood**, a **helmet**, and an automobile **hood**. [2]

---

180. same   同

The primitives in this kanji show us *one* and *mouth* under a *hood*. Let us take the key-word to connote the **sameness** that characterizes the life in community of the monk. They all have the **same** habits, including the "habit" of the monk's robes. Here we see the monk's *cowl,* drawn down over the eyes so that all you can see when you look at him is a *mouth.* But since monks also speak their prayers in common, it is but a short step to think of *one mouth* under a *hood* as the kanji for the **sameness** of monastic life. [6]

181. den   洞

The key-word **den** refers to an animal lair hollowed out in the side of a mountain. Now if we keep to the image of the monastic life as an image for *same,* we can picture a **den** of wild beasts dressed up in habits and living the common life in a mountain cavern. To bring in the element of *water* we need only give them a sacred "puddle" in the center of their **den,** the focus of all their pious attentions. [9]

` ⸴ ⁒ ⟩ ⟩ 汋 汋 洞 洞 洞

182. trunk   胴

The word **trunk** refers to the *part of the body* that is left when you have "truncated" all the limbs. I can hardly think of any reason for doing so, unless one were lumberjacking corpses and needed to have them all properly pruned and made the *same* so they could be floated downstream without causing a *body*-jam. [10]

丿 几 月 月 刖 刖 肌 朋 胴 胴

183. yonder   向

Something referred to as "over **yonder**" is usually far off in the distance and barely within sight—like a wee *drop* in the distance—and is usually an expression used in giving directions or pointing something out. Hence this kanji begins with a *drop.* Then we find a sort of transparent *helmet* with no eyes or nose, but only a prominent *mouth* under it, obviously an extraterrestrial. And what is it jabbering on about with its *mouth* open like that? Why, about his spaceship way over **yonder,** stranded without fuel. [6]

184. esteem

Above we see the primitive for *small* attached to the *glass canopy*, the sort used to display family heirlooms. The *smallness* is important, because what is in fact on display is the shrunken, stuffed, and mounted *mouth* of an **esteemed** ancestor. We may be used to **esteem**ing the words our forebearers leave behind, but here we also **esteem** the very *mouth* that spoke them. I leave it to you to imagine a suitable place in your room for displaying such an unusual conversation piece. [8]

* house

This extremely useful primitive element depicts the roof of a **house**. You can see the chimney at the top and the eaves on either side without much trouble. It is a "crown" element, which means that it is invariably set atop other things. Examples follow immediately. [3]

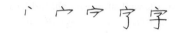

185. character

Here is the character for **character** itself. Not just kanji, but any written character from hieroglyphs to Sanskrit to our own Roman alphabet. It shows us simply a *child* in a *house*. But let us take advantage of the double-meaning of the key-word to note that just as a *child* born to a Japanese *house* is given **characters** for its name, so it is also stamped with the **character** of those who raise it from infancy on. [6]

ヽ　ゝ　宀　字　宁　字

186. guard

The notion of **guarding** something easily brings to mind the image of someone standing **guard**, like the royal soldiers in front of Buckingham Palace or the Pope's Swiss **Guard**. The whole idea of hiring **guards** is that they should stick like *glue* to your *house* to protect it from unwanted molesters. So go ahead and *glue* a **guard** to your *house* in imagination. [6]

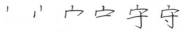

---

187. perfect   完

In order not to confuse the key-word **perfect** with others nearly synonymous in meaning, pull it apart to have a look at its native Latin roots. *Per-factum* suggests something so "thoroughly made or done" that nothing more needs to be added to it. Now look at the kanji, which does something similar. We see a *house* that has been made **perfectly** from its *beginnings* in the foundation to the roof on the top. Now return to Frame 97 and make sure not to confuse this key-word with the kanji for *complete*. [7]

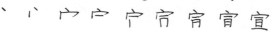

---

188. proclaim   宣

Under the primitive for *house* we meet the kanji for *span*. Think of the key-word in its "evangelical" sense of missionary preaching: **"proclaiming** the good news to all nations" and "shouting it from the *housetops.*" That should be enough to help you remember this simple kanji, used in fact both for advertising and missionary work. [9]

---

189. wee hours   宵

As the key-word hints, the kanji in this frame refers to the late evening or early morning hours, well after one should be in bed asleep. It does this by picturing a *house* with a *candle* in it. The reason is obvious: whoever is living there is "burning the *candle* at both ends," and working night after night into the **wee hours**. [10]

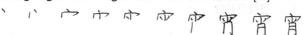

190. relax

To be told that the place of the *woman* is in the *house* may not sit well with modern thought, but like all cultural habits the Chinese characters bear the birthmarks of their age. So indulge yourself in a Norman Rockwell image of **relaxing** after a hard's days work: the scruffy and weary *woman* of the *house* slouched asleep in the living room chair, her hair in curlers and a duster lying in her lap. [6]

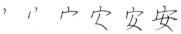

191. banquet

To carry on from the last frame, we note the entire *day* of work that comes between a *woman* and her *house* in preparing for a great dinner **banquet**, pictorially "interrupting" her *relaxation*. [10]

192. draw near

Let the idea of **drawing near** suggest something dangerous or eerie that one approaches with fear and trembling. Here we see a *strange house*—perhaps the haunted *House* of Usher that Edgar Allen Poe immortalized, or the enchanted Gingerbread *House* that lured Hansel and Gretel to **draw near**. [11]

193. wealth

The things we find under the roof of this *house* constitute the family's **wealth**, presumably in an age before banking when people stored their valuables right at home. [12]

194. savings

To avoid confusing this frame with the last one, try to think of
savings as actual money. The only difference is that our currency is
not paper bills but *shells,* a rather common unit of exchange in older
civilizations. The *nail* under the roof of the *house* points to a hiding
place in the rafters on which one strings up one's *shells* for safe
keeping. [12]

丨　冂　冂　月　目　貝　貝　貯`　貯'　貯宀　貯宀　貯宁

LESSON 10

Of the several primitive elements that have to do with plants and grasses,
we introduce two of the most common in this lesson: *trees* and *flowers*. In
most cases, as we shall see, their presence in a "strong" position (to the left
and at the top, respectively) helps give a meaning to the kanji. Where this
is not the case, we shall do our best to MAKE it so.

195. tree   木

Here we see a pictograph of a **tree,** showing the main trunk in the
long vertical stroke and the boughs in the long horizontal stroke. The
final two strokes sweep down in both directions to indicate the roots.
Although it may look similar at first sight to the kanji for *water*
(Frame 130), the order in which it is written is completely different
and this affects its final appearance. [4]

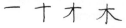

* As a primitive, this kanji can be used to mean *tree* or *wood*. In
those cases where the last two strokes are detached from the trunk
(朩), we shall change its meaning to *pole,* or *wooden pole.*

196. grove

Learn this frame in connection with the next one. A **grove** is a small cluster of *trees*. Hence the simple reduplication of the kanji for *tree* gives us the **grove**. [8]

197. forest 森

A **forest** is a large expanse of *trees*, or "*trees, trees* everywhere," to adopt the expression we used back in Frames 22 and 23. [12]

198. Japanese Judas-tree 桂

Unless you are a botanist, you are not likely to know what a **Japanese Judas-tree** looks like, and probably never even heard of it before, but the name is sufficiently odd to make remembering it easy. Using the primitives as our guide, we define it as a *tree* with *ivy* growing down on its branches in the shape of a hangman's rope. [10]

199. oak

This kanji calls to mind the famous myth of the "golden bough." As you may recall, what made the sacred **oak** in the forest of Diana the Huntress outside of Rome "golden" were the *white* berries of the mistletoe that grew in the branches of the *tree*, presumably appearing yellow when the the light of the sun shone through them. (If you don't know the story, take a break today and hunt it down in a dictionary of myth and fable. Even if you forget the kanji, which of course you won't, the story of the mistletoe and the fate it brought to Balder the Beautiful is most memorable.) [9]

一　十　才　木　术　术　柏　柏　柏

200. frame

枠

You might think of the **frame** this character refers to as the sort of **frame** we have created by drawing a dark line around this kanji and its explanation. Then think of that line as made of very thin *wood;* and finally note how each time the line bends it forms a 90° angle, thus giving us the *nine* and the *ten.* [8]

一 十 オ 才 木 朷 朷 枠 枠

201. treetops

梢

As the days grow shorter and shorter, or so the northern European myth goes, the fear grows that the sun will take its leave of us altogether, abandoning the world to total darkness. Fixing *candles* to the branches of evergreen *trees,* it was believed, would lure the sun back (like things attracting like), whence the custom of the lighted tree that eventually found its way into our Christmas customs. The story is a lot longer and more complex than that, but it should help to fix the image of climbing high up into the **treetops** to fix *candles* on the *tree.* [11]

一 十 オ 才 木 朴 朴 柎 梢 梢 梢

202. shelf

棚

One often thinks of books as "good *companions,*" but here it is the **shelf** we store them on that is the *companion.* The reasons should be obvious: it is made of the same stuff, *wood,* and spends a lot more time with them than we do! Here again, be careful not to let the rationality of the explanation get in the way before you turn it into a proper story. [12]

一 十 オ 才 木 机 枏 枏 棚 棚 棚

203. apricot

杏

Since **apricots** can be eaten just as they fall from the *trees,* picture this *mouth* agape at the bottom of a *tree* (just as the elements have it), waiting for **apricots** to fall into it. [7]

204. paulownia   桐

Since you probably don't know what a **paulownia tree** is, we shall let
the key-word suggest the phrase "the Little Brothers of St. **Paulownia**"
and it is a short step to associate the *tree* with the *monks* to its right.
(For the curious, the name of this oriental *tree* really comes from the
Russian Princess, Anna Pavlovna.) [10]

一 十 才 木 material 机 相 桐 桐 桐

205. plant   植

You have no doubt seen how people practicing the Japanese art of
bonzai take those helpless little saplings and twist them into crippled
dwarfs before they have a chance to grow up as they should. The
more proper way to **plant** a young *tree* and give it a fair shake in life
is to set it into the earth in such a way that it can grow up *straight*. [12]

一 十 才 才 material 材 柿 枯 桔 植 植 植

206. wither   枯

What makes a *tree* begin to **wither** up, and perhaps even die, is a kind
of arterio-sclerosis that keeps its sap from flowing freely. Usually
this is due to simple *old* age, as this character shows us. Be sure to
picture a wrinkled *old tree,* **withering** away in a retirement center so
that the commonsense explanation doesn't take over. [9]

一 十 才 木 material 材 material 枯 枯

207. crude   朴

As all magicians who have passed their apprenticeship know, one
makes one's *wand* out of a hazel branch and is careful not to alter the

natural form of the *wood*. For the magic of the *wand* derives its power from its association with the hidden laws of nature, and needs therefore to be kept in its **crude**, natural state. [6]

---

208. town　村

The character for *village* was associated with *rice fields* (Frame 92). That for **town**, a step up on the evolutionary path to cities, shows a row of *trees* surrounding a certain area to *measure* off the confines of a **town**. [7]

---

209. inter-　相

The prefix **"inter-"** stirs up associations of cooperation among people. From there we read off the elements: *tree . . . eye*. Those two words call to mind the scriptural proverb about first taking the *tree* out of one's own *eye* before helping your neighbors with the splinter in theirs. What more useful rule for **inter**-human relationships, and what more useful tool for remembering this kanji! [9]

一　十　オ　木　木　机　杣　相　相

---

210. desk　机

We need to fix imagination here on two things to learn the kanji for **desk**: the wonderful rough *wood* of which it has been hewn and the *wind* that blows across it, sending your papers flying all over the room. These two elements, written in that order, dictate how to write the character. [6]

一　十　オ　木　朾　机

---

211. book　本

Recalling that **books** are made of paper, and paper made of *trees,* one might think of a **book** as a slice of a *tree*. Can you see the "cross-cut"

in the trunk of the *tree?* Picture it as a chain-saw cutting you out a
few **books** to start your own private library with. [5]

212. tag   札

The **tags** you see hanging on *trees* in public places in Japan are helpful to identify what sort of *trees* they are. Next time you see one,
imagine the bit of wire that fixes the **tag** to the branch as a large *fishhook.* REALLY imagine it, illogical as it is, and you will never have
trouble with this kanji again. [5]

213. calendar   暦

Look at this character in reverse order, from bottom up. First we see
the primitive for *days,* an appropriate enough way to begin a
calendar. Next we see a *grove of trees* growing under a *cliff.* The laws
of nature being what they are, the trees would be stunted under such
conditions, unless they were strong enough to keep growing upwards
until they passed through the layers of rock and soil, right up to the
surface. Now imagine that in those little boxes marking off the *days*
on your wall **calendar,** you see that very process taking place step by
step: 30 or so time-lapse pictures of that *grove of trees* each month,
from January under the *cliff* to December on top of the *cliff.* The
story is not as complex as it sounds, particularly if you happen to
have a **calendar** nearby and can flip through it with this image in
mind. [14]

214. plan   案

Without much effort, the elements *relax . . . tree* suggest a hammock
strung between two *trees* in your back yard, and you stretched out in
it, hands folded behind your head **planning** something or other. After
all, it's something we all do from time to time: kick up our legs on the

nearest piece of furniture and day-dream about the best **plan** of action to take. Only here be sure to relate the *relaxation* to the *tree,* so that you don't end up with something else in its place (like "legs" or "desk" or "table"). [10]

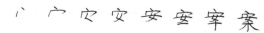

215. parch   燥

Parchment, made from animal skins, was the most common form of writing material used until the beginning of the 19th century. When paper took over, a method was devised to make artificial **parch**ment from *wood* pulp. The fire at the left and in the "strong" position serves to remind us of the root word, **"parch,"** since nothing dries, puckers, wrinkles, and scorches quite like *fire.* And here is how we put it all together. Take a sheet of paper (a *"wood-good,"*), wet it, and hold it over a *hearth* in your mind's eye. Now watch as it **parches** the paper, leaving it with a strange and bumpy surface resembling **parch**ment. [17]

` ˊ 丷 少 火 火 灯 灯 灯 灯 炉 炉 炉
炉 煐 煐 煟 煟 燥 燥

216. not yet   未

As the key-word suggests, this kanji has to do with something not quite over and done with. More concretely, it shows us a *tree* that is **not yet** fully grown. The extra short stroke in the upper branches shows new branches spreading out, leaving one with the feeling that the whole has a ways to go yet before it is completed. In other words, the kanji conveys its meaning pictographically, playing on the previous pictograph of the *tree.* [5]

一 二 十 才 未

217. extremity   末

This character is best learned in connection with that of the previous frame. The first stroke shows a branch that is longer than the main branch, indicating that the *tree* has reached the **extremity** of its growth, so that its branches stop spreading and start drooping downwards. Be sure to keep this imagery in mind, to avoid confusing this key-word with synonyms to appear later. [5]

一 二 十 才 末

218. splash 沫

The **splash** this kanji refers to is the dash of *water* against the rocks, with all the foam and spray that this creates. If you think of a **splash** in this sense as a wave that has run its full course and reached its *extremity,* namely the seashore, and if you think of it pictorially in your mind's eye, this somewhat rare (but oh-so-easy-to-learn) kanji is yours for good. [8]

丶 シ シ シ 氵 汁 沫 沫

219. flavor 味

When a tree has *not yet* finished growing, it produces fruit with a full **flavor**. When the official taster (the professional "*mouth*" to the left) determines that full **flavor** has been reached, the *tree* is pruned back so that it stays permanently *not yet* grown. A neat little agricultural trick and an easy to way see the sense of **flavor** hidden in this character. [8]

丶 口 口 口 叶 吁 吋 味

220. younger sister 妹

The **younger sister** in the family is the *woman* in the family who, like the newest branch in a tree, is *not yet* old enough or mature enough to do everything the elder sister can do (see Frame 413). [8]

く 女 女 女 女 女 妹 妹

221. vermilion 朱

That red-orange color we call **vermilion** is found in nature during the fall when the leaves lose their sugar and begin to change color. This kanji depicts the very last leaf on a tree in the fall (the *drop* hung in the first stroke), the leaf that has *not yet* fallen as it one day must. Look at its color—**vermilion**. (Well, not really. The truth is, **vermilion** is made from a mercuric sulfide, but I'm sure you will agree that autumn leaves are a lot easier to work with.) [6]

ノ　　ト　　ヒ　牛　牛　朱

222. stocks 株

The **stocks** bought and sold on the market by the tens of millions each day get their name from a comparison to a healthy *tree*, in which one takes "**stock**" in the hopes that it will grow and produce more and more *trees* like itself. Usually good **stocks** are referred to as "blue ribbon," but here we are asked to associate the key-word with the color "*vermilion*," as if one could assess the value of a *tree* from the color of its autumn leaves. [10]

一　十　オ　オ　オ゛　木゛　朾　杵　株　株

* flower

We are not yet equipped with all the pieces necessary to study the character for **flower**, so shall have to content ourselves here with the first three strokes, which represent the primitive of the same meaning. Concentrate on the the actual "bloom" of the **flower**, and keep a particular flower in mind—try rose, tulip, or daisy, since none of them will have their own kanji. [3]

一　十　艹

223. young 若

Here we see a *flower* held in the *right* hand. You can imagine yourself in a magic *flower* bed where *flowers* picked with the *right* hand grant eternal **youth**; and those picked with the left, premature senility. Go ahead, pick one with each hand and watch what happens. [8]

一　十　艹　艹　芏　芊　若　若

224. grass   草

Perhaps you know the custom of seeding **grass** randomly or in some
particular pattern with the *flower* called the crocus, which blooms for
a few days *early* each year in spring. As the **grass** begins to turn green
again after winter has passed, these tiny *flowers* dot up here and
there. Now just look out your window at a patch of **grass** somewhere
and think what a nice idea it would be to have your name spelled out
in *flowers* once as a sort of *early* harbinger of spring. [9]

一　十　卄　艹　艹　苧　苩　苩　苴　草

225. suffering   苦

The picture of **suffering** we are given here is that of a *flower* that has
grown *old*. When a *flower* ages, it pales and dries up, and probably
even **suffers**. If you think that plants are incapable of such feelings,
then ask yourself why so many people believe that talking to *flowers*
has a therapeutic effect on them. [8]

一　十　卄　芐　芊　芊　芐　苦

226. tolerant   寛

The *house* of *flowers* or "hothouse" has become a metaphor for a narrow minded, biased, and intolerant attitude distrustful of change.
Tolerance, in contrast, is open-minded and welcomes novelty. The
way to encourage **tolerance** in those who lack it is first to have them
see through their own hothouse attitudes, which is the very counsel
we are given in this kanji. [13]

丶　宀　宀　宀　宁　宁　宁　宵　宵　宵　寏

寏　寛

227. dilute   薄

Take a good look at this kanji: the "strong" element here is really the
flower, not the *water* as you might have thought. In general, things

that "crown" have that privilege. To the right is the *acupuncturist* from Frame 47. Taking the key-word to connote **diluting** the vital humors of the body, we can imagine our *acupuncturist* performing his task with *flowers* in place of needles, and using their hollow stems to pipe *water* into the body of the patient. [16].

一 十 艹 艹 艹 艹 芦 芦 芦 萡 萡 萡 蒲 蒲 薄 薄 薄

228. leaf 葉

Three elements are given here: *flower . . . generation . . . tree.* The first and last seem logical enough, since it is the **leaf** that feeds the *flowers* on a *tree.* The element for *generation* interposed between the two suggests that the movement of a *tree* from one *generation* to the next is like its "turning over a new **leaf.**" [12]

一 十 艹 艹 艹 艹 艹 茁 茁 苹 茸 葉

* graveyard 莫

The element shown here should be taken to represent a modern **graveyard.** Gone are the cobwebs and gnarled trees, the tilted headstones and dark, moonless nights that used to scare the wits out of our childhood imaginations. Instead, we see brightly colored *flowers* placed before the tombstones, the *sun* shining gloriously overhead, and a cuddly great *St. Bernard* sitting at the gate keeping watch. [10]

一 十 艹 艹 芦 芍 苩 苩 莫 莫

229. imitation 模

Ah, but haven't these modern *graveyards* become a parody of their once rich cultural significance! The *flowers* are plastic, the writing on the stones is unimaginative and cold, and the whole thing looks more like a marble orchard than a right and proper *graveyard.* This kanji continues with the modernization trend by picturing **imitation** *trees* in the *graveyard.* But of course, how convenient! They don't need pruning or fertilizing, their leaves don't fall, and they remain the same color all year long. [14]

十 才 才 才 杧 杧 杧 柑 桐 椙 模

模 模

---

230. vague   漠

Think of the key-word as having to do with something viewed
through a haze, or in the twilight and from a distance, so that only its
outlines are **vaguely** discernible. Now we are back again at the
essence of the true *graveyard*. The *water* may be taken as the sound of
waves dashing up against the rocks or the dripping of moisture on
cold rock—anything that helps you associate **vagueness** with the
graveyard and keep it distinct from the *imitation* we met in the last
frame. [13]

丶 丶 氵 氵 氵 汁 汁 沖 洪 消 澊

漠 漠

---

231. grave   墓

The mounds of *soil* with crude wooden crosses set at their head suggests those boot-hill *graveyards* we all know from cowboy lore. The
only odd thing about this kanji is that the *soil* comes UNDER the
graveyard, rather than to its left, where we might expect. Just think
of the bodies as "lying under boot-hill" if you have any trouble.
    By the way, this is not the first time, nor will it be the last, that
we learn whole kanji whose key-words are the same as a primitive
element based on them but whose shape differs somewhat. Again,
there is no cause to worry. By using the primitive in a variety of
other characters, as we have done here, the confusion will be averted
as a matter of course. [13]

一 十 艹 艹 芦 芦 苩 莒 莫 莫 墓

墓 墓

---

232. livelihood   暮

Imagine that you have chosen the occupation of an undertaker or

keeper of a *graveyard* as your life's vocation, the work that will
provide you with a **livelihood**. How odd to make a "livelihood" out of
others' "deadhood"! [14]

一 十 艹 芒 艹 芮 芦 苩 苩 苩 荁 莫 莫 莫 幕

暮 暮

233. membrane   膜

The part of the body first affected by a stroll through a haunted
graveyard is the skin, which gets goose-bumps. But we save the word
"skin" for another kanji, and use the odd word **"membrane"** here.
Think of being so scared through and through that the goose-flesh
moves from the outside in, giving you goose-**membranes**. [14]

丿 几 月 月 月 月 旷 肝 肤 肤 腊

腊 腜 膜

234. seedling   苗

To avoid confusion with the image of rice-planting to appear later
(Frame 1513), we shall take these **seedlings** out of their agricultural
frame into the frame of Brave New World surgery, where "ideas" or
"values" are being implanted into *brains* like **seedlings** to insure a
harmonious society. Then you need only imagine them taking root
and breaking out into *flower* right through of the tops of the skulls of
people walking around on the streets. [8]

一 十 艹 艹 芍 苗 苗 苗

LESSON 11

Now that we are well over 200 characters, it is time to pause and consider
how you are getting on with the method introduced in this book. While this

lesson will be a short one (only 15 new kanji) you might want to spend some time reviewing your progress in the light of the remarks that follow. At the same time, I shall try to draw together the main principles that have been woven into the fabric of the text from frame to frame and lesson to lesson, beginning with some of the problems that can arise:

1. *If you can remember the key-word when you see the kanji, but have trouble remembering the kanji when you have only the key-word to go on . . .*

Probably you did not take seriously the advice about studying these stories with a pad and pencil. If you try to short-cut the process by merely learning to recognize the characters for their meaning without worrying about their writing, you will find that you have missed one bird with two stones, when you could have bagged two with one. Let me repeat: study only from key-word to kanji; the reverse will take care of itself.

2. *If you find yourself having to go back to a kanji, once you have written it, to make corrections or additions . . .*

My guess is that you are asking your visual memory to do the work that belongs to imaginative memory. After Lesson 12, you will be given more leeway to create your own images and stories, so it is important that you nip this problem in the bud before going any further. A small step in the wrong direction on a journey of 2,000 kanji will land you in deep trouble in no time. Here are the steps you should be following each time you come to a new frame:

I   Read the key-word and take note of the **particular connotation** that has been given it. There is only one such meaning, sometimes associated with a colloquial phrase, sometimes with one of the several meanings of the word, sometimes with a widely known cultural phenomenon. Think of that connotation and repeat it to yourself. When you're sure you've got the right one, carry on.

II Read through the particular little story that goes with the key-word and let the **whole picture** establish itself clearly.

III Now close your eyes, focus on those images in the story that belong to the key-word and primitive elements, and **let go of the controls.** It may take a few seconds, sometimes as long as a few minutes, but the picture will start to change on its own. The exaggerated focal points will start to take on a life of their own and enhance the image with your own particular experiences and memories. You will know when this has happened and when you have finally created a memorable image that is both succinct and complete, both faithful to the original story and yet your very own.

IV   Open your eyes and **repeat the key-word and primitive elements,** keeping that image in mind. This will clear away any of the fog, and at the same time make sure that when you let go you didn't let go of the original story too.

V   In your mind, **juxtapose the elements** relative to one another in line with your image or the way they normally appear in the characters.

VI   Take pencil and paper and **write the character once,** retelling the story as you go.

These are basically the same steps you were led through in reading the stories, even though they were not laid out so clearly before. If you think back to the kanji that "worked" best for you, you will find that each of these steps was accomplished perfectly. And if you look back at the ones you forget, you should also be able to locate which step you skipped over. In reviewing, these same steps should be followed, with the only clue to set the imagination in action being the key-word.

3. If you find you are forgetting the relative position of the elements in a kanji . . .

Before all else, go back and re-read the frame for that character to see if there were any helpful hints or explanatory notes. If not, return to the frame where the particular primitives were first introduced to see if there is any clue there. And if this is not the problem, then, taking care not to add any new words or focal points to your story (since they might end up being elements later on), re-think the story in such a way that the image for each element actually takes the position it has in the kanji itself. This should not happen often, but when it does, it is worthwhile spending a few minutes to get things sorted out.

4. If you are confusing one kanji with another . . .

Take a careful look at the two stories. Perhaps you have made one or the other of them so vivid that it has attracted extraneous elements to itself that make the two kanji-images fuse into one. Or again, it may be that you did not pay sufficient attention to the advice about clarifying a single connotation for the key-word.

Whether or not you have had all or only a few of these problems, now is the time to review the first 10 lessons keeping an eye out for them. Put aside any schedule you may have set yourself until you have those lessons down perfectly, that is, until you can run through all 6 steps outlined above for every character, without a hitch. The most important thing in this review is not really to see whether you are remembering the characters, but to learn how to locate problems and deal with them.

One final note before you close the book and run your review. Everyone's imagination works differently. Each has its own gifts and its own defects. The more you pay attention to how you imagine things, the more likely you are to find out what works best for you and why. The one thing you must distrust to make the system outlined in this book work for you is your ability to remember kanji by themselves. Once you start making exceptions for characters you "know" or "have no trouble with" or "don't need to run through all the steps with," you are bound to end up frustrated. In other words, if you start using the method only as a "crutch" to help you only with the kanji you have trouble with, you will quickly be limping along worse than ever. What we are offering here is not a crutch, but a different way to walk.

That having been said, let us pick up where we left off, turning from primitive elements having to do with plants to those having to do with — animals.

---

235. portent   兆

Here we have a pictograph of the back of a turtle, the two sloping vertical strokes representing the central ridge and the four short strokes the pattern. Think of reading turtle-backs as a way to foretell the future, and in particular things that **portend** of coming evils. [6]

丿　丿　丬　兆　兆　兆

* When this character is used as a primitive in its full form, we keep the key-word sense of a *portent*. When it appears to the left in its abbreviated form (namely, the left half only 丬), we shall give it the pictographic sense of a *turtle*.

---

236. peach tree   桃

To associate the **peach tree** with the primitive for a *portent,* recall the

famous Japanese legend of Momo Tarō, the **Peach** Boy. It begins once
upon a time with a fisherman and his wife who wanted badly to have
a child, but none was born to them. Then one day the old man caught
a giant **peach,** out of which jumped a healthy young lad whom they
named **Peach** Boy. Though the boy was fated to perform heroic deeds,
his birth also *portended* great misfortune (else how could he become a
hero?). Thus the *tree* that is associated with a *portent* of coming evil
comes to be the **peach** *tree.* [10]

一 十 才 才 木 朹 村 材 机 桃 桃

237. stare   眺

To give someone the "evil *eye*" is to **stare** at them, wishing them evil.
The roots of the superstition are old and almost universal throughout
the cultures of the world. In this kanji, too, being **stared** at is
depicted as an *eye* that *portends* evil. [11]

丨 冂 冂 月 目 貝 貯 眇 眺 眺 眺

238. dog   犬

We have already learned that the character for *large* takes on the
meaning of the *St. Bernard dog* when used as a primitive. In this
frame we finally see why. The *drop* added as a fourth and final
stroke means that we have to do with a normal-sized **dog,** which compared to the *St. Bernard* is no more than a mere *drop* in the kennel. [4]

一 ナ 大 犬

* As a primitive this character can take two meanings. In the form
  given here it will mean a very small dog (which we shall refer to
  as a *chihuahua* for convenience sake). When it takes the form 犭 to
  the left of a character, we shall give it the meaning of a pack of
  wild dogs.

239. status quo   状

Did you ever hear of the *turtle* who fell madly in love with a
chihuahua but could not have her because their two families did not
like the idea of their children intermarrying? Like all classic stories
of ill-fated love, this one shows how the young upset the **status quo**

with an emotion older and more powerful than anything their elders have devised to counter it: blind love. [7]

丨　忄　扌　丬　丬　汁　状　状

240. silence   黙

Oddly enough, the character for **silence** shows us a *black chihuahua.* Actually, the cute little critter's name is Darkness, as I am sure you remember from the famous song about **silence** that begins, "Hello, Darkness, my old friend..."

Note how the four dots reach all the way across the bottom of the character. [15]

丶　冂　冃　日　甲　里　里　里　野　黙　黙　黙

黙　黙　黙

241. sort of thing   然

The key-word in this frame refers to a suffix that gives the word before it an adjectival quality; hence we refer to it as **"sort of thing."** Reverting to the time when dog was more widely eaten than it is today (see frame Frame 121), we see here a large cauldron boiling over an *oven flame* with the butchered *flesh* of a *chihuahua* being thrown into the whole concoction to make it into a "hot-diggity, dog-diggity" **sort of thing.** [12]

丿　ク　夕　夗　夗　外　状　状　然　然　然　然

242. reed   荻

You've heard of cat-tails, those swamp **reeds** with a furry *"flower"* to them like the tail of a cat. This might just turn out to be a good way to get rid of a troublesome pack of *wild dogs:* lure them into a swamp of these **reeds** with the cat-tail *flowers* on them, and then set *fire* to it. Take care to focus on the *flower* rather than the "cat-tail" to avoid confusion with Frame 244 below. [10]

一　十　艹　艹　艻　荻　荻　荻　荻　荻

243. hunt   狩

One of the worst problems you have to face when you go **hunting** is to
guard your take from the *wild dogs*. If you imagine yourself failing
at the task, you will probably have a stronger image than if you try to
picture yourself succeeding. [9]

丶 丁 丬 犭 犭 犷 犷 狩 狩

244. cat   猫

Knowing how much dogs love to chase cats, picture a pack of *wild
dogs* planting "**cat**-*seedlings,*" watering them, and fertilizing them
until they can be harvested as a crop of **cats** to chase and torment. If
you begin from the key-word and think of a "crop of **cats**," you will
not confuse this story with the apparently similar story of two
frames ago. [11]

丶 丁 丬 犭 犷 犷 犷 猫 猫 猫 猫

245. cow   牛

Why not see this kanji as a "doodle" showing a **cow** that has just been
run over by a steamroller. The small *dot* in the first stroke shows its
head turned to one side, and the next two strokes, the four legs. [4]

丿 ⺊ 二 牛

* As a primitive, the same sense of *cow* is kept. Note only that when
  it is placed OVER another element, its tail is cut off, giving us ⺧.

246. special   特

Despite the strong phonetic similarity, there will be no problem
keeping the key-word **special** distinct from the character we met
earlier for *specialty* (Frame 46), since the latter has immediate connotations lacking in the former. Anyway, let **special** refer to something in a **special** class all its own—like the sacred *cows* of India that

wander freely without fear of being butchered and ground into hamburger. Though the practice is a Hindu one, the Buddha's refusal to take the life of any sentient being makes it only fitting that the *cows* should be placed on the sacred grounds of a *Buddhist temple* in this kanji. [10]

丿 ㇄ 牛 牛 牜 牜 牜 牜 特 特

247. revelation   告

Folklore throughout the world tells us of talking animals who show a wisdom superior to that of human beings, and that same tradition has found its way into television shows and cartoons right into our own century. This character depicts **revelation** through the *mouth* of a *cow*, suggesting oracular utterances about truths hidden to human intelligence. [7]

丿 ㇒ 牛 生 牛 告 告

248. before   先

Take this key-word in its physical, not its temporal, sense (even though it refers to both). If you have a *cow* with *human legs,* as the elements show us here, it can only be because you have two people in a *cow*-suit. It has always seemed to me that I should prefer to be the one standing **before**, rather than hold up the rear and become the "butt" of everyone's laughter. [6]

丿 ㇒ 牛 生 牛 先

249. wash   洗

This character is so logical that one is tempted to let the elements speak for themselves: *water . . . before.* But we have already decided we shall not do that, not even once. So let us imagine a character like Peanuts' "Pigpen" who is always preceded by a little cloud of dust and grime, and call him "Wash-Out." Everywhere he walks, a spray of *water* goes *before* him to sanitize everything he touches. [9]

丶 冫 氵 氵 汁 汼 洗 洗 洗

LESSON 12

In this the final lesson of PART ONE we introduce the useful compound primitive for metals and the elements needed to form it, in addition to picking up a number of stray characters that have fallen by the wayside.

---

* umbrella

The actual character on which this primitive meaning **umbrella** is based we shall not meet until Frame 1026. We may think of it as a large and brightly-colored beach **umbrella**. If you compare this with Frame 8, you will notice how the two strokes touch here, while the kanji for *eight* would leave a gaping leak in the top. [2]

---

250. jammed in 介

The idea of something getting **jammed into** something else is depicted here by having a *walking cane* get **jammed inside** an *umbrella* frame by someone shoving it into an already occupied slot in the *umbrella* stand at the door. First notice the vertical strokes: on the left is the curved *umbrella* handle, and on the right the straight *walking stick*. Now try to imagine the two parties tugging at their respective properties like two kids on a wishbone, creating a scene at the entrance of an elegant restaurant. [4]

---

251. world 界

As the **world** gets *jammed* with more and more people, there is less and less space. Imagine yourself taking an air flight over a **world** so densely populated that every bit of it is sectioned off like a gigantic checkerboard (the *rice fields*). If you look closely at the character, you should be able to see a kind of movement taking place as still more is being *jammed into* that already narrow space. [9]

252. tea

As everyone knows, **tea** is made from **tea** leaves. But the **tea** plant itself has its own *flowers,* which can be quite beautiful and add a special flavor to the **tea,** as the Chinese found out already over 4,600 years ago. With the image of a terrace of *flowering* **tea** bushes in mind, picture very l-o-n-g *wooden poles* (Frame 195) placed here and there in their midst, with a tiny *umbrella* at the top, like a parasol shading the delicate-tasting **tea**-*flowers.* [9]

* meeting

This compound primitive depicts a **meeting** as a massive gathering of people under *one umbrella.* The full kanji from which this derives will be introduced later in Frame 752. The important thing here is to picture the scene just described and associate it with the word **meeting.** [3]

253. fit

The kanji for **fit** reads literally, top to bottom, as a *meeting* of *mouths*—which is a rather descriptive way of speaking of a romantic kiss. We know what happens when there is no *meeting* of minds and when people's ideas don't **fit,** but try to imagine what would happen to a poor couple whose *mouths* didn't **fit.** [6]

254. pagoda

On the left we see a mound of *dirt,* and to the right *flowers* made to *fit* together. The two sides combine to create a great **pagoda** made of *dirt,* with *flowers* by the tens of thousands made to *fit* together for the roofing of each of the layers. Be sure to put yourself in the scene and *fit* a few of the *flowers* in place yourself so that the image works its way into memory with full force. [12]

255. king 王

See what you can do to come up with a pictograph of a **king's** sceptre here that suits your own idea of what it should look like. (You might even begin with the basic element for *crafted* and then try to fit the remaining third stroke in somehow.) [4]

> * As a primitive, this can mean either *king* or *sceptre,* but it will usually be taken as an abbreviation of the character in the next frame.

256. jewel 玉

Note the *drop* here in the king's *sceptre,* which is exactly what you would expect it to be: a precious **jewel** handed down from one generation to the next as a symbol of his wealth and power. [5]

一 丁 干 王 玉

> * As a primitive, we can use this to mean either *jewel* or *ball.* When it appears anywhere other than on the left side of a kanji, it takes the same shape as here. On the left, it will be lacking the final stroke, making it the same as the character in the previous frame, 王.

257. treasure 宝

Every *house* has its **treasure,** as every thief knows only too well. While the things we **treasure** most are usually of sentimental value, we take the original sense of the term **treasure** here and make it refer to *jewels* kept in one's *house.* [8]

丶 宀 宀 宀 宀 宀 宝 宝

258. pearl 珠

Take care to keep the meaning of this kanji distinct from that for *jewel*. Think of the most enormous *pearl* you have ever seen, a great *vermilion*-colored *ball* sitting on the ring of your beloved and making it extremely difficult to move without falling over for the weight of the thing. [10]

一 丁 干 王 玎 圹 珎 玞 珜 珠

259. present 現

Do not think of a "gift" here, but of the **present** moment, as distinct from the future and the past. The kanji gives us a *ball* into which we *see* the **present**—obviously a crystal *ball* that enables us to *see* things going on at the **present** moment in places far away. [11]

一 丁 干 王 玎 玏 玒 玥 玴 玥 珇 現

260. lunatic 狂

A **lunatic** is literally one driven mad by the light of the moon, and the most famous of the "looneys" are the legendary lycanthropes or "wolfmen." Sometimes the transformation is only a temporary phenomenon, sometimes it is permanent. In the latter cases, the poor chap takes off on all fours to live with the beasts. Imagine one of these lycanthropes going **looney** and setting himself up as *king* of a pack of *wild dogs* that roams about and terrorizes innocent suburban communities. [7]

ノ 丬 犭 犭 狆 狌 狂

261. emperor 皇

An **emperor**, as we all know, is a ruler: something like a *king* but higher in status. The *white bird* perched above the *king*, elevating him to **imperial** heights, is the messenger he sends back and forth to the gods to request advice and special favors, something that *white birds* have long done in folklore throughout the world. [9]

丿 亻 忄 白 白 白 阜 阜 皇

262. display 呈

The trick to remembering this character lies in associating the key-word with the line from the nursery rhyme about 4 and 20 blackbirds baked in a pie: "Wasn't this a dainty dish to set before the *king*?". If we think of **display** in terms of that famous line, and the *king* with his head thrown back and his *mouth* wide open as 4 and 20 blackbirds fly in one after the other, we shall have satisfied both the elements and their position. [7]

丶 冂 口 曰 早 早 呈

263. whole 全

Wholeness suggests physical and spiritual health, "having your act together." The kanji-image for **wholeness** depicts being "*king* under your own umbrella"—that is, giving order to your own life. I know it sounds terribly abstract, but what could be more abstract than the word **whole**? [6]

丿 入 △ 全 全 全

264. plug 栓

Here we think of **plug** in the sense of a cork or stopper used to seal the mouth of a bottle, water faucet, or something with liquid running out of it. Forgetting the abstract picture of the former frame, let us work with all the primitive units: *tree . . . umbrella . . . ball.* Imagine a *tree* with a faucet in the side out of which tennis *balls* are flowing, bouncing all over the ground by the hundreds. You fight your way up to it and shove your giant beach *umbrella* in the *tree* to **plug** it up. [10]

一 十 才 木 朴 朴 朴 栓 栓 栓

265. logic 理

We first referred to this character back in Frame 173, which you might want to return to have a peek at. The image of **logic** we are given is something like a central *jewel* in a *computer,* like the *jewels* in old clocks that keep them running smoothly. Try to picture yourself making your way through all the RAMS and ROMS and approaching this shining *jewel,* a chorus of voices and a blast of trumpets in the background heralding the great seat of all-knowing **logic.** [11]

一 丁 干 王 尹 玎 珂 珥 珇 理 理

---

266. lord   主

"A man's home is his castle," goes the proverb from an age where it was the male who was **lord** of the household. Fundamentally, it means only that every person is a bit (or *drop*) of a *king* in one's own environment. If you take care to "read off" the primitives in this way, you won't end up putting the *drop* down below, where it turns the kanji into a *jewel.* [5]

丶 亠 十 丰 主

* As a primitive element, we set the key-word aside entirely and take it as a pictograph of a solid brass *candlestick* (with the *drop* representing the flame at the top).

---

267. pour   注

Picture **pouring** *water* from a lighted *candlestick.* What could be more ridiculous, and simpler as a way to recall this kanji? [8]

---

268. pillar   柱

The **pillar** referred to here is the *wooden* beam that stands at the entrance to a traditional Japanese house. Carve it in imagination into the shape of a gigantic *candlestick* and your work is done. [9]

269. gold

If this were not one of the most common characters you will ever have to write, I would apologize for having to give the explanation that follows. Anyway, we want to depict bars of **gold** bullion with an *umbrella* overhead to shade them from the heat (and perhaps to hide them as well). The bullion is made by melting down all the *sceptres* of the kingdom, *drop* by *drop* and shaping them into bars. [8]

* As a primitive, it means not only *gold* but any *metal* at all.

270. pig-iron

Pig-iron refers to iron in the crude form in which it emerges from the smelting furnaces. Of all the various forms *metal* can take, this one shows us *metal before* it has been refined. Imagine two photographs labeled "*before*" and "after" to show the process. [14]

271. bowl

Let **bowl** suggest a large and heavy *metal* **bowl** into which you are throwing all the *books* you own to mash them into pulp, for what outrageous reason you will have to decide yourself. [13]

272. copper

Picture an order of *monks* serving as chaplains for the police force. Their special habit, made of protective *metal*, is distinguished by a row of **copper** buttons just like the "cops" they serve. [14]

／ ／ ㇀ ㇀ ㇀ 牟 牟 希 金 釦 釦 釦 銅

銅 銅

273. angling

釣

The character we learned for *fishing* (Frame 172) refers to the professional, net-casting industry, while the **angling** of this character refers to the sport. The odd thing is that your **angling** rod is a *ladle* which you are using to scoop *gold*-fish out of a river. [11]

／ ／ ㇀ ㇀ 牟 牟 希 金 釗 釣 釣

274. needle

針

In Frame 10 we referred ahead to this full character from which the primitive for **needle** to the right, derives. Since we already expect that **needles** are made of *metal*, let us picture a set of solid *gold* darning **needles** to complete the kanji. [10]

／ ／ ㇀ ㇀ 牟 牟 希 金 金一 針

275. inscription

銘

Take **inscription** in the sense of the *name* you ask the jeweler to carve on a *gold* bracelet or inside a *gold* ring to identify its owner or communicate some sentimental message. It will help if you can recall the first time you had this done and the feelings you had at the time. [14]

／ ／ ㇀ ㇀ 牟 牟 希 金 金 釙 釼

釗 銘 銘

276. tranquillize

鎮

The first lie-detector machines of twentieth century psychology worked by wiring pieces of *metal* fixed to the body to measure the amount of sweat produced when questions were asked. It was dis-

covered that nervousness produced more sweat, indicating sub-
conscious reactions when the *truth* was getting too close for comfort.
Nowadays, people can take drugs that **tranquillize** them in such a
way as to neutralize the effect of the device, which is why other
means have had to be developed. [18]

ノ 八 ヘ 伫 牟 牟 全 金 金 金 釒 釘 鈩
鈩 鈰 鎮 鎮 鎮 鎮

With that, we come to the end of PART ONE. Before going on to PART
TWO, it would be a good idea to return now to the INTRODUCTION and
read it once again. Anything that did not make sense at first should
now be clear.

By this time, too, you should be familiar with the use of all the
INDICES. If not, take a few minutes to study them, since you will no
doubt find them useful in the pages ahead.

Part Two:

PLOTS

By this time, if you have been following along methodically frame by frame, you may find yourself growing impatient at the thought of having to read through more than 2,000 of these little stories. By now you probably want to move at a quicker pace and in your own way. Take heart, for that is precisely what we are going to start doing in PART TWO. But if you happen to be one of those people who are quite content to have someone else do all the work for them, then brace yourself for the task that lies ahead.

We begin the weaning process by abbreviating the stories into simple plots, leaving it up to you to patch together the necessary details in a manner similar to what we did in PART ONE. As mentioned in the INTRODUCTION, the purpose of the longer stories was to impress on you the importance of recreating a complete picture in imagination, and to insure that you did not merely try to associate words *with words* but with *images*. The same holds true for the kanji that remain.

Before setting out on our way again, a word of caution is in order. Left to its own, your imagination will automatically tend to add elements and see connections that could prove counter-productive in the long run. For example, you might think it perfectly innocent and admissable to alter the primitive for old to old man, or that for cliff to cave. In fact, these changes would be confusing when you meet the kanji and primitives with those meanings later on. You would return to the earlier kanji and find that everything had gotten jumbled up.

It may be that you have experienced this problem already on one or the other occasion when you decided to alter a story to suit your own associations. That should help you appreciate how hard it is to wipe out a story once you have learned it, particularly a vivid one. To protect yourself against this, stick faithfully to the key-words as they are given, and try not to move beyond the range of primitive-meanings listed. Where such confusion can be anticipated, a longer story will be presented as a protective measure, but you will have to take care of the rest.

LESSON 13

We begin PART TWO with a group of 23 kanji having to do with travel, and the primitives that accompany them: a road, a pair of walking legs, and a car.

* road   辶

The **road** envisioned here is a road for traffic, or a path or walkway. The natural sweep of these three simple strokes should be easy to remember, especially since we will be using it so often. [3]

277. road-way   道

The key-word carries both the sense of a *road* for transit and a *way* or method of doing something, but the former is better for forming an image. The primitives read: the *neck* of a *road*. Think of a crowded **road-way** where traffic has come to a standstill—what we commonly refer to as a "bottle-*neck*." [12]

丶 丷 丷 䒑 丷 𦣞 𦣞 首 首 首 道 道

278. guidance   導

When we accept someone's **guidance**, we permit ourselves to be *glued* to a certain *road* or *way* of doing something, and try to "stick" to it. [15]

丶 丷 丷 丷 丷 𦣞 𦣞 首 首 首 道 道

道 導 導

279. crossing   辻

Take the first two strokes in the sense we gave them back in Frame 16, as the pictograph of a **cross**, and set it on a *road* to create a "**crossing**." [5]

一 十 十 辻 辻

280. swift   迅

Here we see a *crossing* in the form of a barbed *fishhook*, suggesting a

swifter alternate not only to the old roundabouts but to the "clover-leaf" pattern used on today's super highways. [6]

乁 乁 卂 卂 讯 迅

281. create   造

Think of **creating** as making something out of nothing. Then recall how the *way* of *revelation* laid out in the bible begins with the story of how God **created** the world out of a dark and chaotic nothingness. [10]

丿 丄 屮 牛 牛 告 告 告 浩 造

282. urge   迫

To **urge** someone to do something, you make the *way* as appealing as possible, perhaps even *white* washing it a bit. [8]

丿 亻 冇 白 白 白 泊 迫

283. escape   逃

When **escaping** from something or someone, one always feels as if one is not going fast enough, like a *turtle* on a super-highway. (Since the *turtle* is on the *road* and not on the left, it can keep its full kanji shape as in Frame 235.) [9]

丿 丿 兆 兆 兆 兆 逃 逃

284. environs   辺

To keep the **environs** clean and safe, you could cement *daggers* in the *road,* blades pointed upwards, so that no pollution-producing traffic could pass by. You could, if you were an ecologically-minded terrorist. [5]

刁 刀 刀 刃 辺 辺

285. patrol   巡

A virtual *deluge* of motorcycle police washing down a *road* is this kanji's image for a **patrol**. [6]

〈　《　《〈　`《〈　氵《〈　巡

286. car   車

You may keep the whole range of connotations for this key-word, **car**, provided it does not interfere with the pictograph. Look for the front and back wheels (the first and last horizontal strokes) and the seat in the carriage in the middle. As an exercise, try to isolate the primitives on your own and make a story out of them. [7]

一　厂　冂　百　百　亘　車

* *Car, cart, wagon,* and *vehicle* are all possible primitive meanings.

287. take along   連

What you are meant to **take along** in this kanji are not things but people. The image of the *car* on the *road* should ground your image for picking up your friends to **take** them **along** to wherever you are going. [10]

一　厂　冂　百　百　亘　車　`車　連　連

288. rut   軌

Combine the primary and secondary meanings of this key-word to form your story. Begin with the *car* whose tires get caught in a **rut**, and then go on to the *baseball team* who can't win a game because it has fallen into a **rut** of losing. [9]

一　厂　冂　百　百　亘　車　車)　軌

289. transport

On the left we see a *vehicle* used for **transport**. On the right, we see a new tangle of elements that need sorting out. The first three strokes, you will remember, are the primitive for *meeting*. Below it we see the elements for *flesh* and *sword*, which combine to create a compound-element for a *butcher* and his trade. Try putting them together in the image of a "trucker's convoy." [16]

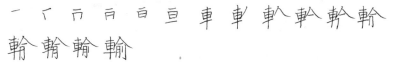

290. in front

We waited to introduce this character until now, even though the pieces have been available for some time, because it helps to reinforce the odd kanji of the last frame. Picture the *butcher* hacking away with his knife at a slab of meat on his table with a pair of ram's *horns* placed **in front** of him.

No need to worry about confusing this kanji with that for *before* (Frame 248), since it will not appear as a primitive in any other character used in this book. [9]

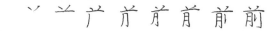

* walking legs

We call this element **walking legs** because it indicates "legs in motion," whether you want to think of them as jogging or walking in long strides, as the shape seems to suggest. Be careful how you write it, with the first two strokes like a "7." [3]

291. each

"Suum cuique" goes the popular Latin proverb. A certain disease of the English language makes it almost impossible to translate the phrase without bias. In any event, here we see someone walking with his/her *mouth* between his/her *walking legs*, giving us an image of "To **each** his/her own." [6]

* The sense of the proverb should help when using this kanji as a primitive; otherwise, reduce it to its original elements. But do NOT associate it in any way with the word "every," which we shall meet later in another context.

292. status

If you can imagine *trees* as **status** symbols (as they might well be for those living in Japan's congested modern cities), then *each* might be aiming to have his/her own *tree,* just to keep up with the Suzukis. [10]

293. abbreviation

Each field has its own **abbreviations** (chemistry, philosophy, sports, etc.). Needless to say, the stronger primitive goes to the left, even though the story would read them off the other way around. [11]

294. guest

When you are a **guest** in a courteous town, *each household* has its own way of welcoming you, and *each house* becomes your home. [9]

295. forehead

Out of respect, you do not look straight in the eyes of your *guest,* but look at the part of the *head* just above that, namely the **forehead,** when you must look in that direction. [18]

丶 丷 冖 宀 灾 灾 宓 客 客 客 額
額 額 額 額 額 額

296. summer   夏

In the **summer**, fatigued by the heat, your *head* hangs down nearly as
far as your *walking legs*, or rather, your "dragging legs." Note how the
new legs here substitute for the old "animal legs" in the element for
head. [10]

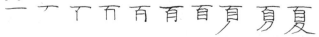 一 丆 丁 而 而 百 百 戸 夏 夏

297. dispose   処

Both the stretching out of the *walking legs* and the little bit of *wind*
tucked into the right suggest using one's legs to kick something out of
the way, or **dispose** of it. [5]

ノ 夕 夂 処 処

298. twig   条

Geppetto made *walking legs* for his little Pinocchio from two **twigs** of
a *tree,* giving him a set of "**twiggy**" shanks. [7]

ノ 夕 夂 夂 冬 条 条

299. fall   落

When *water* **falls**, it splats and splashes; when *flower*-petals fall, they
float gently in the breeze. To *each* thing its own way of **falling.** [12]

一 十 艹 艹 艾 艾 芝 芝 莈 茨 落 落

LESSON 14

We may now go a step further in our streamlining, this time in the area of the stroke-order of the kanji. From here on in, only the order in which the composite primitive elements are written will be indicated; if you are not sure of the writing of any of the particulars in a given character, you will have to hunt it down yourself. New primitives and unusual writings will be spelled out as before, however. At any rate, you should ALWAYS count the strokes of the character when you learn it, and check your results against the number given in square brackets in each frame.

The next group of primitives, around which this lesson is designed, have to do with lids and headgear.

---

* crown ⌐

This pictograph of a simple **crown** is distinguished from the *roof* only by the absence of the chimney (the first *drop* at the top). It can be used for all the principal connotations of the word **crown**. We will meet the full character from which this element is derived later on, in Frame 304. [2]

---

300. superfluous 冗

Picture a *weather-vane* on top of a regal *crown,* spinning round and round. It is not only **superfluous** but makes a perfect ass out of the one that wears it. [4]

⌐ 冗

---

301. army 軍

The *crowned vehicle* depicted here is a "chariot," symbol of an **army**. [9]

* Used as a primitive this kanji means only *chariot*.

302. radiance 輝

Take advantage of the first syllable of the key-word to think of the *ray* of light to the left. Now add the glittering chariot which is emitting those *rays* and you have **radiance**. [15]

303. carry 運

A long string of "sweet" *chariots* "swinging low" to our *roads* is a sure sign that the Lord is "comin' for to **carry**" someone home. [12]

304. crown 冠

By having the **crown** pass from one age to the next, a people keeps itself *glued* to its *beginnings*. [9]

305. dream 夢

To have a **dream** after going to bed is really the *crown* to a perfect *evening*. The *flower*-petals over the *eyes* (instead of the "sand" that Westerners are used to finding there when they awake in the morning) only confirms the image of a pleasant **dream** suggested by the rest of this somewhat unusually complex kanji. [13]

*   tophat 亠

The broad rim and tall top of the **tophat** is pictured graphically here in these two simple strokes.

At this point, by the way, you can revert back to Frame 6. If you have had any trouble with that character, you now have the requisite elements to make a story: SIX suggests the number of spider's *legs;* just set a tall silk *tophat* on the crawling creature and you have your character. [2]

---

* whirlwind   兀

A formal high silk *tophat* resting atop an eddy of *wind* represents a **whirlwind.** To keep it distinct from *wind,* try to picture the vortex, or tornado-like spinning movement, of a **whirlwind.** The next frame should help. [4]

一   兀

---

306. pit   坑

A *whirlwind* begins to dig its way into the *soil* like a drill until it makes a deep **pit.** [7]

土   坑

---

307. tall   高

Recalling an image from Frame 183, first see the *mouth* under the extraterrestrial's glass *hood,* and then the *mouth* under the *tophat* of one of his mates who has tried on the strange earthling's headgear only to find that it makes him look much, much **taller** than everyone else. [10]

古   高

* As a primitive, this character keeps its sense of *tall* and its position at the top of other primitives, but its writing is abbreviated to the first 5 strokes: .

---

308. receive   享

Tall children **receive** more attention. *Tall children* grow up to make better **receivers.** Take your pick, depending on whether you prefer child psychology or American football. At any rate, be sure you have some particular *tall child* in mind, because he or she may come in handy in the next two frames. [8]

309. cram school

Cram schools are after-hours educational institutions where kids can **cram** for coming examinations or drill what they missed during **regular class hours. The exception are the** *tall children* **who are also** *fat* **and therefore need to be out there on the school grounds burning off calories. So this character depicts those who do** NOT **go to the cram schools, rather than those who do. [14]**

310. mellow

These same *tall children* from the last frame who are also *fat* are here cast into a cauldron over an open *flame* until they have sufficiently **mellowed** that they can return to the normal life of a student. [15]

311. pavilion

Think of all the **pavilions** at some world Expo you have attended or followed in the media, and you will no doubt see rising up among them that familiar gigantic, *tall crowned nail* (the *crown* being a revolving restaurant)—that architectural monstrosity that has become a symbol of science and technology at such events. [9]

312. capital

Think of some *tall,* domed **capital** building with swarms of *small* folks gathered around its base, probably demonstrating for their government's attention. [8]

古 京

313. refreshing   涼

Since few things are as **refreshing** on a warm day as a cool shower (the *water*), here we picture a *capital* building treating itself to one, and in full view of everyone. [11]

氵 涼

314. scenery   景

Scenery is depicted as a *sun* rising over a *capital,* which is as close as some city-dwellers get to natural **scenery** for years at a time! [12]

日 景

315. whale   鯨

The **whale** swallows a whole school of fish, who turn their new abode into a proper little *fish-capital.* [19]

魚 鯨

* lidded crock   吉

Soil over the *mouth* of a container gives us a piece of clay pottery with its *lid*. Behold the **lidded crock.** [6]

土 吉

316. cottage   舍

A *lidded crock* with an *umbrella* overhead gives us a mixture of the modernistic and the nostalgic in this design for a **cottage.** [8]

 舍

317. circumference   周

Look more closely at your *lidded crock* and you will see little ruler marks along its bottom edge. This is so you can use it to calculate the **circumference** of your *pheasant glass*: just begin at a fixed point and turn the *lidded crock* around and around, keeping it flush against the side of the *pheasant glass*, until you come back to your starting point. If you kept track of how many turns and part-turns your *lidded crock* made, you now know the **circumference**. [8]

* As a primitive, this character can take the added significance of a *lap*.

318. week   週

Picture a circular *road* with 7 markers on it, one for each day of the **week**. When you have walked one complete *lap* on this *road,* you shall have completed one **week**. [11]

319. gentleman   士

The shape of this kanji, slightly differing from that for *soil* by virtue of its shorter final stroke, hints at a broad-shouldered, slender-waisted warrior standing at attention. When feudalism collapsed, these warriors became Japan's **gentlemen**. [3]

* The primitive meaning reverts to the more colorful image of the *samurai,* Japan's warrior class.

320. good luck   吉

Here we see a *samurai* standing on a street with his *mouth* open, which people walk up to and look down deep inside of for **good luck**. [6]

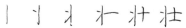

* As a primitive, we shall take this shape to mean an *aerosol can*,
from the *mouth* and the very tightly-fitting *lid* (note how it
differs here from the *lidded crock*).

321. robust   壮

Robust is seen as a *turtle* turned *samurai.* [6]

丨 丬 丬 壮 壮 壮

322. villa   荘

The **villa** pictured here is filled with exotic *flowers* at every turn, and
has a pair of *turtle-samurai* standing before its gates. [9]

一 一 艹 丬 丬 丬 丬 荘 荘

323. sell   売

A *samurai,* out of a job, is going door-to-door **selling** little wind-up
crowns with *human legs* that run around on the floor looking like
headless monarchs. [7]

一 十 士 声 声 声 売

LESSON 15

In this Lesson we consider a group of primitives associated one way or
another with schooling. Be sure to give the story enough time to come to
life in imagination, because you will need more vividness than these brief
"plots" allow for. You know that you are NOT giving enough time when you
find yourself memorizing definitions rather than playing with images.

*   school house

Here we see a little red **school house** with the 3 dots on the roof. As you write it in the following frames, you should acquire a "feel" for the way the first two short strokes move left to right, and the third one right to left. Write it twice now, saying to yourself the first time as you write the first 3 strokes, "In the **school house** we learn our A-B-Cs," and the second time, "In the **school house** we learn our 1-2-3s." [5]

`丶   丷   丷   丷   丷`

324. study

The *child* in the little red *school house* is there for one reason only: to **study**. Anyone who has gone through the schooling system knows well enough that **study** is one thing and *learning* quite another again. In the kanji, too, the character for *learning* (Frame 574) has nothing to do with the *school house*. [8]

325. memorize

The idea of **memorizing** things is easily related to the *school house*; and since we have been at it for more than a hundred pages in this book, the idea that **memorizing** involves *seeing* things that are not really there should make it easy to put the two elements together. [12]

326. flourish

The botanical connotations of the word **flourish** (to bud and burst into bloom, much as a *tree* does) are part of the ideal of the *school house* as well. [9]

*   brush

This primitive element, not itself a kanji, is a pictograph of a writing **brush.** Let the first 3 strokes represent the hairs at the tip of the **brush,** and the following two strokes the thumb and forefinger that guide it when you write. Note how the long vertical stroke, cutting through everything, is drawn last. This is standard procedure when you have such a stroke running the length of a character. However, as we saw in the case of *cow,* when this primitive appears on top of another primitive, its "tail" is cut off, giving us 聿 . [6]

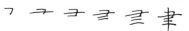

327. write

The sage *talks rapidly* with his *tongue wagging in his mouth,* while the *brush* of the scribe runs apace to **write** down the master's words. [10]

328. haven

Seeing the tiny boats of poor mortals tossed about in a stormy sea like so many corks, the All-Merciful took its *brush* and drew little inlets of *water* where the hapless creatures might seek shelter. And so it is that we have **havens.** [9]

*   taskmaster

First find the long rod (the first stroke), held in the hand of someone seated (the next 3 strokes, not unlike the pictograph for *woman,* but quite different from that for *walking legs* introduced in the last lesson). The only thing left to do is conjure up the memory of some **taskmaster** (or taskmistress) whom you will "never forget." [4]

329. breed 牧

When it is time to **breed** new cattle, the bull is usually willing but the *cow* is often not. Thus the *taskmaster* to the right forces the *cow* into a compromising position, so to speak, so that she can **breed**. [8]

牛 牧

330. aggression 攻

The special *craft* of the successful *taskmaster* is his ability to remain constantly on the **aggressive**, never allowing his underlings a moment to ponder a counter-**aggression** of their own. [7]

工 攻

331. failure 敗

The *taskmaster* is acknowledging the **failure** of a *clam* to make the grade in some marine school or other. [11]

丨 冂 冃 月 目 貝 貝 貝 貯 敗 敗

332. sheet of... 枚

English counts thin, flat objects, like bed linen and paper, in *sheets*. The kanji does this with a *taskmaster* whipping a *tree* into producing *sheets* against its will. [8]

一 十 才 木 术 杧 杧 枚

333. happenstance 故

Call it fate or providence or just plain old Lady Luck, **happenstance** is the *oldest taskmaster* we know. It always has its way. [9]

一 十 十 古 古 古 扗 故 故

334. awe

敬

Standing in **awe** of someone, you get self-conscious and try to speak in *flowery phrases* out of veneration or fear. The *taskmaster* at the right is drilling you in the practice of your "honorifics." [12]

335. say

言

Of all the things we can do with our *mouths,* speech is the one that requires the greatest distinctness and clarity. Hence the kanji for say has four little sound-waves, indicating the complexity of the achievement. [7]

* This kanji, which appears often as a primitive, can mean **saying,** *speech,* or *words,* depending on which is most useful.

336. admonish

警

Here you have a perfect example of how an apparently impossible kanji to learn becomes a snap once you know its elements. The idea of being **"admonished"** for something already sets up a superior-inferior relationship between you and the person you are supposed to stand in *awe* of. While you are restricted to answering in honorifics, the superior can use straightforward and ordinary *words.* [19]

337. plot

計

Words and a compass *needle* combine to form the sense of **plot:** to talk over plans and to calculate a course of action. [9]

338. prison

Although we didn't make note of it at the time, the kanji for *dog* is also a low-grade term for a spy. And later (Frame 1414) we will meet another association of criminals with *dogs*. The **prison** here depicts a pack of *wild dogs* (the long-timers and hardened criminals) into which the poor little *chihuahua* (first-offender) has been cast. The only thing he has to protect himself against the pack are his shrill and frightened *words*. [14]

犭 猚 獄

339. revise

After completing the first draft, you **revise** it by *nailing* down your *words* and "hammering" them into shape. [9]

言 訂

340. chastise

Words spoken to **chastise** us stick to us like *glue* in a way no other *words* can. [10]

言 討

341. instruction

The personalism connoted by the word **instruction**, as opposed to "teaching" or "discipline," suits the picture here of *words* guiding one's progress like the gentle flowing of a *stream*. [10]

言 訓

342. imperial edict 詔

The **imperial edict**, spoken with the force of unquestionable law, is made up of *words* intended to *seduce* the masses—be it through fear or respect—to follow obediently. [12]

言　詔

---

343. packed   詰

A piece of writing that is pregnant with meaning and needs to be re-read several times to be understood we refer to colloquially as **"packed."** The character sees the *words* as sealed tightly inside of an *aerosol can.* [13]

言　詰

---

344. tale   話

That the *words* of the *tongue* should come to mean a **tale** is clear from the etymology: a **tale** is something "talked," not something read from a book. [13]

言　話

---

345. recitation   詠

Listening to the *words* of poets **reciting** their poetry is like being transported for a moment into *eternity* where the rules of everyday life have been suspended. [12]

言　詠

---

346. poem   詩

Since silence is treasured so highly at a *Buddhist temple* the *words* spoken there must be well-chosen. This is why the records of the monks often read to us like **poetry**. Before going on, back up a frame and make sure you have kept **poetry** and *recitation* distinct in your mind. [13]

言　詩

347. word

Whereas the character for *say* focused on the actual talking, that for **words** stresses the fact that although it is *I* who *say* them, the *words* of a language are not my own. You should see the tension between *I* and *words* just by looking at the kanji. [14]

348. read

In the age of advertising, most *words* we **read** are out to *sell* some product or point of view. [14]

349. tune

A complete **tune** is composed not only of a succession of notes but also of one *lap* of the *words* that go with it. [15]

350. discuss

In almost every attempt to discuss an issue, the fervor of one's convictions comes to the surface and creates an *inflammation* of *words* (if you will, the "cuss" in "**discuss**"). [15]

351. consent

The *words* of the *young* do not have legal validity unless backed up by "parental **consent**." [15]

352. rebuke

The stern tone of a **rebuke** is seen here in the image of *words* spoken at a *meeting* of *butchers* (see Frame 289) waving their choppers at one another and "cutting one another down" as only *butchers* can. [16]

LESSON 16

In this short lesson of 17 characters we come to an interesting cluster of primitive elements—unique among all those we have met or will meet throughout this book—built up step by step from one element. Be sure to study this lesson as a unit in order to appreciate the similarities and differences of the various elements, which will appear frequently later on.

*   arrow

Here we see a pictograph of a long and slightly warped **arrow**. By extending the short final stroke in both directions, you should see the **arrowhead** without any difficulty. The hook at the bottom represents the feathers at the butt end. When it serves as a semi-enclosure for other primitives, the first stroke is drawn longer, as we shall see in the following frames. [3]

353. style

Take **style** in its sense of some fashion design or model. Then let the elements, *arrow-craft* stand for the well known **style** of shirts known as "*Arrow*" shirts" because of the little *arrow* sewn on each one. [6]

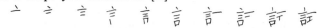

354. test

When a manufacturer produces a new *style* for the market, the first thing that is done is to run a **test** on consumers, asking them to *speak* their opinions frankly about the product. Never mind the anachronism (the kanji was there well before our capitalistic market-system) if it helps you remember. [13]

* quiver

This primitive is easy to remember as depicting something used to bring all one's *arrows* together into *one* handy place: the **quiver**. [4]

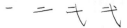

355. II

We use the Roman numeral "II" here to stress that this kanji is an older form of the kanji for *two*. Think of *two arrows* in a *quiver*. [6]

* fiesta

The picture in this primitive is what we may call a "tassled *arrow.*" A decorative tassle is strung on the shaft of an *arrow* to indicate that it is no longer a weapon any longer but a symbol of a **fiesta** As before, the first stroke is extended when it serves as a quasi-enclosure. [4]

356. range

From its original meaning of a defined area or zone, a **range** has also taken on the sense of grazing *land* where cowboys roam and do whatever it is they do with cows. When the herds have all been driven to market, there is a great homecoming *fiesta* like that pictured here. As soon as the cowboys come home, home on the **range,** the first thing they do is kiss the ground (the *mouth* on the *floor*), and then get on with the *fiesta.* [11]

土　坦　坦　域

357. burglar   賊

From a **burglar's** point of view, a *fiesta* is an occasion to take out the old lockpicking *needle* and break into the unattended safe filled with the family *shells* (the *money,* as we saw in Frames 80 and 194). [13]

丨　冂　冃　月　目　貝　貝　貯　財　賊

* Thanksgiving   戈

I choose the word **Thanksgiving** as only one possible way of making this primitive more concrete. The sense, as its composite primitives make clear, is of a *"land fiesta,"* or a harvest feast. If you choose a word of your own, make sure it does not conflict with *fiesta.* [6]

一　十　土　弍　戈　戈

358. plantation   栽

On a **plantation** it is the *trees* that one is particularly grateful for at the time of *Thanksgiving.* Imagine yourself inviting a few representative *trees* from the fields and orchards to join you around the table to give thanks. [10]

一　十　土　圭　丰　耒　耒　栽　栽　栽

359. load   載

One **loads** bales on a wagon or *cart* in preparation for the great Hay Ride that follows the *Thanksgiving* dinner each year. [13]

車 載

---

* parade   戊

Note first the order of the writing. The first stroke gives us a full-fledged enclosure, because of which we should always think of this as a **parade** OF something or other, namely whatever is inside the enclosure. [5]

丿 厂 仄 戊 戊

---

360. overgrown   茂

The sense of the key-word **overgrown** is of something growing luxuriantly, in this case a whole *parade* of weeds (outcaste *flowers*). By way of exception, the *flowers* take their normal place OVER the enclosure. [8]

一 十 艹 芦 芦 芪 茂 茂

---

361. turn into   成

Let the phrase **"turn into"** suggest some sort of a magical change. What happens here is that the *parade* marching down main street **turns into** a *dagger*-throwing bout between competing bands. Note how only one stroke has to be added to make the change. [6]

丿 厂 历 成 成 成

---

362. castle   城

In this frame, we see a mound of *dirt* which is being *turned into* a **castle** (the way children do at the beach with the sand). [9]

一 十 土 圹 圹 圹 城 城 城

363. sincerity 誠

The sure sign of **sincerity** is that one's mere *words* are *turned into* deeds. [13]

言　誠

* march 戌

As distinct from the *parade,* the **march** points to a formal demonstration, whose emotions are generally a far cry from the happy spirit of the *parade.* The inclusion of the *one* gives the sense of the singlemindedness and unity of the group joined in the **march.** As before, the primitive inside the enclosure indicates who or what is **marching.** [6]

丿　厂　厂　戊　戌　戌

364. intimidate 威

Here we see a *march* of *women* demonstrating on behalf of equal rights, something extremely **intimidating** to the male chauvinist population. [9]

丿　厂　厂　厈　反　厔　威　威　威

365. destroy 滅

Picture a *march* of *flames* demonstrating against the Fire Department but being doused with *water* by the police riot squads. [13]

氵　滅　滅

366. dwindle 減

A group of unquenchable *mouths* sets out on a *march* across the country, drinking *water* wherever they find it until the *water*-supply has **dwindled** to a trickle, triggering a national disaster. [12]

* float

The **floats** that are such an important part of a *fiesta* are shown here by the addition of the two extra horizontal strokes, which you may take as a quasi-pictographic representation of the platform structure of a **float**. [6]

367. scaffold

Prior to the use of metal, *trees* were once cut down and bound together for use as **scaffolding** material. In this case, what is being constructed is not a skyscraper but a simple *float*. [10]

368. coin

Those special *gold*-colored tokens minted each year for the Mardi Gras and thrown into the crowds from people on the *floats* give us the kanji for **coins**. [14]

369. shallow

An entourage of *floats* going from one town to the next must always seek a **shallow** place to cross the *water*. Try to picture what happens if they don't. [9]

LESSON 17

Because of the rather special character of that last group of primitives (8 in all), it might be a good idea not to rush too quickly into this lesson until you are sure you have them all learned and fitted out with good images. Now we will take another set of primitives built up from a common base, though fewer in number and lacking the similarity of meaning we saw in the last lesson.

370. stop 止

This character is easiest to learn as a pictograph. Take it as a rather crude drawing of a footprint: the first 3 strokes represent the front and the last the heel. The big toe (stroke 1) on the right indicates that this is a left foot. [4]

丨 ├ ㅑ 止

* Although the meaning of *stop* will be retained, we will return occasionally to the pictographic meaning of *footprint*.

371. walk 歩

Footprints that follow one another a *few* at a time indicate **walking**. [8]

丨 ├ ㅑ 止 讣 步 步 步

372. ford 渉

To **ford** a body of *water* means to *walk* across it. [11]

丶 丶 氵 沪 沪 沖 沖 沖 渉 渉 渉

373. repeatedly 頻

The image of something occurring **repeatedly**, over and over again, is of having one's *head walked* on. [17]

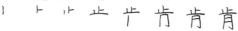

374. agreement

Seeing *footprints* on someone's *flesh* indicates a rather brutal way of having secured that person's **agreement**. [8]

375. undertake

To **undertake** a project is take some idea and *stop* it from floating around freely in the air so that it can become a reality. Here we see some **undertaking** made to *stop* under a beach *umbrella*. [6]

376. curriculum

That same *grove of trees* we met in Frame 213 shows up here in the character for **curriculum** (in the sense of a record of one's life or academic achievements, the **curriculum** vitae). Instead of the *grove* making its way slowly through the surface of the *cliff* as before, here we see it *stopped,* much the same as a **curriculum** *vitae* calls a halt to the calendar and talks only about the past. [14]

厂 麻 歷

377. warrior 武

With a *quiver* of *arrows* set on one's back, the goal of the **warrior** depicted here is not to attack but merely to *stop* the attack of others: the oldest excuse in history! [8]

378. levy 賦

A certain portion of *shells* (money) is collected by the *warrior* from the local villages as he passes through to defray the costs of keeping the land safe, and this is called a **levy**. [15]

貝 賦

379. correct 正

"A journey of a thousand miles begins with a single step," says the Chinese proverb. Here we see *one footprint*, complementing that proverb with the sound advice that if the first step is not made **correctly**, the whole point of the journey will be forfeited. This is the ideal that teachers are supposed to have in **correcting** their students, and parents in **correcting** their children. [5]

一 丁 下 正 正

380. evidence 証

Words that testify to the *correctness* of some fact are classified as **evidence**. (Here we see a good example of how the more common primitive element takes the "strong" position to the left, even though it has more strokes.) [12]

381. politics 政

To the many definitions for **politics** that already exist, this character offers yet another: *correct taskmastering*. Pull the pieces apart. On the one hand, we see the pessimistic wisdom that **politics** has to do with *taskmastering,* maneuvering people with or without their will. And on the other, we see the campaign assurances that this duty can be performed *correctly* if only the right candidate is given a chance. [9]

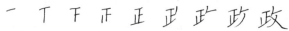

* ## mending   疋

This primitive differs from the kanji for *correct* only by the movement added to the last two strokes, the "-ing" of **mending** if you will. But take a more concrete sense, like **mending** holes in socks. [5]

382. determine   定

Determination, in the sense of settling on a certain course of action, is likened here to *mending* one's *house.* [8]

383. lock   錠

Metal of itself doesn't **lock.** It needs to be so *determined* by a **lock**smith. Now make a concrete image of that. [16]

384. run   走

Running, we are told here, *mends* the *soil.* Observe in the following frames how this kanji can embrace other elements from below, much the same way as the element for *road* does; and to do this, the final stroke needs to be lengthened. [7]

385. transcend   超

When one is *running* after something, the goal that *seduces* one on is said to **transcend** the seeker. [12]

386. proceed

赴

In **proceeding** to a new city or a new job, something in you *runs* ahead with excitement, and something else holds you back, like a *divining rod* built into your psyche warning you to check things out carefully before rushing in too wildly. [9]

387. surpass

越

Here we see two *parades* in competition with one another, each trying to **surpass** the other by *running* at high speed from one town to the next. Note the little "hook" at the end of the first stroke of the element for *parade*. This is the ONLY time it appears in the kanji. [12]

388. just so

是

In this kanji we are shown someone spending an entire *day* at *mending* one stocking, because they want the job done "**just so**." [9]

389. topic

題

In many kinds of research, one can find information on a given **topic** only if the *headings* are prepared *just so*. [18]

是 題

390. dike

堤

A **dike** is a successful bit of engineering only if the amount of *earth* piled up is measured *just so* for the height and pressure of the water it is meant to contain. [12]

土 堤

---

* stretch   　　夂

The primitive meaning to **stretch** might at first seem similar to that for *road.* Take a moment to study it more carefully and you will no doubt notice the difference. Like *road,* however, this character holds other primitives above its sweeping final stroke. [3]

７   ３   夂

---

391. build   建

To construct a **building,** you first draw a set of plans (the writing *brush)* and then *s-t-r-e-t-c-h* your drawing out to scale in reality. [9]

聿   建

---

392. prolong   延

This character is a kind of pictographical image of how **prolonging** is a clever way of *stopping* things by trying to *stretch* them out just the tiniest bit (the extra *drop* at the top of *stop*). Be sure to get a concrete image of this process, by **prolonging** something you can really, physically *stretch*. [15]

正   延

---

393. nativity   誕

The key-word of course calls to mind the feast of Christmas. As the famous poem at the start of St. John's gospel tells us, the **nativity** we celebrate at Christmas had its origins at the very start of time and governs all of human history: it represents the *prolongation* of the eternal *Word* in time and space. [15]

言   誕

* ZOO

This primitive refers to animals in general, but we shall refer to it as a **zoo**, to avoid confusion with some of the other animals that appear elsewhere. Were it not for the downward hook at the end of the first stroke, it would be indistinguishable from *mend*. Perhaps by now you have developed an eye for such details. If not, don't worry. It will come in time if you pay attention each time one of them shows up. [5]

394. cornerstone

This character depicts a **cornerstone** as a *stone* set at the end of a wildlife preserve (the *"zoo* in the *grove"*). [18]

395. bridegroom

What makes a man a **bridegroom** is obviously a *woman* and her dowry, here presented as a small *zoo* (animals were often used for this purpose in earlier societies) and a *month* away from it all (the "honeymoon"). [12]

LESSON 18

The three groups of characters brought together in this rather long lesson are clustered around three sets of primitives dealing respectively with cloth and clothing, weather, and postures.

396. garment   衣

At the top we see the *tophat,* and at the bottom a pictographic representation of the folds of a **garment.** If you break the "4-fold" part into 2 sets of 2 strokes, you will find it easier to remember. [6]

* Used as a primitive, the additional meanings of *cloak, scarf,* or simply *clothing* will come in handy. What has to be noted particularly are the changes in shape the kanji can undergo when it becomes an element in other kanji. In fact, it is the most volatile of all the kanji we shall treat, and for that **reason** deserves special attention here. When it appears to the left, it looks like this: 衤 and we shall take it to mean *cloak.* At the bottom, when attached to the stroke immediately above it, the first two strokes (the *tophat*) are omitted, giving us: 𧘇 which we shall take to mean a *scarf.* On rare occasions, the element can be torn right across the middle, with the first 2 strokes appearing at the top and the last 4 at the bottom of another primitive or cluster of primitives: 衣 in which cases we shall speak of a *tophat* and *scarf.* And finally, of course, it can keep its kanji shape, and its meaning of *clothing* in general. Examples of each of these shapes will appear in the following frames.

397. tailor   裁

Think here of *clothes* that have been specially **tailored** for **Thanksgiving** celebrations to look like traditional Pilgrim garb. [12]

一　十　土　牛　耂　丰　耒　耒　表　裁　裁　裁

398. attire   装

The character for **attire** can be remembered as a picture of what we may call a *"turtle-samurai"* sweater. At the top we see the *turtle-samurai* and at the bottom the element for clothes. [12]

丨　丬　爿　壮　壮　壮　壮　壯　装　装　装　装

399. back

A perfectly innocent looking *tophat* and *scarf* lying there in front of you, turned over, reveal a hidden *computer* on the backside: obviously the tools of a master spy. Such experiences teach one always to have a look at the **back** side of things. [13]

400. demolition

The right half of this character shows *cloth* woven so thin that it can pass through the *eye* of a *needle,* fittingly draped around the slithering, ethereal form of a poltergeist. In this frame, our eerie visitor brushes its robes against a nearby block of apartments and completely **demolishes** them, razing them to the *ground.* [16]

401. pathetic

A drunken son in a tattered *tophat* and soiled silk *scarf* with a giant *mouth* guzzling something or other gives us a **pathetic** character-role in which W. C. Fields might find himself right at home. [9]

402. distant

A **distant** figure is coming at you on the *road* ahead but is so far away that you can't make it out to be anything but a *lidded crock* wearing a silk *scarf.* [13]

403. monkey

This clever little **monkey** has captured an entire pack of *wild dogs,* locked them inside a *lidded crock,* and wrapped the whole thing up in a silk *scarf* to make a present to the dog-catcher. [13]

---

404. first time   初

The primitives here take care of themselves: *cloak* and *dagger*. What I leave to you is to decide on an appropriate connotation for **"first time"** to take advantage of them. [7]

---

* towel   巾

The basic meaning of this primitive is a **bolt of cloth,** from which we derive the meaning of a **towel.** [3]

---

405. linen   布

The maid, *towels by her side* distributes the linen. [5]

---

406. sail   帆

A **sail** made of a *towel* distinguishes a clearly **mediocre** vessel. [6]

---

407. hanging scroll   幅

A *towel* owned by the *wealthiest* tycoon in the world is made into a **hanging scroll** after his death and sold to the highest bidder. [12]

408. cap 帽

Because of the *risk* involved (of getting the *sun* in one's *eyes*), one puts together a make-shift **cap** out of a dirty old *towel*. [12]

409. curtain 幕

The *bolt of cloth* draped over the entrance of the old *graveyard* is painted to look like the **curtain** of death that leads to the other world. [13]

410. canopy 幌

The *bolt of cloth* stretched overhead with only a few of the *sun's rays* breaking through represents a **canopy** over one's bed. [13]

411. brocade 錦

A strip of *white towel* and some scraps of *metal* have the makings of a primitive kind of **brocade**. [16]

412. market 市

Dressed in nothing but a bath-*towel* and *tophat,* one sets off to the **market**place in search of a bargain or two. [5]

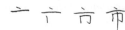

413. elder sister   姉

Of all the *women* of the family, it is the **elder sister** who has the duty to go to *market* to do the shopping. [8]

414. lungs   肺

One is surprised, strolling through the *market,* to find among the *meats* hung out for sale a slab marked: **lungs.** [9]

*   apron   帗

The *bolt of cloth* with edges jagged like little *crowns* is the cook's **apron.** [5]

415. sash   带

The part of the *apron* where one finds the buckle or fastener (represented pictorially by the first 5 strokes) is on the **sash.** [10]

416. stagnate   滞

People that have been *"sashed"* to something (whether their mother's apron strings or a particular job) for too long become like *water* that has stopped moving: they start to **stagnate.** [13]

* belt   冂

This primitive, clearly derived from that for *towel,* is always hung on another vertical stroke, and takes the meaning of a **belt.** [2]

丨　冂

417. thorn   刺

Thorns grow on a bush here that has wrapped itself around a *tree* like a *belt,* and sting the poor *tree* like a thousand *sabres* [8]

418. system   制

Remember this kanji as a unique **system** for leading cows to the slaughterer's *sword:* one ties a *belt* about their waist and fixes that *belt* to an overhead cable, pulling the *cow* up into the air where it hangs suspended, helpless against the fate that awaits it. [8]

丿　ﾉ二　ﾆﾟ　ﾄﾟ　ﾄﾞ　缶　制　制

419. made in...   製

A label indicating that a piece of *clothing* was **made in** U.S.A. or Taiwan or Japan is itself a symbol for the *systematization* of the *clothing* industry. [14]

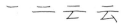

* rising cloud   云

This primitive is meant to depict in graphic fashion a **cloud** of something or other **rising** upwards, like vapor or smoke or dust. [4]

一　二　云　云

420. revolve

As the wheels of the *car* **revolve**, they kick up small *rising clouds* of dust and debris behind them. [11]

421. technique

The secret **technique** of making a *rising cloud* of smoke turn into a bouquet of *flowers* is shown here. [7]

422. rain

This kanji, also a primitive, is one of the clearest instances we have of a complex pictograph. The top line is the sky, the next 3 strokes a pair of clouds, and the final 4 dots the **rain** collected there and waiting to fall. [8]

* As a primitive it can mean either **rain** or *weather* in general. Because it takes so much space, it usually has to be contracted into a crown by shortening the second and third strokes into a *crown* like this: 雫

423. cloud

雲

Here is the full character for **cloud** from which the primitive for a *rising cloud* derives. **Clouds** begin with vapors *rising* up in small *clouds* from the surface of the earth, and then gathering to make **clouds** that eventually dump their *rain* back on the earth. [12]

424. cloudy weather

We refer to days when the *sun* is covered by the *clouds* as **cloudy weather**. [16]

425. thunder

The full noise and terror of **thunder** is best felt not with your head tucked under your pillow safe in bed, but out in an open *rice field* where you can get into the full spirit of the *weather*. [13]

426. frost

Think of **frost** as a cooperative venture, an *inter*-action of the forces of *weather* that sit around a conference table and finally decide to allow a very light amount of moisture to fall just before a short and sudden freeze. [17]

* ice

The condensation of the three drops we have been using to mean *water* into two drops signals the solidifying of *water* into **ice**. Note that when this primitive appears to the left, it is written like the last two strokes of the element for *water,* ⺀ , whereas under another primitive, it is written like the first two strokes of the *water* primitive: ⼀ . [2]

427. winter

Walking legs slipping on the *ice* are a sure sign of **winter**. [5]

---

428. heavens   天

This character is meant to be a pictograph of a great man, said to represent the Lord of the **Heavens**. (You may, of course, use the elements *ceiling* and *St. Bernard* instead.) [4]

> * The primitive can mean either the **heaven** of eternal bliss or the general term for sky, the **heavens**. Pay special attention to the fact that in its primitive form the first stroke is written right to left, rather like the first stroke of *thousand* (Frame 40), ratheı than left to right, giving us: 天 .

---

*   angel   喬

The sense of the primitive, **angel,** derives from the primitive for *heavens* replacing the *tophat* in the character for *tall.* [12]

---

429. bridge   橋

The **bridge** shown here is made of *trees* in their natural form, except that the trunks have been carved into the forms of *angels,* a sort of "Ponte degli Angeli." [16]

---

430. attractive   嬌

Associating a particularly **attractive** *woman* you know with an *angel* should be no problem. [15]

431. stand up

This picture of a vase **standing up** has its meaning extended to represent the general posture of anything **standing up**. [5]

> * Used as a primitive, it can also mean *vase*. In taking its kanji-meaning, it is best to think of something **standing up** that is normally lying down, or something standing up in an unusual way.

432. cry

One **cries** and **cries** until one is *standing up* knee-deep in *water* (or until one has a *vase*-full of *water*). [8]

433. badge

Try to imagine a club **badge** pinned to your lapel in the form of a mammoth *sunflower* protruding from a wee little *vase*. [11]

434. vie

Two *teenagers* are seen here *standing up* to one another, **vying** for the attention of their peers. [20]

435. sovereign

An uncommon, but not altogether unlikely picture of a reigning **sovereign** has him *standing up* in his *apron,* presumably at the behest of HIS **sovereign** who needs help with washing the dishes. [9]

436. juvenile

This frame shows up the image of a **juvenile** genius *standing* on top of a *computer,* or rather jumping up and down on it because it couldn't come up with the right answer. [12]

437. pupil

Begin with the double meaning of the key-word: "student" and "the apple of one's *eye*." Now all you have to do is dwell on the phrase *"juvenile* of one's *eye"* (the meaning here) until it provides you with an image. [17]

438. bell

A **bell** is made of *metal* and makes a noise like the **"bellowing"** of *juveniles* who aren't getting their own way. [20]

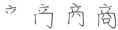

439. make a deal

See the peddlar *standing* atop a *pheasant-glass* as if it were a soap-box, hawking his wares to passers-by. The *legs* and *mouth* represent the tools of his trade, to **make a deal** anyway he can. [11]

*   antique   商

The primitive meaning **antique**, not itself a kanji, depicts a *vase* kept under a *glass hood* because it is very, very *old.* [11]

---

440. legitimate wife

The phrase **legitimate wife** would have no meaning if there were not such things as "illegitimate wives," taken because one's legal *woman* has turned into an *antique*. [14]

---

441. suitable

Can you imagine anything less **suitable** to do with one's precious *antiques* than to display them in the middle of a crowded *roadway?* [14]

---

442. drip

Picture *water* dripping on what you thought were precious *antiques,* only to find that the artificial marks painted on them are running! [14].

---

443. enemy

Picture your most precious *antique* (it doesn't matter how old it really is, so long as it is the oldest thing YOU own) being knocked over by your most unlikeable *taskmaster,* and you have a good picture of how people make themselves **enemies** for life. [15]

商 敵

---

444. spoon   匕

This character, a pictograph of a **spoon,** is easy enough to remember, provided you keep it distinct from that for *seven.* The difference, of course, is that the first stroke does not cut across the second here. [2]

ノ ヒ

* As a primitive, this kanji can take on the additional meaning of someone *sitting on the ground,* of which it can also be considered a pictograph.

---

445. north   北

The cold air from the **north** is so strong that we see *two people sitting on the ground* back to back, their arms interlocked so they don't blow away. (Pay special attention to the drawing of the first 3 strokes.) [5]

---

446. stature   背

One's stature is measured according to the *"northern*-most" *part of the body.* [9]

---

447. compare   比

With *two spoons*, one in each hand, you are comparing your mother's cooking with your mother-in-law's. [4]

上 比

---

448. descendants   昆

By *comparing* apes with anthropoids, we not only discover the latter have **descended** from those progenitors educated in the higher branches, but that the very idea of seeing everything **descended** from everything else, one way or another, means that there is "nothing new UNDER the *sun.*" [8]

449. all

Think of the housewives in TV commercials *"comparing* the *whiteness"* of their laundry across the fence, a typical advertisement for the popular detergent known as **All**. (If you don't know the brand, surely you've heard the phrase **"all**-purpose detergent" or **"all**-temperature detergent.) [9]

450. mix

Mixed marriages, this character suggests, *water* down the quality of one's *descendants—the* oldest racial nonsense in the books! [11]

* siesta

Conjure up the classic portrait of the Latin **siesta**: a muchacho *seated on the ground*, propped up against some building, *bound up* from neck to ankles in a sarape, one of those great, broad-rimmed Mariachi hats pulled down over his face, and the noonday *sun* beating down overhead. Always use the complete image, never simply the general sense of **siesta**. [8]

451. thirst

As you pass by the muchacho taking the *siesta,* he cries out that he is **thirsty** and you turn the *water*-hose on him. [11]

452. audience

Imagine an **audience** with the emperor or the pope in which all those in attendance are sitting down, leaning against the wall, sleeping like our muchacho on *siesta* as the honored one gives his *speech*. [15]

---

453. brown   褐

The color of the sarape or *cloak* of our muchacho on *siesta* is a dull **brown**, the color this kanji indicates. [13]

---

454. hoarse   喝

When the muchacho on *siesta* looks up at you and opens his *mouth* to talk, his voice is so **hoarse** that you cannot understand him. [11]

---

455. delicious   旨

Something is so downright **delicious** that one spends the entire *day* with a *spoon* in hand gobbling it up. [6]

---

456. fat   脂

This kanji tells us that if you feed the *flesh* with too many *delicious* things, it soon gets **fat**. [10]

---

457. I (one)   壱

The Roman numeral I, like that for *II* we met earlier in Frame 355—is only rarely used now. In the midst of all the *samurai,* we notice one in particular *seated on the ground* with a *crown* on his head, indicating that he is "number **one**" in the current rankings. [7]

士 声 壱

*   reclining   ⼇

The picture is obvious: the first stroke represents the head, and the
second the body of someone **reclining**. You may also use the synonyms
lying or *lying down*. [2]

丿 ⼇

458. every   每

"Behind **every** successful person *lies* a woman . . . ," who usually turns
out to be one's *mother!* [6]

⼇ 每

459. cleverness   敏

Behind *every* successful *taskmaster,* the **cleverness** of a fox to outwit
his charges. [10]

 敏

460. plum   梅

Behind *every* Jack Horner's piemaker, a **tree** full of **plum**. [10]

木 梅

461. sea   海

Behind every *drop of water*, a **sea** from which all *water* originally
came. [9]

氵 海

462. beg 乞

See someone *lying down* in a public place with a *hook* in place of a hand, **begging** a morsel of rice or a few pence. [3]

463. drought 乾

In times of **drought** anything at all will do. Here we see the victims *begging* for just a little *mist* for relief. [11]

卓 乾

* double back 复

Either the connotations of turning around and heading back during one's travels, or folding an object in half will do here. It pictures someone **doubling back** to the nearest inn to *lie down* and rest a weary pair of *walking legs* after a full *day's* voyage. [9]

⺊ 旬 复

464. abdomen 腹

If you *double back* (fold over) most animals in the middle, the *part of the body* where the crease comes would be the **abdomen**. [13]

月 腹

465. duplicate 複

In its original and etymologically transparent sense, to **duplicate** something means to *double* it *back* with a fold, like the fold of a *cloak*. [14]

466. lack

The pictograph hidden in this character is of someone yawning. The first stroke shows the head thrown back; the second, the arm bent at the elbow as the hand reaches up to cover the mouth; and the last two, the legs. Since yawning shows a **lack** of something (psychologically, interest; physiologically, sleep), the connection is plain to see. [4]

* As a primitive, it can mean either *yawn* or *lack*.

467. blow

To **blow** is really no more than a deliberate effort to make one's *mouth lack* all the air that is in it. [7]

468. cook

Better to picture what happens when you do not pay attention to your work in the kitchen. Here we see a blazing *fire* and an inattentive, *yawning* **cook** who let things get out of control. [8]

469. song

The **song** in this kanji is being sung by a chorus line of *can-can* girls. Why it should be eliciting nothing but *yawning* from the audience, I leave to you to decide. [14]

470. soft   軟

If the cushions of one's *car* are too **soft**, one may begin *yawning* at the wheel. [11]

471. next

This key-word connotes the **"next** in line" of a succession of people or things. Let there be a shortage of *ice* on the hottest day of summer, and you stand in line, *yawning* and impatiently waiting for the distributor to call out "Next!" [6]

* As a primitive, this character can either retain its key-word meaning of *next* or the related meaning of *second*.

472. briar

Earlier we made mention of the story of **Briar** Rose (or "Sleeping Beauty," as we called her in Frame 154) and drew attention to the **briar** hedge that grew up all about her castle. But in the *second* part of the story, these **briars** blossomed into *flowers*. Hence her name, **Briar** Rose. Be careful not to confuse this character with that for *thorn* (Frame 417). [9]

473. assets

The first *shells* (money) you earn, you use to pay your debts. From then on, the *next shells* you accumulate become your **assets**. [13]

474. figure

This kanji depicts a woman's **figure** as a sort of *second* self. [9]

475. consult with

To seek the *words* of a *second mouth* is to **consult** with someone about something. [16]

LESSON 19

We conclude PART TWO by picking up most of the remaining primitives that can be built up from elements already at our disposal, and learning the kanji that are based on them. When you have completed this section, run through all the frames from LESSON 13 and jot down notes at any point you think helpful. That way, even if you have not made any notations on your review cards, you will at least have some record of the images you used.

* muzzle

The element for **muzzle** shows a *vase* fixed over a *mouth,* perhaps with a rubber band running around the back of the head to keep it in place. [8]

476. compensation

Picture a *clam* used as a *muzzle* to quiet the complaints of a fisherman's widow asking **compensation** for her husband lost at sea. [15]

貝　賠

477. cultivate 培

The barrel hoops used by many Japanese farmers to stretch clear plastic over a garden patch in order to **cultivate** bigger and bigger vegetables is a way of *muzzling* the *soil*. [11]

478. divide 剖

To "**divide** and conquer" you use a *sabre* and a *muzzle*. [10]

479. sound 音

The kanji for **sound** depicts something *standing* in the air over a *tongue wagging in a mouth*, much the same as *a* **sound** does for the briefest of moments before disappearing. [9]

立 音

* The primitive from this kanji also means simply a *sound*.

480. darkness 暗

When "**darkness** covered the earth" at the beginning of time, there was neither *sun* nor *sound*. [13]

日 暗

481. rhyme 韻

Poetry restricted to verses which **rhyme** often finds it has to abandon clarity of thought in order to make the **rhyme** of the words work. In this kanji's picture, one becomes a kind of "*sound-employee*." [19]

*   kazoo

This primitive's special usefulness lies not in its frequency but in its simplification of a few otherwise difficult kanjis. It pictures the *sound* of a *fiesta,* namely a **kazoo**. [12]

482. discriminating

A person of **discriminating** intellect can tell the difference between the mere *kazoo*-buzzing and *words* spoken wisely. [19]

*   mirror

This primitive gets its meaning from the following frame. It shows a pair of *human legs* and a *tongue-wagging mouth* looking at a **mirror** *standing* on the wall, asking perhaps who might be the fairest of them ·all. [11]

483. mirror

After lakes but before glass, polished *metal* was used for **mirrors**. These *metal* **mirrors** are recalled in this character for *a* **mirror**. [19]

484. boundary

Imagine the **boundary** of a plot of *land* marked with gigantic *mirrors* enabling the landowner to keep trespassers in sight at all times. [14]

485. deceased

A *tophat* hanging on a *hook* in the front hall, right where the **deceased** left it the day he died, reminds us of him and his kanji. [3]

* In addition to *deceased*, the primitive meaning of *to perish* shall also be used for this character.

486. blind

If one's *eyes perish* before death, one remains blind for the rest of life. [8]

487. delusion

The "ideal *woman*" one daydreams about is no more than a **delusion**. Hence, *perish* the thought of her. [6]

488. laid waste

The *flowers* which *perish* in the *flood* are taken here as symbols of an area that has been **laid waste**. [9]

489. ambition

The story of **ambition** talks of a *king* walking under the *perishing* (or "waning") *moon* dreaming great dreams about his kingdom. (The roots of ambition are from the same word as "ambulate," meaning to walk about.) [11]

亡　汐　望

490. direction　　　方

Spinning a *dagger* about on its hilt on the top of a *tophat*—waiting to see in which **direction** it points when it comes to rest—one leaves to fate where one is going next. Take care in writing this character. [4]

一　方

* As a primitive, this character will take the sense of a *compass,* the instrument used to determine *direction.*

491. disturb　　　妨

Imagine a *compass* that is **disturbed** every time a *woman* passes by, sending the needle spinning madly round and round. [7]

女　妨

492. boy　　　坊

The character for a **boy** shows us a **boy**-scout cleaning the *dirt* out of his *compass*—the more *dirt* you can imagine, the better. [7]

坊

493. perfume　　　芳

Here we see a special *compass* used to pick out those *flowers* most suited for making good **perfumes.** [7]

艹　芳

494. obese　　　肪

When one eats too much, one needs a *compass* to find one's way around the **obese** mass that accumulates in the mid-section. Compare this with your stories for *round* (Frame 44) and *fat* (Frame 456), similar in meaning but distinct in imagery. [8]

月　肪

---

495. call on

訪

When making a courtesy **call on** a dignitary, one has to gauge one's *words* with great care. Hence the need for a *compass*. [11]

言　訪

---

496. set free

放

The *taskmaster* **sets** an unruly slave **free**, giving him no more than a quick glance at the *compass* and a boot from behind. [8]

方　放

---

497. violent

激

Some cosmic *taskmaster* hovering overhead whips up the waves to make them dash **violently** against the shore. In the *white* foam that covers the *water* we see a broken *compass* floating, all that remains of a shipwreck. [16]

氵　沪　澊　激

---

*   devil

The two *horns* on the head of the *teenager* are enough to suggest to most parents of adolescents a good picture of the **devil**. [7]

ソ　兑

---

498. undress

脱

To **undress** is to expose the *flesh* and tempt the *devil* in one's companion. Ignore the moral if you want, but not the *devil*. [11]

月　脱

---

499. rumor 　　　　　　　　　　説

Not inappropriately, this character likens a **rumor** to the *devil's* own
words. [14]

言　説

---

500. pointed 　　　　　　　　　　鋭

Metal which has been **pointed** (as an awl, a pick, a nail, or a knife)
tends to serve the *devil's* purposes as well as civilization's: our tools
are also our weapons. [15]

金　鋭

---

501. formerly 　　　　　　　　　　曾

This primitive (named for its associations with the kanji of the
following frame) is composed of a pair of *horns* growing out of a
brain with a *tongue wagging in the mouth* beneath. Think of **"former"**
in connection with administrators or heads of state who have just left
office but continue to make a nuisance of themselves by advertising
their opinions on public policy. [11]

丷　曲　曾

* The primitive meaning, *increase,* comes from the next frame.
Always think of of something multiplying wildly as you watch.

---

502. increase 　　　　　　　　　　増

This kanji depicts an **increase** of *soil,* multiplying so fast that it literally buries everything in its path. [14]

土　増

503. presents

The **presents** offered here are *money* that *increases* each time you give it away. Do not confuse with the temporal word *present* (Frame 259). [18]

貝　贈

504. east 東

As a "Western" language, English identifies the **east** with the rising *sun*. In more fanciful terms, we see the *sun* piercing through a *tree* as it rises in the **east**. [8]

* Both the direction *east* and the part of the world called "the *East*" are primitive meanings of this character.

505. ridgepole

If the piece of *wood* in the roof known as the **ridgepole** points *east*, the sunrise will be visible from the front door. [12]

才　棟

506. frozen 凍

The whole secret to breaking the *ice* with the *East* is to peek behind those mysteriously **"frozen smiles."** [10]

冫　凍

* porter

Let the extended dot at the top represent the load which the *samurai* is carrying in his role as the master's **porter**. [4]

ノ 壬

507. pregnancy   妊

A *woman* who is in her **pregnancy** is a bit like a *porter,* bearing her new companion wherever she goes. [7]

女 妊

508. courts   廷

Those who rule the **courts,** the *porters* of justice and order, are often found to *stretch* the law to suit their own purposes. Recall the kanji for *prolong* from Frame 392 and keep it distinct. [7]

壬 廷

Part Three:

———————

ELEMENTS

We come now to the third major step in our study of the kanji: the invention of plots from primitive elements. From now on, the ordering of the remaining   characters according to their primitives will be taken care of, but the reader will be required to do most of the work. As before, particularly difficult kanji will be supplied with supplementary hints, plots, or even whole stories.

By now you will have a feel for the way in which details can be worked into a kanji story so as to create a more vivid ambience for the primitive elements to interact. What may be more difficult is experimenting with plots and discarding them until the simplest one is fixed on, and then embellished and nuanced.

You may find it helpful occasionally to study some of the earlier stories which you found particularly impressive, in order to discover precisely why they struck you, and then to imitate their vitality in the stories you will now be inventing. Equally instructive will be any attention you give to those characters whose stories you have found it difficult to remember, or have easily confused with those of other characters. As you progress through this final section, you may wish even to return and amend some of those earlier stories. But do it with the knowledge that it is generally better to review a story and perhaps repair it slightly than to change it entirely, once it has been learned.

LESSON 20

To begin our work with the primitives by themselves, let us take six kanji of varied difficulty which use primitives we have already learned, and which have been kept apart deliberately for the sake of this initial sally into independent learning.

509. dye

Water . . . nine . . . tree. From those elements you must compose a plot for the key-word, **dye**. Here, as elsewhere, any of the alternate meanings of the primitives may be used, provided they do not require a position other than that of the kanji in question. [9]

510. burn

Hearth . . . sort of thing. Beware letting the very reading of the primitive elements do your work for you. Unless you make a vivid image of something **burning** and relate it just as vividly to those primitive meanings, you can count on forgetting this character very soon. [16]

511. V.I.P.

The **V.I.P.** indicated here is an important guest making a visit. The elements are: *house . . . ceiling . . . few . . . shells.* [15]

512. year-end

Stop . . . march . . . small. Be sure not to forget that final dot! [13]

止 广 炭 歳

513. prefecture 県

Above, the *eye;* and below two primitives **attached to one another: the** *fishhook* and *small.* Although apparently the simplest of these first six kanji, when you begin to work on its plot and story you will quickly find out that the number of strokes and visual complexity of a kanji does not make it easier or harder to remember. It is the primitives with which one has to work that are the critical factor, as in this case where the meaning of the key-word is so seemingly distant from the obvious elements, *eye, fishhook,* and *small,* that we decided to break the kanji down further. [9]

且 県

---

514. horse chestnut　　　　　　　　栃

A tree . . . cliff . . . ten thousand. [9]

 木 术 栃

LESSON 21

If you have found some of the characters in the last brief lesson difficult to work with, I can only assure you that it will get easier with time, indeed already with this long lesson. More important is to take heed that as it does get easier you don't skip over the stories too quickly, trusting only in the most superficial of images. If you spend up to five minutes on each character focusing on the composition of the primitives into a tidy plot, and then filling out the details of a little story, you will not be wasting time, but saving yourself the need to relearn it later.

---

*　scorpion　　　　　　　　也

This primitive is a pictograph of the **scorpion**, the first 2 strokes representing its head and pincers, the last stroke its barbed tail, in which you may recognize the *fishhook*. [3]

 𠃌 也 也

---

515. ground　　　　　　　　地

Soil and a *scorpion* (an "earth animal"). This is, of course, the full character from which the primitive of the same meaning derives. [6]

 土 地

516. pond   池

Water . . . scorpion. It would be easy to slip into a "lazy image" in cases like this one, picturing, let us say, a *scorpion* near the *water*. But if you picture rather a *scorpion* letting its venom out *drop by drop* until it has made a whole **pond** of the stuff, the image is more likely to remain fixed. [6]

氵 池

517. insect   虫

Work with the pictograph as you wish. [6]

口 中 虫 虫

* As a primitive, this insect will refer to the whole *insect* kingdom, so that it can be specified anew in each kanji that contains it.

518. lightning-bug   蛍

Schoolhouse . . . insect. [11]

⺌ 蛍

519. snake   蛇

Insect . . . house . . . spoon. [11]

虫 虴 蛇

520. rainbow   虹

Insect . . . craft. [9].

虫 虹

521. butterfly 蝶

Insect . . . generation . . . tree. [15]

522. single 独

Think of this key-word in connection with "a bachelor." The elements: *wild dogs . . . insect.* [9]

523. silkworm 蚕

Heavens . . . insect. Be sure to do something about the position of the two elements. [10]

524. wind 風

Windy . . . drops of . . . insects. Hint: think of the last two primitives as representing a swarm of gnats, those tiny *drops of insects* that are such pests. [9]

525. self 己

The kanji carries the abstract sense of the **self**, the deep-down inner structure of the human person that mythology has often depicted as a *snake*—which is what it depicts pictographically. Be sure to keep it distinct from the similar key-words, *oneself* (Frame 36) and *I* (Frame 17). [3]

* As a primitive element, this kanji can be used for the *snake*—of which it is a pictograph—or any of the various concrete symbolic meanings the *snake* has in popular myth and fable. [3]

526. rouse

起

Run . . . snake. [10].

527. queen

妃

Woman . . . snake. [6]

528. reformation

改

Pluralizing the *snake* and focusing on a single *taskmaster* may help recommend the image of Ireland's most famous **reformer**. [7]

529. scribe

記

Words . . . snake. [10]

530. wrap

包

Bind up . . . snake. [5]

* The primitive meaning of *wrap* should always be used with the *snake* in mind to avoid confusion with similar terms. Just let "*wrap*" mean "with a snake coiled about it."

531. placenta

胞

Part of the body . . . wrap. [9]

---

532. cannon

砲

Stones . . . wrap. [10]

石 砲

---

533. bubbles

泡

Water . . . wrap. [8]

氵 泡

---

534. tortoise

亀

This is not a *turtle* (see Frame 235) but a **tortoise,** however you wish to picture the difference. Let the "*bound-up*" at the top refer to the head, and the two *suns,* with a long tail running through it, to the shell. [11]

* As a primitive, this kanji is abbreviated to its bottom half, 电 , and comes to mean *eel.* (If it is any help, this kanji in its full form can also be remembered through its abbreviation's primitive meaning.)

---

535. electricity

電

Rain/weather . . . eel. [13]

536. dragon

Vase . . . eel. In order not to confuse this kanji with the zodiacal *sign of the dragon*, which we will meet later (Frame 2008) and use as a primitive, you might think here of a paper parade **dragon**. [10]

537. waterfall

Water . . . vase . . . eels. As explained in the previous frame, the character learned there for *dragon* should not be used as a primitive. [13]

*   sow

Let this primitive represent a fat **sow**. Easier than pulling it apart into smaller elements is remembering its shape as a highly stylized pictograph. Practice its 7 strokes a few times before going on to examples of its use in the following frames. [7]

538. pork

Flesh . . . sow. [11]

539. pursue

Sows . . . road. [10]

540. consummate

The *horns* atop the *sow* suggest a boar at work. Add the element for a *road*. Now create a story whose meaning is: **consummate.** [12]

541. house

This is the full character whose primitive form we learned already. To help a little, this kanji recalls the times when the "domestic" animals were, as the word itself suggests, kept in the **house**. Hence: *house . . . sow* [10]

542. marry into

The kanji in this frame betrays the traditional Japanese approach to marriage: it is the *woman* who leaves her family for another *house*hold, thus **marrying into** a man's family. [13]

543. overpowering

Tall . . . crowned . . . sow. [14]

* piglets

This abbreviation of the full primitive for a *sow,* quite naturally, means **piglets.** [5]

* piggy bank   昜

This very helpful primitive element is worth the few moments it takes to learn it. Just remember that each *day* a few pence are put into the little *piggy* on your bureau whom you call a **piggy bank**. [9]

日   昜

---

544. intestines   腸

Flesh . . . piggy bank. [13]

月   腸

---

545. location   場

Soil . . . piggy bank. [12]

土   場

---

546. hot water   湯

Water . . . piggy bank. [12]

氵   湯

---

547. sheep   羊

This pictograph shows the animal *horns* at the top attached to the head (3rd stroke), the front and back legs (strokes 4 and 5) and body (final stroke). [6]

丷   兰   羊

* The primitive meaning of *sheep* can add the further connotations given in the following frame. As we saw with the *cow,* the "tail" is cut off when it is set immediately over another element.

548. beauty

美

Try to think of what the Chinese were on to when they associated the idea of **beauty** with a *large sheep*. [9]

549. ocean

洋

Water . . . sheep. Be sure to keep the stories and key-word of this kanji distinct from those for *sea* (Frame 461). [9]

550. detailed

詳

Words/speaking . . . sheep. [13]

551. fresh

鮮

Fish . . . sheep. [17]

552. accomplished

達

The key-word is meant to connote someone "skilled" at something. On the *road* we find *soil* OVER *a sheep*. You may have to work with this one a while longer. [12]

553. envious

羨

Sheep . . . water . . . yawn. Although this character looks rather simple,

special care should be taken in learning it because of the proximity
of the final two elements to the character for *next,* which we learned
in Frame 471. Note, too, that the *water* comes UNDER the *sheep,* rather
than to the left. [15]

羊 羊 羡

---

* wool   关

This rather uncommon primitive is made by pulling the tail of the
sheep to one side to create a semi-enclosure. The meaning of **wool** is
derived from the fact that the shearer is holding the *sheep* by the tail
in order to trim its **wool.** [7]

羊 羊

---

554. distinction   差

Wool . . . craft. [10]

产 差

---

555. don   着

I cannot resist doing this one for you, since it clearly describes
donning (putting on) one's clothes as "pulling the *wool* over one's
eyes." [12]

羊 着

---

* turkey   隹

This primitive is best remembered as an old **turkey,** complete with
pipe and monocle. Its writing is somewhat peculiar, so take note of
the order of the strokes. Let the first four strokes stand for the
turkey's head, neck, and drooping chin. The remainder can then be
pictographic of the plumage. [8]

ノ イ 亻 仁 什 仹 佳 隹

556. solely

唯

Mouth . . . turkey. [11]

口　唯

557. char

焦

Turkey . . . oven-fire. [12]

佳　焦

558. reef

礁

Rocks . . . char. [17]

石　礁

559. gather

集

Turkeys . . . atop a tree. [12]

隹　集

560. quasi-

准

Ice . . . turkey. [10]

冫　准

561. advance

進

Turkey . . . road. [11]

佳　進

562. miscellaneous   雑

Baseball . . . trees . . . turkey. [14]

九　杂　雑

563. feminine   雌

This character for **feminine** forms a pair with that for *masculine* (Frame 743). The elements: *footprint . . . spoon . . . turkey.* [14]

止　此　雌

564. semi-   準

Think of this in terms of the **semi**-finals of some sports competition. *Water . . . turkeys . . . needle.* [13]

氵　準

565. stirred up   奮

St. Bernard dog . . . turkey . . . rice field/brains. [16]

大　奞　奮

566. rob   奪

Whereas *burglary* (Frame 357) implies clandestine appropriation of another's property, **robbery** refers to taking by force. The primitive elements: *St. Bernard dog . . . turkey . . . glue.* [14]

大　奞　奪

567. assurance   確

On the left you see the *rock,* which is familiar enough. But pay attention to the right. Taking careful note of the unusual stroke order which has the "chimney" on the *house* doubled up with the first stroke of the *turkey,* we may see the right side as a *turkey-house* (or "coop"). We shall see this pattern only on one other occasion (Frame 1943), but even for these two characters it is well worth the trouble. [15]

石　厂　碓

568. noon 午

With a bit of stretching, you might see a horse's head pointing leftwards in this character. That gives the primary meaning of the Chinese zodiacal sign of the horse, which corresponds to the hour of **noon**. Note how this kanji-primitive differs from that for *cow* (Frame 245). [4]

丿　ﾉ　ﾉ　午

* As a primitive, this character gets the meaning of the *horse*. Any *horse*-image will do, except that of a *team of horses*, which will come later (Frame 1978) and get its own primitive.

569. permit 許

Words . . . horse. [11]

言　許

* Pegasus 隹

By combining the *horse* (and twisting its final stroke to the left a bit) with the *turkey,* we get a *flying horse* or **Pegasus**. Be sure you do not confuse with the *turkey-house* from Frame 567. [11]

 隹

570. delight 歓

Again I cannot resist sharing my own associations. If you've ever seen

Disney's animated interpretation of classical music, "Fantasia," you will recall what was done there with Beethoven's "Pastoral Symphony" (the 6th), and the *flying horses* that figured in it. The mares are bathing in the stream and the stallions begin to gather. As dusk sets in, the *flying horses* all start *yawning* and pair off: a perfectly delightful portrait of **delight**. [15]

隹 歓

571. authority   権

Tree . . . Pegasus. [15]

木 権

572. outlook   観

Pegasus . . . see. [18]

隹 観

573. feathers   羽

From the pictograph of two bird-wings, we get **feathers**. [6]

コ ヨ ヨ 羽

* The related image of *wings* can be added as a primitive meaning.

574. learn   習

Feathers . . . white bird. [11]

羽 習

575. the following   翌

Feathers . . . vase. Be sure to contrast the connotation of this key-word with that for *next* (Frame 471). [11]

羽 翌

576. weekday   曜

Day . . . feathers . . . turkey. [18]

日　日羽　曜

577. laundry   濯

Water . . . feathers . . . turkey [17]

氵　氵羽　濯

LESSON 22

This is a good time to stop for a moment and have a look at how primitive elements get contracted and distorted by reason of their position within a kanji. Reference has been made to the fact here and there in passing, but now that you have attained greater fluency in writing, we may address the problem more systematically.

1. At the left, a primitive will generally be squeezed in from the sides and slanted upwards. For instance, *gold* 金 comes to be written 金 when it functions as the primitive for *metal*. Or again, *tree* has its kanji form 木 flattened into 木 when it comes to the left.

2. Long strokes ending in a hook, which would normally flow out gracefully are squeezed into angular form when made part of a primitive at the left. We see this in the way the kanji for *ray* 光 gets altered in the kanji for *glitter* 光 . In like manner, the *spoon* that is spread out on the right side of *compare* 比 is turned in on itself on the left.

3. Certain characters are pressed down and widened when weighted down by other elements from above. Such is the case, for example, with *woman* 女 when it appears in the lowest position of *banquet* 宴 .

4. The long vertical stroke cutting through a series of horizontal lines is often cut off below the lowest horizontal line. We saw this in changing the *cow* 牛 to fit it into *revelation* 告 , and in the *brush* 聿 which appeared in the kanji for *write* 書 .

5. The long downward swooping stroke that we see in *fire* is an example of another group of distortions. Crowded in by something to its right, it is turned into a short stroke that bends downwards. Hence *fire* 火 and *a lamp* 灯 .

6. Again, we have noted how horizontal lines can double up as the bottom of the upper primitive and the top of the lower primitive. For instance, when *stand* 立 comes in the primitive for *make a deal* 商 .

7. Finally, there are situations in which an entire kanji is changed to assume a considerably altered primitive form. *Water* 水 , *fire* 火 and *portent* 兆 thus become 氵 , 灬 , and 兆 in other characters. Because the full forms are ALSO used as primitives, we have altered the meaning or given specified distinctions in meaning so as to assure that the story in each case dictates precisely how the character is to be written.

From this chapter on, the stroke-order will not be given unless it is entirely new, departs from the procedures we have learned so far, or might otherwise cause confusion. With that, we carry on.

* pent in □

This primitive depicts a corral or pen surrounding something. [3]

| ⌐ 冂 □

578. sayeth 曰

Pent in . . . one. The key-word refers to famous sayings of famous people, and is the origin for the primitive meaning of a *tongue wagging in the mouth* which we leaned in Frame 12. The size of this kanji, a relatively rare one, is what distinguishes it from *day*. [4]

579. quandary   困

Pent in . . . trees. [7]

丨　冂　冂　困　困　困　困

580. harden   固

Old . . . pent up. Leave the people out of your story to avoid complications later when we add the element for *person* to form a new kanji (Frame 973). [8]

581. country   国

Jewels . . . pent up. [8]

582. group   団

Glued . . . fenced in. [6]

583. cause   因

St. Bernard dog . . . fenced in. [6]

584. matrimony   姻

Woman . . . cause. Think here of the "state of **matrimony**" and you will not confuse it with other characters involving marriage, one of which we have already met (Frame 542). [9]

585. park   園

Fenced in . . . lidded crock . . . scarf. [13]

586. -times

The suffix **"-times"** refers to a number of repetitions. Its elements: *a mouth . . . pent up*. Hint: you may find it more helpful to forget the primitives and think of one circle revolving inside of another. [6]

冂 冃 回

587. podium

Soil/ground . . . tophat . . . -times . . . nightbreak. With kanji as difficult as this one, it generally pays to toy around with the various images belonging to its primitives before settling on one image. Aim for as much simplicity as you can. [16]

*　cave 广

This primitive combines the *cliff* (the last 2 strokes) with the first dot we use on the roof of the *house*. Together they make a "cliff-house" or **cave**. It "encloses" its relative primitives beneath it and to the right. [3]

丶 亠 广

588. store

Cave . . . fortune-telling. [8]

广 店

589. warehouse 庫

Cave . . . car. [10]

590. courtyard 庭

Cave . . . courts. [10]

591. government office   庁

Cave . . . a spike. [5]

592. bed   床

Cave . . . tree. [7]

593. hemp   麻

Cave . . . grove. Literally, the "hemp" marijuana comes from. [11]

594. grind   磨

Hemp . . . stone. [16]

595. heart   心

This character, a pictographic representation of the **heart,** is among
the most widely used primitives we shall meet. [4]

l   心 心 心

* As a primitive, it can take three forms to which we shall assign
three distinct meanings. In its kanji-form, it appears BENEATH or
to the RIGHT of its relative primitive and means the physical organ
of the *heart.* To the LEFT, it is abbreviated to three strokes, 忄 , and
means a wildly emotional *state of mind.* And finally, at the very
BOTTOM, it can take the form 小 , in which case we give it the
meaning of a *valentine.*

596. forget   忘

Perish . . . heart. [7]

597. endure   忍

Blade . . . heart.   **Endure** here means longsuffering patience. [7]

598. acknowledge   認

Words . . . endure. [14]

599. mourning   忌

Snake . . . heart. [7]

600. intention   志

Heart . . . samurai. [7]

601. document   誌

Words . . . intention. [14]

602. loyalty   忠

In (the middle of) . . . heart. [8]

603. shish kebab   串

This pictograph of two pieces of meat on a skewer, a **shish kebab**,
will help us in the next frame. [7]

丶　　冂　　冂　　尸　　吕　　吕　　串

604. afflicted   患

Shish kebab . . . heart. [11]

605. think   思

Brains . . . heart. [9]

---

606. grace   恩

Take **grace** in its sense of a favor freely bestowed, not in its meaning
of charming manners or fluid movement. The primitives: *cause . . .
heart.* [10]

---

607. apply   応

The sense of the key-word here is of something appropriate that fills
a particular need, and hence **"applies."** The elements you have to work
with are: *cave . . . heart.* [7]

---

608. idea   意

Sound . . . heart. [13]

---

609. concept   想

To distinguish this kanji from that of the previous frame, focus on
the sense of the "con-" in the word **"concept."** Its elements are: *inter- . . .
heart.* [13]

---

610. breath   息

Nose . . . heart. [10]

---

611. recess   憩

Tongue . . . nose . . . heart. The sense of *breath* from the last frame does
not figure here since it might lead us later to put only the *nose* over
the *heart* and leave the *tongue* off to one side. [16]

612. favor 恵

Ten . . . fields (or: *needle . . . brains*) *. . . heart.* [10]

613. fear 恐

Craft . . . mediocre . . . heart. [10]

614. beguile 惑

The first three elements, *fiesta . . . mouth . . . floor*, appeared together once already in Frame 356. Beneath them, once again, the *heart*. [12]

615. emotion 感

Mouths . . . marching . . . heart. [13]

616. melancholy 憂

Head . . . crowned . . . heart . . . walking legs. Two things merit mention here. First, the "doubling-up" of the last stroke of *head* with the top of the *crown* serves to make the whole more aesthetically beautiful. It happens so rarely that the exceptions are easily learned. Second, try to make a single image out of the four elements. (Religious statuary should offer plenty of suggestions.) [15]

617. widow 寡

House . . . head . . . dagger. Immediately we get another instance of a very odd exception. Notice how the final stroke of the *head* is stretched out, giving the final two strokes a chance to stretch out and make room for the *dagger* that fits in beneath. [14]

618. busy   忙

Perish . . . state of mind. [6]

619. ecstasy   悦

State of mind . . . devil. [10]

620. constancy   恒

State of mind . . . span. [9]

621. lament   悼

To keep this character distinct from others of similar connotation, one need only think of the Prophet Jeremiah whose poetry gave an *eminence* to *the state of mind* we call **lamentation**. [11]

622. enlightenment   悟

I know of one Indian sect which teaches that **enlightenment** is to be had by covering the eyes with one's index fingers, the ears with the thumbs, and the mouth with the little fingers. While these differ a bit from the *five holes* which we used to represent the *"I"* (Frame 17), the idea of achieving a special *state of mind* by covering those five places can help you learn this kanji. Try the position out while you are learning this character. [10]

623. dreadful   怖

State of mind . . . linen. [8]

624. disconcerted   慌

State of mind . . . laid waste. [12]

625. repent   悔

Every (see Frame 458) . . . state of mind. [9]

626. hate   憎

State of mind . . . increase. [13]

627. accustomed   慣

State of mind . . . pierce. [14]

628. pleasure   愉

State of mind . . . butchers (see Frame 289). [12]

629. lazy   惰

State of mind . . . left (i.e. "sinister") *. . . flesh.* [12]

630. humility   慎

State of mind . . . truth. [13]

631. remorse   憾

State of mind . . . emotion. Hint: the etymology of **"remorse"** indicates a
memory that returns again and again to "bite at" one's conscience and
disturb one's peace of mind. [16]

632. recollection   憶

State of mind . . . idea. [16]

633. pining

Graveyard . . . valentine. Note carefully the stroke order of the *valentine* primitive. [14]

634. annexed

Water . . . heavens . . . valentine. [11]

635. invariably

First note the stroke-order of this character, which did not really evolve from the *heart,* even though we take it that way. If one takes it as a pictograph "dividing" *the heart* in half, then one has one of those **invariably** true bits of human anatomy: the fact that each *heart* is divided into two halves. [5]

636. ooze 泌

Water . . . the "invariably" divided heart. [8]

LESSON 23

With this lengthy lesson we shall have passed well beyond one-third of our way through this book. Its main focus is on elements having to do with *hands* and *arms.* As always, the one protection you have against confusing them is to form clear and distinct images the first time you meet a primitive. If you make it through this chapter smoothly, the worst will be behind you and you should have nothing more to fear the rest of the way.

637. hand

Any way you count them, there are either too many or too few fingers to see a good pictograph of a **hand** in this character. But that it is, and so you must. [4]

* Keep to the etymology when using this kanji as a primitive: a single *hand* all by itself.

638. watch over

Hand . . . eyes. [9]

639. chafe

Hemp . . . hand. [15]

640. ego

Hand . . . fiesta. Note how the second stroke of the *hand* is stretched across to double up as the first stroke of the tassled arrow we use for *fiesta*. Compare this with Frames 17, 36, and 525. [7]

641. righteousness

義

Sheep . . . ego. [13]

642. deliberation

議

Words . . . righteousness. [20]

643. sacrifice 犠

Cow . . . righteousness. Do NOT use the image of an animal sacrifice here, since that has its own character, to appear later on. [17]

* fingers 扌

This alternate form of the primitive for *hand* we shall use to represent **finger** or **fingers**. It invariably appears at the left of other primitives. [3]

644. rub 抹

Fingers . . . extremity. [8]

645. embrace 抱

Finger . . . wrap. [8]

才　抱

646. board 搭

The key-word refers to **boarding** vessels for travel. Its elements are: *finger . . . flowers . . . fit together* (see Frame 254). [12]

647. extract 抄

Fingers . . . a few. [7]

648. confront 抗

Fingers . . . a whirlwind. [7]

649. criticism

批

Finger . . . compare. [7]

650. beckon

招

Finger . . . seduce. [8]

651. clear (the land)

拓

Fingers . . . rocks. [8]

652. clap

拍

Fingers . . . white. [8]

653. strike

打

Finger . . . spike. [5]

654. arrest

拘

Fingers . . . phrase. [8]

655. discard

捨

Fingers . . . cottage. [11]

656. kidnap

拐

Finger . . . mouth . . . dagger. [8]

657. pinch   摘

Finger . . . antique. [14]

658. challenge   挑

Fingers . . . portent. [9]

659. finger   指

Finger . . . delicious. [9]

660. hold   持

Fingers . . . Buddhist temple. [9]

661. fasten   括

Finger . . . tongue. [9]

662. brandish   揮

Finger . . . chariot. [12]

663. conjecture   推

Fingers . . . turkey. [11]

664. hoist   揚

Fingers . . . piggy bank. [12]

665. propose   提

Fingers . . . just so. [11]

666. damage   損

Finger . . . employee. [13]

667. pick up   拾

Fingers . . . fit together. Compare Frame 646. [9]

668. shouldering   担

The key-word of this frame refers to **shouldering** a burden of some
sort. Its elements are: *fingers . . . nightbreak.* [8]

669. foothold   拠

Fingers . . . dispose. [8]

670. sketch   描

Fingers . . . seedling. [11]

671. maneuver   操

Fingers . . . goods . . . tree. [16]

672. touch   接

Fingers . . . vase . . . woman. [11]

673. put up (a notice)   掲

Fingers . . . siesta. [11]

674. hang   掛

Fingers . . . ivy . . . magic wand. [11]

*   two hands   开

Let this primitive represent a stylized union of **two hands**, so that its meaning is related to using both hands at the same time. Note that whenever this element appears at the bottom of its relative primitive, the top line is omitted, whether or not there is a horizontal line to replace it. [4]

一　二　于　开

675. polish   研

Stone . . . two hands. [9]

676. commandment   戒

Two hands . . . fiesta. [7]

一　开　戒

677. contraption   械

Tree . . . commandment. [11]

678. nose   鼻

Let me share a rather grotesque image to help with this kanji. Imagine taking your *two hands* and reaching up into someone's *nose.* Once inside you grab ahold of the *brain* and yank it out. At the end, you would have a picture something like that of this character, the full kanji for **nose.** [14]

---

679. punish

Two hands . . . sabre. [6]

---

680. mould

型

Punish . . . soil. In cases like this, you might find it easier to break the character up into its more basic elements, like this: *two hands . . . sword . . . soil.* [9]

---

681. genius

才

Whatever one is particularly adept at—one's special "genius"—one can do very easily, "with one finger" as the phrase goes. This kanji is a pictograph of that one finger. Note how its distinctive form is created by writing the final stroke of the element for *fingers* backwards. [3]

  * The primitive meaning, *genie*, derives from the roots of the word *genius*. Use the *genie* out in the open when the primitive appears to the right of or below its relative primitive; in that case it also keeps its same form. At the left, the form is altered to 扌, and the meaning should be changed to a *genie in the bottle*.

---

682. property

財

Clam . . . genie. [10]

---

683. lumber

材

Tree . . . genie. [7]

684. suppose 存

Genie in the bottle . . . a child. Hint: focus on the key-word's connotation of "make-believe". [6]

一 ナ 存 存

685. exist 在

Genie in the bottle . . . soil. [6]

686. from 乃

This pictograph of a clenched fist, is another of the "hand-primitives". Take note of its rather peculiar drawing. Try to think of drawing a *fist* (the primitive meaning) "**from**" this character to give yourself a connotation for the key-word. [2]

丿 乃

* The primitive meaning is taken from the pictograph: a *fist*.

687. portable 携

Fingers . . . turkey . . . fist. [13]

688. reach out 及

The addition of a final stroke transforms this character from the primitive for a clenched *fist* into the kanji for **reaching out,** much as a stroke of kindness can often turn anger into acceptance. [3]

丿 乃 及

* As a primitive, this shall stand for *outstretched hands.* Only take care not to confuse it with that for *beg* (Frame 462).

689. suck   吸

Mouth . . . outstretched hands. Hint: use the image of a nursing baby. [6]

690. handle   扱

Finger . . . outstretched hands. [6]

* arm   人

The picture of an **arm** dangling from the trunk of the body gives us the element for **arm**, or *tucked under the* **arm** (relative, of course, to the element below it). Examples of both usages follow. Unlike most primitives, the kanji that bears the same meaning (Frame 1418) has absolutely no connection with it. [2]

691. length   丈

The **length** whose measure this kanji depicts extends from the tip of one hand to the tip of the other with the *arms* outstretched. Notice the final stroke, which cuts across the vertical second stroke to distinguish it from *large* (Frame 107). [3]

692. history   史

A mouth . . . tucked under one's arm. [5]

693. officer   吏

One . . . mouth . . . tucked under the arm. [6]

694. grow late

Ceiling . . . sun . . . tucked under the arm. [7]

695. stiff

Rocks . . . grow late. [12]

696. or again

又

Like the several abbreviations in Roman script to indicate "and" (+, &, etc.), this short two-stroke kanji is used for the similar meaning of **or again**. [2]

ㄱ 又

* As a primitive, it will mean *crotch,* as in the *crotch* of the arm. Or whatever.

697. pair

The *crotch* reduplicated gives us a **pair**. [4]

698. mulberry

桑

Crotches, crotches everywhere . . . *tree.* Hint: think of a group of children playing an original version of "Here We Go 'Round the **Mulberry** Bush." [10]

699. vessels

The key-word indicates the Japanese generic term for counting *ships.* Its elements: *turkey . . . crotch.* [10]

700. safeguard 護

Words . . . flowers . . . vessels. [20]

701. seize 獲

A pack of *wild dogs . . . flowers . . . vessels.* Do not confuse this with the character for *arrest* (Frame 654). [16]

702. guy 奴

Woman . . . crotch. [5]

703. angry 怒

Guy . . . heart. [9]

704. friend 友

By one's side . . . crotch. [4]

705. slip out 抜

Fingers . . . friend. [7]

* missile 殳

Although modern connotations are more suggestive, this primitive simply refers to something thrown as a weapon. Its elements: *wind . . . crotch.* [4]

706. throw   投

Fingers . . . missile. [7]

707. drown   没

Water . . . missile. [7]

708. establishment   設

Words . . . missile. [11]

709. beat   撃

Car . . . missile . . . hand. [15]

車　軹　撃

710. husk   殻

Samurai . . . superfluous . . . missile. [11]

土　売　殻

711. branch   支

Needle . . . crotch. [4]

十　支

712. skill   技

Branch . . . fingers. [7]

713. bough

枝

Tree . . . branch. Take a moment to focus on the differences between a **bough,** a *branch,* and a *twig* (Frame 298). [8]

714. limb

肢

Part of the body . . . branch. [8]

* spool

圣

Here we see a simplified drawing of a **spool** (the element for *earth* at the bottom) with threads being wound about it tightly (the *crotch* at the top). You may remember it either pictographically or by way of the primitives. [5]

715. stalk

茎

Flower . . . spool. [8]

716. suspicious

怪

State of mind . . . spool. [8]

717. lightly

軽

Car . . . spool. [12]

718. uncle

叔

Above . . . small . . . crotch. [8]

719. coach   督

Uncle . . . eye. [13]

---

720. loneliness   寂

House . . . uncle. [11]

---

721. graceful   淑

Water . . . uncle. [11]

---

722. anti-   反

Cliff . . . crotch. [4]

---

723. slope   坂

Ground . . . anti-. [7]

---

724. plank   板

Tree . . . anti-. [8]

---

725. return   返

Anti- . . . road. [7]

---

726. marketing   販

Shells/money . . . anti-. [11]

727. claw

This character is a pictograph of a bird's **claw**, and from there comes to mean animal **claws** in general (including human fingernails). [4]

* As a primitive, we shall use the graphic image of a *vulture,* a bird known for its powerful *claws.* It generally appears above another relative primitive element, where it is squeezed into the form ⼱ .

728. gentle

妥

Vulture . . . woman. [7]

* fledgling

孚

The *vulture* and *child* combine to create the image of an aerie full of **fledglings.** [7]

729. milk

乳

Fledglings . . . hook. [8]

730. floating

浮

Water . . . fledglings. [10]

731. leader

将

Turtle . . . vulture . . . glue. [10]

732. exhort

Leader . . . St. Bernard dog. Do not confuse with *urge* (Frame 282). [13]

733. pick

Unlike *pick up* (Frame 667), this character is used for **picking** fruits from trees. Its elements: *finger . . . vulture . . . tree.* [11]

734. vegetable

Flower . . . vulture . . . tree. [11]

*   birdhouse

The *claw* and crown of the roof of a *house* (whose chimney is displaced by the *claw*) combine to give us a **birdhouse.** [6]

735. accept

Birdhouse . . . crotch. [8]

736. impart

Fingers . . . accept. [11]

737. love

Birdhouse . . . heart . . . walking legs. [13]

* elbow   ム

This pictograph of an arm bent at the **elbow** is obvious. [2]

ㄥ   ㄙ

738. pay   払

Finger . . . elbow. [5]

739. wide   広

Cave . . . elbow. [5]

740. broaden   拡

Fingers . . . wide. The connection with the previous character is very close. Beware. [8]

741. mineral   鉱

Metal . . . wide. [13]

742. valve   弁

Elbow . . . two hands. [5]

743. masculine   雄

By one's side . . . elbow . . . turkey. Its match is in Frame 563. [12]

744. pedestal   台

Elbow . . . mouth. [5]

745. neglect   怠

Pedestal . . . heart. [9]

---

746. reign   治

Water . . . pedestal. [8]

---

747. commence   始

Woman . . . pedestal. [8]

---

748. womb   胎

Part of the body . . . pedestal. [9]

---

749. window   窓

House . . . human legs . . . elbow . . . heart. [11]

宀　穴　窓　窓

---

750. gone   去

Soil . . . elbow. [5]

土　去

---

751. method   法

Water . . . gone. [8]

---

*   wall   厶

The *elbow* under a *ceiling* will become our element for a **wall**. [3]

752. meeting   会

Meeting . . . wall. This is the full character from which the abbreviated primitive for **meeting**, which we met back in LESSON 12, gets its name. [6]

753. climax   至

Wall . . . soil. The key-word is chosen so as to preserve the variety of connotations: to peak, to arrive at the end, and the like. [6]

754. room   室

Climax . . . house. [9]

755. arrival   到

Climax . . . sabre. [8]

756. doth   致

The archaic English form for "does" indicates a humble form of the verb "to do." It is made up of *climax* and *taskmaster.* [10]

757. mutually   互

When you draw this character think of linking two *walls* together, one right side up and the other upside down. [4]

* **infant**   去

This primitive can be seen as an abbreviation of the full primitive for *child,* the second stroke dividing the head from the body much as it does in 子 ; and the other strokes condensing the long form so that it can be used atop its relative primitive. We change the meaning to **infant** to facilitate keeping the full form and its abbreviation distinct. [4]

758. abandon   棄

Infant . . . buckle (see Frame 415) *. . . tree.* [13]

759. bring up   育

Since the key-word has to do with raising children to be strong both in mind and body, it is easy to coordinate the primitive elements: *infant . . . meat.* [8]

760. remove   撤

Fingers . . . bring up . . . taskmaster. [15]

761. allot   充

Infant . . . human legs. [6]

762. gun   銃

Metal . . . allot. [14]

763. sulphur   硫

Rock . . . infant . . . flood. [12]

764. current   流

Water . . . infant . . . flood. Be sure to distinguish the two water-
primitives from one another in making your story. [10]

765. license   允

Elbow . . . human legs. [4]

766. tempt   唆

Mouth . . . license . . . walking legs. [10]

LESSON 24

After that long excursus into hand-primitives we may take a rest with the
far easier group built up from *exit* and *enter.*

767. exit   出

The kanji for **exit** pictures a series of mountain peaks coming out of
the *earth.* Learn it together with the following frame. [5]

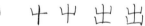

768. mountain 山

Note the clearer outline of a triangular **mountain** here. [3]

｜ 凵 山

769. bungling 拙

Fingers . . . exit. [8]

770. boulder 岩

Mountain . . . rock. [8]

771. charcoal 炭

Mountain . . . ashes. [9]

772. branch off 岐

Mountains . . . branch. [7]

773. mountain peak 峠

Mountain . . . above . . . below. [9]

山 屵 峠

774. crumble 崩

Mountain . . . companion. [11]

775. secrecy 密

House . . . invariably . . . mountain. [11]

776. honey

House . . . invariably . . . insect. [14]

777. storm

Mountain . . . winds. [12]

嵐

778. promontory

Mountain . . . strange. Hint: you might save yourself the trouble of a story here simply by recalling the kanji for *cape* (Frame 153) and toying around with the differing images suggested by the key-words **promontory** and *cape*. [11]

779. enter

入

This character is meant to be a picture of someone walking leftwards, putting one leg forward **so as to enter** someplace. Since the "in" side of a character is the left, it should be easy to remember the writing of this character. [2]

ノ　入

* As a primitive, the meaning of the key-word is expanded to include: *to go in, to put in, to come in,* and the like. It generally appears atop its relative primitive where, unlike the element for *umbrella* ⌒ , the two strokes do not touch one another here, making it virtually the same as the kanji for *eight*. When it appears elsewhere, however, it retains its original form.

780. crowded

Enter . . . road. [5]

781. part   分

Go in . . . dagger. [4]

八 分

782. poverty   貧

Part . . . shells/money. [11]

783. partition   頒

Part . . . head. [13]

784. public   公

Come in . . . elbows. (Use the adjectival sense of the key-word.) [4]

785. pine tree   松

Tree . . . public. [8]

786. venerable old man   翁

Public . . . feathers. [10]

丿 八 公 公 夻 夻 夻 翁 翁 翁

787. sue   訟

Words . . . public. [11]

788. valley   谷

Go in . . . an *umbrella . . .* a *mouth.* Because of space restrictions, the element for *go in* is shortened in this character. Hint: If you turn this kanji upside down (just this once, then never again), the image of a **valley** stands out: the *mouth* of the river whose water flows down at the intersection of the two mountains, with the final two strokes adding the element of perspective. Now turn the kanji right-side up again and see if the image still remains clear. If not, then return to the primitives and make a story in the usual way. [7]

---

789. bathe

Water . . . valley. [10]

---

790. contain

This character depicts a *house* so large that it can **contain** an entire *valley.* [10]

---

791. melt

Water . . . contain. [13]

---

792. longing

Valley . . . yawn. Be sure to keep the key-word distinct from *pining* (Frame 633). [11]

---

793. abundant

This character shows the *clothing* of *valley*-folk which, unlike that of city-folk, is loose-fitting and baggy. Hence, **abundant**. [12]

---

* gully

As an abbreviation of the kanji for a *valley,* this primitive gets its meaning as a small *valley* or **gully**. [5]

794. lead (metal)   鉛

Metal . . . gully. [13]

795. run alongside   沿

Water . . . gully. The key-word is meant to refer to things like rivers and railway tracks that **run alongside** something else. [8]

LESSON 25

The following group of kanji revolve about primitive elements having to do with human beings. We shall have more to add to this set of primitives before we are through, but even the few we bring in here will enable us to learn quite a few new characters. We begin with another "roof" primitive.

* outhouse   尚

The combination of the element for *small,* the basic *roof*-structure (in which the chimney was displaced just as in the element for *vulture),* and the "window" (*mouth*) below gives this element its meaning of **outhouse**. Although the window is not an essential part of an **outhouse,** I think you will agree that its inclusion is a boon to imagination—not to mention the fact that it greatly simplifies the learning of the characters in which it appears. [8]

ハ → ハ → 尚

796. prize   賞

Outhouse . . . shellfish. [15]

797. party   党

Think of this key-word as referring to a political **party**, not a gala affair. Its elements: *human legs* . . . sticking out of an *outhouse* window. [10]

798. public chamber   堂

Outhouse . . . *land.* [11]

799. usual   常

Outhouse . . . *towel.* [11]

800. skirt   裳

The key-word refers to an ancient **skirt** once used as part of a woman's costume. The primitives you have to work with are: *outhouse* . . . *garment.* [14]

801. manipulate   掌

Outhouse . . . *hand.* [12]

802. pelt   皮

The simplest way to remember this character is to see it as built up from that for *branch.* The first stroke can then stand for something "hanging" down from the *branch,* namely its bark or **pelt**. The barb at the end of the second stroke is the only other change. Merely by concentrating on this as you write the following small cluster of characters should be sufficient to fix the form in your mind. By way of exception, you might doddle around with the kanji-form to see what you can come up with. [5]

丿　厂　广　皮　皮

803. waves   波

Water's . . . pelt. [8]

804. old woman   婆

Waves . . . woman. [11]

805. expose   披

Fingers . . . pelt. [8]

806. rend   破

Rock . . . pelt. [10]

807. incur   被

Cloak . . . pelt. [10]

衤　被

* bone   歹

This character is meant to be a pictograph of a **bone** attached to a piece of flesh (or vice-versa.) The first stroke serves to keep it distinct from the character for *evening* (Frame 109). [4]

一　丁　歹　歹

808. remainder   残

Bones . . . (parade) float. [10]

809. martyrdom   殉

Bones . . . decameron. [10]

810. particularly   殊

Bones . . . vermilion. [10]

811. augment   殖

Bones . . . straightaway. [12]

812. file   列

Bones . . . sabre. The sense of the key-word is of people or things lined up in a row. [6]

813. split   裂

File . . . garment. [12]

814. ardent   烈

File . . . oven fire. [10]

815. death   死

Bones . . . spoon. Note how the first stroke is extended to the right, forming a sort of overhead "roof." [6]

816. interment   葬

Flowers . . . death . . . two hands. Compare *bury* (Frame 179). [12]

* sunglasses   舛

These two elements are actually an abbreviation of the character for
measuring box which we learned in Frame 42. To the left, we see the
familiar shape of *evening,* and to the right a completely new shape.
The meaning we have assigned, **sunglasses**, is entirely arbitrary. [7]

ノ　ク　タ　タ丆　タヒ　タヒ　舛

---

817. wink   瞬

Eye . . . birdhouse . . . sunglasses. [18]

---

818. ear   耳

The pictograph for the **ear** looks much like that for *eye,* but note how
the stroke-order gives it a different look. [6]

一　丁　下　F　E　耳

---

819. take   取

Ear . . . crotch. [8]

---

820. gist   趣

Run . . . take. [15]

---

821. utmost   最

Sun . . . take. [12]

---

822. snapshot   撮

Finger. . . utmost. This is the character used for taking pictures; hence the element for *"take"* is hidden in it. [15]

---

823. shame   恥

Ear . . . heart. It is most rare to have the *heart* at the right, rather than at the bottom. Take advantage of this fact when you compose your story. [10]

---

824. post   職

The key-word refers to one's occupation or position of employment. Its elements: *ear . . . kazoo.* [18]

---

825. holy   聖

Ear . . . mouth . . . king. [13]

---

826. daring   敢

Spike . . . ear . . . taskmaster. [12]

---

827. listen   聴

Ear . . . needle . . . eye . . . heart. Compare Frame 400 for this and the following kanji, and again when you get to Frame 885. [17]

---

828. pocket   懐

State of mind . . . needle . . . eyes . . . garment. [16]

---

* mandala   曼

Sun . . . eye . . . crotch. [11]

---

829. ridicule

慢

State of mind . . . mandala. [14]

---

830. loose

漫

Water . . . mandala. [14]

---

831. buy

買

Eye . . . shellfish. [12]

---

832. placement

置

Eye . . . straightaway. [13]

---

833. penalty

罰

Eye . . . words . . . sabre. [14]

---

834. rather

寧

House . . . heart . . . eye . . . spike. [14]

---

835. voiced

濁

The key-word for this kanji connotes the "muddying" effect on a soft consonant brought about by vibrating the vocal chords. For example, in English a "j" is **voiced** while a "sh" is unvoiced. In Japanese, the し is changed to じ when it is **voiced**. The primitives are: *water... eye... bound up . . . insect.* [16]

---

836. ring

環

Jewel . . . eye . . . ceiling . . . mouth . . . scarf. The number of elements is large here, so take extra care with this kanji. It is best to learn it in conjunction with the following frame, since these are the only two cases in this book where the combination of elements to the right appears. [17]

---

837. send back　　　　　　　　　還

Road . . . eye . . . ceiling . . . mouth . . . scarf. [16]

---

838. husband　　　　　　　　　夫

The kanji for *a* **husband** or "head of the family" is based on the kanji for *large* and an extra line near the top for the "head." Do not confuse with *heavens* (Frame 428). [4]

一　二　尹　夫

---

839. aid　　　　　　　　　　　扶

Fingers . . . husband. [7]

---

840. mountain stream　　　　　渓

Water . . . vulture . . . husband. [11]

---

841. standard　　　　　　　　規

Husband . . . see. [11]

---

842. exchange　　　　　　　　替

Two husbands . . . day. [12]

---

843. approve　　　　　　　　　賛

Two husbands . . . shells. [15]

844. submerge   潜

Water . . . exchange. [15]

---

845. lose   失

"To **lose**" here takes the sense of "misplace," not the sense of *defeat*, whose kanji we learned in frame Frame 63. It pictures a *husband* with something falling from his side as he is walking along, something he **loses**. [5]

丿 失

* As a primitive, this character can also mean "*to drop.*"

---

846. iron   鉄

Metal . . . to drop. [13]

---

847. transfer   迭

To drop . . . road. [8]

---

848. retainer   臣

This kanji is actually a pictograph for an eye, distorted to make it appear that the pupil is protruding towards the right. This may not be an easy form to remember, but try this: draw it once rather large, and notice how moving the two vertical lines on the right as far right as possible gives you the pictograph of the eye in its natural form. The "pop-eye" image belongs to an Emperor's **retainer** standing in awe before his ruler. [7]

* As a primitive, the meaning of the key-word becomes *slave.*

849. princess   姫

Woman . . . slave. [10]

850. storehouse   蔵

Flowers . . . parade . . . slaves. [15]

艹 莊 蔵

851. entrails   臓

Part of the body . . . storehouse. [19]

月 臓

852. intelligent   賢

Slave . . . crotch . . . shellfish. [16]

853. strict   堅

Slave . . . crotch . . . soil. [12]

854. look to   臨

Slave . . . reclining . . . goods. The key word suggests both **looking**
ahead **to** something and "seeing to" what **is** at hand. Consistent with
everything we have learned about the role of the key-word, this
means that you must choose ONE meaning and stick to it. [18]

855. perusal   覧

Slaves . . . reclining . . . floor . . . see. [17]

856. gigantic   巨

This kanji depicts a **gigantic** "pop-eye," which accounts for its shape. Be sure not to confuse it with the *slave* (*retainer*) we just learned. [5]

丨 厂 厈 厈 巨

857. repel   拒

Fingers . . . gigantic. [8]

858. power   力

With a little imagination, one can see a muscle in this simple, two-stroke character meaning **power**. [2]

フ 力

* As a primitive, either *muscle* or *power* can be used.

859. male   男

Rice fields . . . power. [7]

860. labor   労

School house . . . power. [7]

861. recruit   募

Graveyard . . . power. [12]

862. inferiority   劣

Few . . . muscles. [6]

863. achievement   功

Craft . . . power. [5]

864. persuade   勧

Pegasus . . . power. [13]

865. toil   努

Guy . . . muscle. [7]

866. encourage   励

Cliff . . . ten thousand . . . power. [7]

867. add   加

Muscles . . . mouth. This is the only case in which the primitive for *muscle* appears on the left; note should be taken of the fact in composing one's story. [5]

868. congratulations   賀

Add . . . shells. [12]

869. erect   架

Add . . . trees. Hint: if you ever had an "Erector Set" or "Tinker Toys" as a child, don't pass up the opportunity to relate it to this kanji's key word and the element for *trees.* [9]

870. armpit   脇

Part of the body . . . muscles (three of which give us *"triceps"* or *"muscles* on top of *muscles").* You will want to keep the kanji distinct from the one that follows by paying attention to the positioning of the elements. [10]

871. threaten   脅

Triceps . . . meat. [10]

872. co-   協

This prefix should be kept distinct from *inter-* (Frame 209) and *mutual* (Frame 757). Its elements: *needle . . . triceps.* [8]

873. going   行

By joining the top four strokes, you should get a picture of the front-wave of a river, the stream trailing behind. Hence the character for **"going."** [6]

ノ　イ　彳　彳　行　行

* As a primitive, this character has two forms. Reduced to the left side only, 彳 , it can mean a *column, going,* a *line.* When the middle is opened up for other elements, it means a *boulevard.*

874. rhythm   律

This character depicts a calligrapher's *brush* and its **rhythmic** sway as it flows down *a column,* writing kanji on the way. [9]

875. restore   復

Going . . . double back. [12]

876. gain   得

Column . . . nightbreak . . . glue. [11]

877. accompany   従

Column . . . animal horns . . . mending. [10]

878. junior   徒

Line . . . run. [10]

879. wait   待

Line . . . Buddhist temple. [9]

880. journey   往

Column . . . candlestick. This character has the special sense of **journeying** to someplace or other. [8]

881. subjugate   征

Column . . . correct. [8]

882. diameter   径

Line . . . spool. [8]

883. he   彼

Going . . . pelt. This kanji refers to the third person singular personal pronoun, generally in its masculine form. [8]

884. duty   役

Going . . . missile. [7]

885. benevolence   德

Going . . . needle . . . eye . . . heart. [14]

886. penetrate   徹

Line . . . bring up . . . taskmaster. [15]

887. indications   徵

Line . . . mountain . . . king . . . taskmaster. [14]

彳 彳 徔 徵

888. penal   懲

Indications . . . heart. [18]

889. delicate   微

Line . . . mountain . . . ceiling . . . human legs . . . taskmaster. [13]

890. boulevard   街

This is the character from which the sense of **"boulevard"** mentioned in Frame 873 derives. Its elements: **boulevard** . . . *ivy.* [12]

891. equilibrium   衡

Boulevard . . . bound up . . . brains . . . St. Bernard dog. [16]

彳 彳 徇 徨 衡

LESSON 26

We return once again to the world of plants and growing things, not yet to complete our collection of those primitives, but to focus on three elements which are among the most commonly found throughout the kanji.

Now and again, you will no doubt have observed, cross-reference is made to other kanji with similar key-words. This can help avoid confusion if you check your earlier story and the connotation of its respective key-word before proceeding with the kanji at hand. While it is impossible to know in advance which key-words will cause confusion for which readers, I will continue to point out some of the likely problem cases.

---

* wheat 禾

This primitive element, not a kanji by itself, shall be made to stand for **wheat**. It connotes a special grain, more expensive than ordinary rice and so reserved for special occasions. Alternatively, it can mean *a cereal*. Its form is like that for *tree*, except for the dot at the top to represent a spike of **wheat** blowing in the wind. [5]

ノ 二 千 禾 禾

---

892. draft 稿

The key-word connotes the preliminary composition of a plan or manuscript. Its elements: *wheat . . . tall.* [15]

---

893. earnings 稼

Wheat . . . house. [15]

---

894. extent 程

Wheat . . . display . Do not confuse with *extremity* (Frame 217) or *boundary* (Frame 484). [12]

895. tax   税

Wheat . . . devil. [12]

896. immature   稚

Wheat . . . turkey. [13]

897. harmony   和

Wheat . . . mouth. [8]

898. shift   移

Wheat . . . many. [11]

899. second   秒

The reference here is to a **second** of time. The elements: *wheat
. . . few.* [9]

900. autumn   秋

Wheat . . . fire. [9]

901. distress   愁

Autumn . . . heart. [13]

902. private   私

Wheat . . . elbow. Like the characters for *I* (Frame 17) and *ego* (Frame
640), this kanji is also representative of the subject, with the special
connotation of privacy. [7]

903. regularity 秩

Wheat . . . drop. [10]

904. secret 秘

Cereal . . . invariably. [10]

905. appellation 称

Wheat . . . reclining . . . small. [10]

906. profit 利

Wheat . . . sabre. Be careful not to confuse with *gain* (Frame 876) or *earnings* (Frame 893). [7]

907. pear tree 梨

Profit . . . tree. [11]

908. harvest 穫

Wheat . . . flowers . . . vessels. Compare Frames 700 and 701 for the right side. [18]

909. ear (of a plant) 穂

Wheat . . . favor. [15]

910. rice plant 稲

Wheat . . . vulture . . . olden times. [14]

911. incense 香

Wheat . . . sun. [9]

912. seasons 季

Wheat . . . child. [8]

913. committee 委

Wheat . . . woman. [8]

914. excel 秀

Wheat . . . fist. [7]

915. transparent 透

Excel . . . road/way. [10]

916. entice 誘

Words . . . excel. Compare *beckon* (Frame 650), *to urge* (Frame 282), *seduce* (Frame 86), and *encourage* (Frame 866) when choosing your connotation. [14]

917. cereals 穀

Samurai . . . crown . . . wheat . . . missile. [14]

918. germ 菌

Flowers . . . pent up . . . wheat. [11]

919. rice

This kanji has a pictographic resemblance to a number of grains of **rice** lying on the ground in the shape of a star. [6]

`      ` ` `   ` ` `   丷   半   米   米

* As a primitive, it keeps its meaning of *rice*, and is meant to connote a very ordinary, commonplace grain in contrast to the primitive for *wheat* which we just learned. (This meaning accords well with Japan where the output of *rice* far exceeds that of *wheat.*) It occasionally takes the shape 米, which can best be remembered by having it refer specifically to *grains of rice*. This primitive is not to be confused with the similar looking primitive for *water*. While the stroke-orders are nearly alike, *grains of rice* has 5 strokes, while *water* only has 4 because it joins the second and third strokes into one. Finally, we may note that by itself the kanji for *rice* is an abbreviation used for the *United States*, which can then also serve as an alternate reading for the main primitive form, if you so wish.

920. flour

粉

Rice . . . part. [10]

921. sticky

粘

Rice . . . fortune-telling. [11]

922. grains

粒

Rice . . . vase. [11]

923. cosmetics

粧

Rice . . . cave . . . soil. [12]

924. astray   迷

Road . . . U.S.A. [9]

925. chic   粋

Rice . . . baseball team . . . ten/needles. [10]

926. provisions   糧

Rice . . . quantity. [18]

927. chrysanthemum   菊

Flower . . . bound up . . . rice. [11]

928. core   奥

A drop . . . pent up . . . rice . . . St. Bernard dog. Notice that the
horizontal line of the bottom primitive doubles up as the final stroke
for *pent up.* [12]

929. number   数

Rice . . . woman . . . taskmaster. [13]

930. watchtower   楼

Tree . . . rice . . . woman. [13]

931. sort   類

Rice . . . St. Bernard dog . . . head. [18]

932. lacquer 漆

Water . . . tree . . . umbrella . . . rice-grains. [14]

933. Esq. 様

The abbreviation **"Esq."** will help associate this character with the honorific form of address to which it belongs. Its elements are: *tree . . . sheep . . . grains of rice.* Note that the final vertical stroke in the element for *sheep* is extended to form the first stroke for *grains of rice.* [14]

才　样　様

934. request 求

Let the *drop* in the upper right-hand corner of this character close the right angle off to make an *arrowhead.* Whenever we find the *needle* with that *drop* in an element that has no other special meaning, we will take advantage of this primitive meaning. At the bottom, we see the *grains of rice*, the vertical line doubling up for the two elements. Do not confuse with *petition* (Frame 135). [7]

935. ball 球

Ball . . request. [11]

936. salvation 救

Request . . . taskmaster. [11]

937. bamboo 竹

Bamboo grows upwards, like a straight *nail,* and at each stage of its growth (which legend associates with the arrival of the new moon) there is a jointed rootstock (the first stroke). Two such **bamboo** stalks are pictured here. [6]

丿 ├ ≮ ≮ ≮ 竹

* As a primitive, the meaning remains the same, but the vertical lines are severely abbreviated so that they can take their place at the top where, like *flowers,* they are always to be found.

---

938. laugh   笑

Bamboo . . . heavens. [10]

---

939. bamboo hat   笠

Bamboo . . . vase. [11]

---

940. bamboo grass   笹

Bamboo . . . generation. [11]

---

941. muscle   筋

Bamboo . . . part of the body . . . power. Here we see how the primitive meaning of **muscle was derived** from the kanji for *power.* [12]

---

942. box   箱

Bamboo . . . inter-. [15]

---

943. writing brush   筆

Bamboo . . . brush. [12]

---

944. cylinder   筒

Bamboo . . . monk. [12]

945. etc.   等

Bamboo . . . Buddhist temple. [12]

946. calculate   算

Bamboo . . . eyes . . . two hands. [14]

947. solution   答

Bamboo . . . fit. [12]

948. scheme   策

Bamboo . . . belted tree (see Frame 417). [12]

949. register   簿

Bamboo . . . water . . . acupuncture specialist. [19]

950. fabricate   築

Bamboo . . . craft . . . mediocre . . . wood/tree. [16]

LESSON 27

This lesson will take us beyond the half-way mark. From there on, it will all be downhill. The final uphill push will involve what appears to be the simplest of primitive elements but was withheld until now because of the difficulty it would have caused earlier on.

951. person

While the character for *enter* (Frame 779) showed someone walking inwards (in terms of the direction of writing), that for **person**, shown here, represents someone walking outwards. [2]

* As a primitive, it can keep its kanji form except when it appears to the left (its normal position), where it is made to stand up in the form 亻 .

  The primitive meaning is another matter. The abstract notion of *person* so often has a relation to the meaning of the kanji that confusion readily sets in. So many of the previous stories have included people in them that simply to use *person* for a primitive meaning would be risky. We need to be more specific, to focus on one particular *person*. Try to choose someone who has not figured in the stories so far, perhaps a colorful member of the family or a friend whom you have known for a long time. That individual will appear again and again, so be sure to choose someone who excites your imagination.

952. assistant   佐

Person . . . left. [7]

953. however   但

Person . . . nightbreak. [7]

954. dwell   住

Person . . . candlestick. [7]

955. rank   位

Person . . . vase. [7]

956. go-between   仲

Person . . . in. [6]

957. body   体

Person . . . book. [7]

958. permanence   悠

Person . . . walking stick . . . taskmaster . . . heart. [11]

959. affair   件

Person . . . cow. [6]

960. attend   仕

Person . . . samurai. The key-word means to wait on someone or serve them. [5]

961. other   他

Person . . . scorpion. [5]

962. prostrated   伏

Person . . . chihuahua. [6]

963. transmit   伝

Person . . . rising cloud. Hint: the American Indians' smoke signals can help provide a good image for this kanji, which has to do with **transmissions** of all sorts. [6]

964. Buddha 仏

Person . . . elbow. [4]

965. rest 休

Person . . . tree. Be sure not to confuse with *relax* (Frame 190). [6]

966. sham 仮

Person . . . anti-. [6]

967. chief 伯

Person . . . white/dove. [7]

968. vulgar 俗

Person . . . valley. The key-word should be taken in its older sense of "popular" or "commonplace." [9]

969. faith 信

Person . . . words. [9]

970. excellent 佳

Person . . . ivy. To distinguish from *excel* (Frame 914), *eminent* (Frame 51), *esteem* (Frame 184), and *exquisite* (Frame 123), give the key-word its own unique connotation. [8]

971. reliant 依

Person . . . clothing. [8]

972. example   例

Person . . . file. [8]

973. individual   個

Person . . . harden. [10]

974. healthy   健

Person . . . build. [11]

イ 律 健

975. side   側

Person . . . rule. See Frame 88 for help. [11]

976. waiter   侍

Person . . . Buddhist temple. The key-word is deceptively modern, but the character itself is another way of writing "samurai." [8]

977. halt   停

Person . . . pavilion. [11]

978. price   値

Person . . . straightaway. [10]

979. emulate   倣

Person . . . set free. [10]

980. overthrow

倒

Person . . . arrival. [10]

---

981. spy

偵

Person . . . upright. [11]

---

982. Buddhist priest

僧

Person . . . increase. [13]

---

983. hundred million

億

Person . . . idea. [15]

---

984. ceremony

儀

Person . . . righteousness. [15]

---

985. reparation

償

Person . . . prize. [17]

---

986. hermit

仙

Person . . . mountain. [5]

---

987. sponsor

催

Hermit . . . turkey. Note what has happened to the *mountain* in the element for *hermit*. In order to make room for the *turkey*, it was raised and condensed. [13]

988. humanity   仁

To refer to the fullness of **humanity**, which one only achieves in dialogue with another (*person . . . two*), Confucius used this character. [4]

989. scorn   侮

Every . . . person. [8]

990. use   使

Person . . . officer. [8]

991. convenience   便

Person . . grow late. Hint: this kanji also means that unmentionable material which one disposes of when one goes to the **"conveniences."** [9]

992. double   倍

Person . . . muzzle. Do not confuse with duplicate (Frame 465). [10]

993. tenderness   優

Person . . melancholy. [17]

994. fell   伐

Person . . . fiesta. Hint: recall the German legend of the English Saint Boniface who **felled** the sacred oak tree dedicated to Thor at Geismar (in lower Hessia), occasioning a great *fiesta* for the Christians in the neighborhood to mark the end of their pagan competition. Be sure to fit your special *person* into the story if you use it. [6]

995. inn   宿

House . . . person . . . hundred. [11]

---

996. wound   傷

Person . . . reclining . . . piggy bank. [13]

---

997. protect   保

Person . . . mouth . . . tree. [11]

---

998. praise   褒

Tophat and scarf . . . protect. [15]

---

999. greatness   傑

Person . . . sunglasses . . . tree. [12]

1000. adhere   付

Person . . . glue. The few cases in which this character serves as a primitive should include some connotation of **"adhering to"** which distinguishes it from *"glued to."* Two examples follow. [5]

1001. token   符

Bamboo . . . adhere. [11]

1002. borough   府

Cave . . . adhere. [8]

1003. responsibility 任

Person . . porter. [6]

1004. fare 賃

Responsibility . . . shells/money. [13]

1005. substitute 代

Person . . . arrow. [5]

1006. sack 袋

Substitute . . . garment. [11]

1007. lend 貸

Substitute . . . shells/money. [12]

1008. change 化

Person . . . spoon. [4]

1009. flower 花

Flower . . . change. [7]

1010. freight 貨

Change . . . shells. [11]

1011. lean

傾

Change . . . head. The key-word has the sense of **leaning** on someone or something. [13]

1012. what

何

Person . . . can. [7]

1013. baggage

荷

Flowers . . . what. [10]

1014. sagacious

俊

Person . . . license . . . walking legs. [9]

1015. bystander

傍

Person . . . stand . . . crown . . . compass. [12]

1016. long time

久

This character uses the diagonal sweep of the second stroke to double up for *bound up* and a *person*. Think of a mummy, and the key-word will not be far behind. [3]

1017. furrow

畝

Think of the three kinds of "furrows" shown here in this character—a *tophat's* rim, a *rice field's* ridges, and the wrinkles that show you've been around a *long time*. [10]

1018. captured

Person . . . pent up. [5]

1019. inside

Person . . belt. Note that we cannot use the primitive meaning of *hood* here because the *person* runs THROUGH the element, not under it. [4]

1020. third class

冂

Those no-frills flights the airlines offer to attract customers should help create an image from *ceiling . . . person . . . belt.* The kanji meaning *"inside"* should not be used because of its proximity to the element for *"in."* [5]

1021. design

柄

Tree . . . third class. [9]

1022. meat

Let this doubling of one of the elements for *"inside"* yield the sense of *"insides"* to approach the key-word, **meat.** The abbreviated form of this character **had the** primitive meaning of *flesh* or *part of the body* for the element 月 . [6]

1023. rot

腐

Borough . . . meat. [14]

* assembly line

从

The duplication of the kanji for *person* gives us this primitive for

assembly line. Perhaps you can imagine clones of your *person* rolling off an **assembly line** in a factory. [4]

1024. squat   座

Cave . . . assembly line . . . soil. [10]

1025. graduate   卒

Tophat . . . assembly line . . . needle. [8]

1026. umbrella   傘

Umbrella . . . two assembly lines . . . needle. [12]

LESSON 28

In this lesson we pick up a group of unconnected characters and elements that have fallen between the cracks of the previous lessons, mainly because of the rarity of the characters themselves, of their primitive elements, or of the way in which they are written. In a later lesson, near the end of the book, we will do this once again.

1027. monme   匁

This character obliges us to compromise the promise made earlier (Frame 178) to avoid Japanese in the key-words. It refers to an old unit of weight, equal to about 3.75 grams. The word is only slightly more useful in modern Japanese than cubits and kites are in modern English. Its primitives, if you look closely, are: *bound up . . . arm.* [4]

* plow

上

Take this as a pictograph of a **plow**. [1]

1028. by means of

以

Picture a *person* dragging a *plow* behind, and the *drop of* sweat which falls from his brow as he does his work. Think of him (or her, for that matter) making a living "*by means of* the sweat of his brow." [4]

1029. becoming

似

"Becoming" here means fitting or well-suited. Keep it distinct from *suitable* (Frame 441). Its elements: *person . . . by means of.* [6]

* puzzle

并

Think of this element as a picture **puzzle** in which the pieces interlock. Its elements: *horns . . . two hands.* [6]

1030. join

併

The sense of the key-word is one of **joining** things together that were previously separate. Its elements: *person . . . puzzle.* [8]

1031. tile

瓦

Ceiling . . . cane . . . fishhook . . . ice. Note how the last stroke of the final element, *ice,* is stretched out to close the bottom of the **tile.** [5]

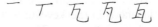

1032. flower pot

瓶

Puzzle . . . tile. [11]

1033. Shinto shrine   宮

Way back in LESSON 2 we learned the character for *spine*. The three characters in which it is used we can now learn together in this and the following two frames. Here a **Shinto shrine** is composed of *house* and *spine*. [10]

1034. occupation   営

Schoolhouse . . . spine. [12]

1035. virtuous   善

Sheep . . . horns . . . mouth. Pay special attention to the writing of this character. [12]

1036. year   年

In an odd fashion, the kanji for **year** joins together the element for *horse* (on the top) and the right half of the element for *sunglasses*. Think of it as a *horse* wearing *sunglasses* with one of the lenses popped out. We will use this latter image again, so learn it now and save yourself the trouble. [6]

1037. night   夜

First of all, be sure not to confuse the connotations of **night** with those of *evening* (Frame 109) and nightbreak (Frame 30). Its elements: *tophat . . . person . . . .walking legs . . . drop.* [8]

1038. fluid

液

Water . . . night. [11]

1039. hillock

塚

Soil . . . crown . . . sow. (Compare Frame 543.) [12]

*   shredder

敝

The element on the left looks like *rice* with a *belt* running through it, but we would do best to think of it in terms of its writing order: *small . . . belt . . . small.* On the right, of course, the *taskmaster.* [12]

屮　屵　屵　敝

1040. cash

幣

Shredder . . . towel. [15]

1041. abuse

弊

Shredder . . . two hands. [15]

1042. yell

喚

The *mouth* on the left is obvious. The rest is harder; try this: *four St. Bernard dogs bound up* in a bunch. Together they should provide a clear enough portrait of *a yell,* provided you are careful to see all *four* of them. Note how the final stroke of the *four* is supplied by the long horizontal stroke of the *St. Bernard.* [12]

1043. interchange

換

Fingers . . . four St. Bernard dogs bound up. [12]

1044. dissolve   融

Ceiling . . . mouth . . . hood . . . human legs . . . spike . . . insect. This is the maximum number of elements to any story in the book. [16]

丹 鬲 鬲 融

LESSON 29

We come now to a rather simple group of primitives, built up from the three elements which represent banners, knots, and flags.

* banner   方

Here we have a unique enclosure made up of two elements: *compass* and *reclining*. Think of the **banner** as a standard for rallying around; then imagine a crowd *reclining* before a *compass* (to give them a "direction" in life). [6]

1045. alms   施

Banner . . . scorpion. [9]

1046. rotation   旋

A banner . . . a zoo. Hint: think of a merry-go-round. [11]

1047. play   遊

Banners . . . children . . . road. [12]

1048. trip

旅

Let the last two strokes, which are also the concluding strokes to the character for *garment,* represent a *rag* as its primitive meaning. We shall meet this only on one other occasion. This gives us as our elements: *banner . . . person . . . rag.* [10]

旅 旅

1049. not

勿

First take the primitive meaning of this character: *knot.* Think of it as the *piglet* minus its body (the first horizontal stroke), that is, the curly tail that looks like a *knot.* As an exception, we will use the homonym to remember the abstract key-word, **not.** [4]

⼃ 勹 勺 勿

1050. thing

物

Cow . . . knot [8]

1051. easy

易

Sun . . . knot. [8]

1052. grant

賜

Shells . . . easy. [15]

* flag

尸

The pictographic representation of this element is obvious. Provided you can hold your imagination in check for the first example, you might best imagine your own national **flag** in composing your stories. [3]

ㄱ ㄱ ㄕ

1053. urine

尿

Flag . . . water. [7]

1054. nun

尼

Flag . . . spoon. [5]

1055. mud

泥

Water . . . nun. [8]

1056. fence

塀

Soil . . . flag . . . puzzle. [12]

1057. footgear

履

Flag . . . restore. [15]

1058. roof

屋

Flag . . . climax. Since this kanji has no relation to the primitive for roof, we cannot use it as a primitive in the next frame. [9]

1059. grip

握

Fingers . . . flag . . . climax. [12]

1060. yield

屈

Flag . . . exit. [8]

1061. dig   掘

Fingers . . . yield. [11]

1062. ditch   堀

Soil . . . yield. [11]

1063. reside   居

Flag . . . old. Do not confuse with *dwell* (Frame 954). [8]

1064. set   据

Fingers . . . reside. [11]

1065. stratum   層

Flag . . . increase. [14]

1066. bureau   局

Flag . . . phrase. Note how the *flag's* long stroke doubles up for the
first stroke of *phrase.* [7]

1067. slow   遅

Flag . . . sheep . . . road. [12]

1068. leak   漏

Water . . . flag . . . rain. [14]

1069. printing
刷

Flag . . . towel . . . sabre. [8]

1070. shaku
尺

The key-word **shaku** has actually come into English in the word **shaku**-hachi, the ancient Japanese flute that measured "one shaku and eight." Since the **shaku** is about one foot in length, this makes about 12 inches. Let the final sweeping stroke be like a tape measure added to the *flag.* [4]

   * As a primitive, this will mean the *shaku-hachi* flute.

1071. exhaust
尽

Shaku-hachi . . . ice. [6]

1072. swamp
沢

Water . . . shaku-hachi. [7]

1073. translate
訳

Words . . . shaku-hachi. [11]

1074. choose
択

Fingers . . . shaku-hachi. [7]

1075. daytime
昼

Shaku-hachi . . . nightbreak. [9]

1076. door   戸

One . . . flag. [4]

1077. shoulder   肩

Door . . . flesh. [8]

1078. tassel   房

Door . . . compass. [8]

1079. fan   扇

Door . . . wings. [10]

1080. hearth   炉

Hearth-fire . . . door. [8]

1081. re-   戻

The key-word signals a "coming back" or return to some place or activity. Its elements: *door . . . St. Bernard dog.* [7]

1082. tears   涙

Water . . . re-. Do not confuse with the character for *cry* (Frame 432). [10]

1083. employ   雇

Door . . . turkey. Be sure to keep distinct from both *employee* (Frame 56) and *use* (Frame 990). [12]

1084. look back   顧

Employ . . . head. [21]

1085. disclose   啓

Taskmaster . . . door . . . mouth. [11]

LESSON 30

In this lesson we pick up a series of primitives related pictographically to one another and based upon the image of a seed. But first we include a stray element that does not really fit in any of our other categories but is very useful in forming some common and elementary kanji: the *altar*.

1086. show   示

Although the elements *two* and *small* are available for the using, it may be easier to remember this character as a picture of an altar. Something placed atop the altar is put on **show** for all to see. [5]

* As a primitive, this kanji means *altar*. At the left, the abbreviated form which this element takes is made by chopping the *altar* in half and leaving only one dot behind to represent the right side. The new appearance of the primitive, , should not be confused with the primitive for *garment,* similar except for the one final short stroke: .

1087. salute   礼

This key-word refers to the polite bows and ceremonious forms of **salute** so important in Japanese culture, principal among which is the bow. Its elements: *altar . . . fishhook.* [5]

1088. auspicious   祥

Altar . . . sheep. [10]

1089. celebrate   祝

Altar . . . teenager. [9]

1090. blessing   福

Altar . . . wealth. [13]

1091. welfare   祉

Altar . . . footprint. [8]

1092. company   社

Altar . . . soil. The **company** referred to here is that of the modern business world. [7]

1093. inspection   視

Altar . . . see. [11]

1094. Nara   奈

We choose the city of **Nara** as the key-word in this case because this kanji, frequently used in proper names, appears in **Nara**; and also because of **Nara**'s famed religious monuments, which help us with the primitives: *St. Bernard dog . . . altar.* [8]

1095. military officer

尉

Flag . . . altar . . . glue. [11]

1096. consolation

慰

Military officer . . . heart. [15]

1097. goodwill

款

Samurai . . . altar . . . yawning. [12]

1098. prohibition

禁

Grove . . . altar. [13]

1099. collar

襟

Cloak . . . prohibition. [18]

1100. religion

宗

House . . . altar. [8]

1101. adore

崇

Mountain . . . religion. [11]

1102. ritual

祭

Flesh . . . crotch . . . altar. Note how the second element is cut short, giving a tent-effect to the character. [11]

1103. guess   察

"Guess" has here the sense of a measured conjecture. Its elements:
house . . . ritual. [14]

1104. grate   擦

Fingers . . . guess. [17]

1105. wherefore   由

The **"wherefore"** of this kanji explains the reason or origin of a thing.
It does this graphically by depicting a seed in a *rice field* sending up a
single sprout, which is the whole why and **wherefore** of the seed's
falling in the earth and dying. (When the *flower* appears, you will
recall from Frame 234, we have a full *seedling.*) [5]

   * As a primitive, in conformity to the explanation above, this kanji
    will be taken to mean *shoot* or *sprout.*

1106. pluck   抽

Fingers . . . sprout. [8]

1107. oil   油

Water . . . sprout. [8]

1108. sleeve   袖

Cloak . . . sprout. [10]

1109. mid-air   宙

House . . . shoot. [8]

1110. deliver

Flag . . . sprout. [8]

1111. flute

Bamboo . . . sprout. [11]

1112. axis

Car . . . shoot. [12]

1113. armor

This kanji reverses the element for *sprout,* giving the image of roots being sent down into the earth by a seed planted in the *rice field.* From there you must invent a connection to the key-word, **armor.** [5]

* The primitive meaning is *roots.* Important to that word is the image of "pushing downwards," as *roots* do.

1114. push

Fingers . . . roots. Compare and contrast with *pluck* (Frame 1106). [8]

1115. headland

岬

Like the *cape* (Frame 153) and the *promontory* (Frame 778), the **headland** refers to a jut of land. Its elements: *mountain . . . roots.* [8]

1116. insert

挿

Fingers . . . thousand . . . roots. Observe how the writing order does not follow the elements in any order, because the final stroke is used for two different elements. [10]

才 扩 挀 挿

1117. speaketh   申

The olde English is used here to indicate a humble form of the verb
"to speak." It is written by a *tongue wagging in the mouth* with a
walking stick rammed through it and coming out at both ends. [5]

日 申

* While this kanji has obvious affinities to the "seed" group, it also
  happens to be the zodiacal sign of the *monkey* (the one who
  speaketh no evil, among other things). We shall therefore take
  monkey as its primitive meaning.

1118. expand   伸

Person . . . monkey. [7]

1119. gods   神

Altar . . . monkey. [9]

1120. search   捜

Fingers . . . monkey . . . crotch. [10]

1121. fruit   果

The final stage of the "seed" is reached when the plant has reached its
full growth (the *tree*) and comes to fruition, producing **fruit** full of
new seeds which can return to the earth and start the process all over
again. The main thing to notice here is the element for *brains* at the
top, which should prove more helpful in creating an image than *rice
field.* [8]

1122. candy *Flowers . . . fruits.* [11]	菓
1123. chapter *Words . . . fruit.* [15]	課
1124. naked *Cloak . . . fruit.* [13]	裸

LESSON 31

By now you will have learned to handle a great number of very difficult kanji with perfect ease and without fear of forgetting. Some others, of course, will take review. But let us focus on the ones you are most confident about and can write most fluently, in order to add a remark about what role the stories, plots, and primitives should continue to play even after you have learned a character to your own satisfaction.

This course has been outlined in such a way as to move from the full-bodied story (PART ONE) to the skeletal plot (PART TWO) to the heap of bones we call primitive elements (PART THREE). This also happens roughly to be the way memory works. At first the full story is necessary (as a rule, for every kanji, no matter how simple it appears), in that it enables you to focus your attention and your interest on the vivid images of the primitives which in turn dictate how you write the character. Once the image has strutted through the full light of imagination, it will pass on, leaving its footprints on the interstices of the brain in some mysterious way. And those footprints are often enough of a clue about the nature of the beast to enable you to reconstruct the plot in broad outlines. Should you need to, you can nearly always follow the tracks back to their source and recall your whole story, but that is generally unnecessary. The third stage occurs when even the plot is unnecessary, and the key-word by itself suggests a certain number of primitive meanings; or conversely, when seeing a kanji at once conjures up a specific key-word. Here again, the plot is still within reach if needed, but not worth bothering with once it has fulfilled its task of providing the proper primitive elements

There is yet a fourth stage to be reached, as you have probably realized by now, but one you ought not trust until you have completed the full list of the kanji given here. In this stage, the primitive elements are suggested according to *form* without any immediate association to *meaning*. Quite early on, you will recall, we insisted that visual memory is to be discarded in favor of imaginative memory. It may now be clear just why that is so. But it should also be getting clear that visual memory deserves a suitable role of some sort or other, once it has a solid foundation. This is a process not to be rushed, however appealing its rewards in terms of writing fluency.

Insofar as you have experienced these things in your own study, fears about the inadequacy of the key-words should be greatly allayed. For in much the same way that the character slowly finds its way into the fabric of memory and manual habits, the key-word will gradually give way to a key-concept distinct from the particular English word used to express it. Hence the substitution of a Japanese word—or even a number of words—will prove no stumbling block. Quite the contrary, it will help avoid confusion between key-words with family resemblances.

In short, the number of steps required to learn the Japanese writing system has not been increased by what we have been doing. It has simply become more pronounced than it is in traditional methods of drawing and redrawing the kanji hundreds of times until they are learned, and in that way the whole process has become much more efficient. Pausing to think about just what your mind has been doing through this book should make the ideas mentioned in the INTRODUCTION much more plausible now than they must have seemed way back then.

But we must be on our way again. We set off this time down a road marked: Tools.

1125. axe

This character represents a picture of an **axe**, the two vertical lines being the handle and the horizontal strokes the blade. Note the writing order carefully. [4]

1126. chop

析

Tree . . . axe. [8]

1127. place

所

Door . . . axe. [8]

1128. pray

祈

Altar . . . axe. [8]

1129. near

近

Axe . . . road. Be careful not to confuse with *draw near* (Frame 192) or *bystander* (Frame 1015). [7]

1130. fold

折

Fingers . . . axe. Hint: make an image out of the Japanese art of "origami" (paper-**folding**). [7]

1131. philosophy

哲

Fold . . . mouth. [10]

1132. departed

逝

The connotation is of a "dearly **departed**" who has passed away. The elements: *fold . . . road.* [10]

1133. vow

誓

Fold . . . words. [14]

1134. temporarily 暫

Car . . . axe . . . days. [15]

1135. steadily 漸

Water . . . car . . . axe. [14]

1136. severance 断

Fishhook . . . rice . . . axe. [11]

1137. substance 質

Two axes . . . shells. [15]

1138. reject 斥

Axe . . . a drop of. [5]

1139. accusation 訴

Words . . . reject. [12]

* saw 乍

The **saw** in this primitive is distinguished from the primitive for *axe* by the extra "teeth" on the blade. [5]

ノ 一 ケ 乍 乍

1140. yesterday 昨

Day . . . saw. [9]

1141. lie

The **lie** in this character refers to falsehoods and fibs. Its elements: *words . . . saw.* [12]

1142. make

Person . . . saw. [7]

* broom

彐

The pictographic representation here is of the bristles on the head of a **broom**. [3]

コ ヨ 彐

1143. snow

Rain which undergoes a change so that it can be swept up with a *broom* is **snow**. [11]

1144. record

Metal . . . broom . . . rice. Note how the final stroke of the *broom* is extended slightly when an element below is attached to it immediately. [16]

1145. inquire

尋

Broom . . . craft . . . mouth . . . glue. [12]

1146. hurry

急

Bound up . . . broom . . . heart. [9]

1147. calm   穏

Wheat . . . vulture . . . broom . . . heart. [16]

1148. encroach   侵

Person . . . broom . . . crown . . . crotch. Try to join together the last three elements into a composite primitive that can serve you in the next two frames. [9]

1149. immersed   浸

Water . . . broom . . . crown . . . crotch. [10]

1150. lie down   寝

Do not confuse this key word either with the element for *reclining* or the character for *prostrated* (Frame 962). Its elements are: *house . . . turtle . . . broom . . . crown . . . crotch.* [13]

1151. lady   婦

Woman . . . broom . . . apron. [11]

1152. sweep   掃

Fingers . . . broom . . . apron. [11]

1153. hit   当

Small . . . broom. [6]

*   rake   尹

This single vertical stroke transforms *broom* into a **rake**. Note that

when an element comes BENEATH the **rake**, the vertical stroke is
shortened, as we have seen before with other similar primitives such
as *sheep* and *cow*. Moreover, when something comes above the **rake**
and joins to it at the top, the vertical stroke is halted at the top
horizontal stroke. [4]

ㄱ　ㅋ　尹

1154. contend   争

Bound up . . . rake. [6]

1155. clean

Water . . . contend. [9]

1156. matter   事

This key-word here refers to abstract **matters**. The elements are: *one .
. . mouth . . . rake*. Note how the *rake* handle reaches the whole length
of the character. [8]

1157. T'ang   唐

The key-word here refers of course to the **T'ang** Dynasty in China. Its
elements: *cave . . . rake . . . mouth.* [10]

1158. sugar   糖

Rice . . . T'ang. [16]

---

*   sieve   隶

A *rake* and the *grains of rice* at the bottom give us a hint of win-
nowing, which relates clearly to the primitive meaning of a **sieve**. [8]

1159. ease

康

Cave . . . sieve. [11]

1160. apprehend

逮

Think of **apprehending** criminals. The elements are: *sieve . . . road.* [11]

* mop

尹

The only thing that distinguishes a **mop** from a *rake* is the bent handle which does not cut through the top horizontal stroke, indicating pictographically the swish-swash motion of a **mop.** [4]

1161. Italy

伊

Used chiefly in proper names, and given the sound "i," we may remember this kanji as an abbreviation of **Italy,** for which it is still used in modern Japanese. Its primitives: *person . . . mop.* [6]

1162. old boy

君

The somewhat high-brow sounding British term of address is chosen here to represent the kanji for a form of address used towards one's juniors. It is composed of: *mop . . . mouth.* [7]

1163. flock

群

Old boys . . . sheep. [13]

* comb

而

The pictograph of **comb** is easily seen in this primitive element. [6]

1164. -proof

The key-word is a suffix used to indicate "safe from" as in the words rust-**proof**, water-**proof**, and fire-**proof**. It is composed of: *comb . . . glue.* [9]

1165. demand

The sense of **demand** is best captured by thinking of the economic principle of "supply and **demand**." The primitives: *rain . . . comb.* [14]

1166. Confucian

Person . . . demand. [16]

1167. edge

Vase . . . mountain . . . comb. [14]

*   shovel

This enclosure—which embraces its relative primitive from the bottom—is a pictograph of the scoop of a **shovel**. When room permits, the arms are extended upwards to nearly the same height as the relative element it holds. [2]

└─   └┘

1168. both 両

Spike . . . belt . . . shovel. Note that the writing order follows the order in which the primitives are given here. [6]

1169. full 満

Water . . . flowers . . . both. Given the abstract nature of this last primitive, you may want to borrow the image from the previous frame. [12]

1170. brush-stroke

In forming an image for the key-word, it is helpful to know that this kanji is used for artistic representations such as completed paintings, as well as for the number of *strokes* in a character. Its elements are: *ceiling . . . sprout . . . shovel.* [8]

1171. tooth

Footprint . . . rice . . . shovel. [12]

1172. bend

Picture yourself grabbing hold of the two strokes poking out the top of the kanji and wrenching them apart, thus giving the sense of **bend**. If you think of them as deriving from the element for *brains* beneath (of course, the middle stroke has been reduplicated and pulled out to where it can be grabbed hold of), you can associate the key-word with *bending* someone's mind to your own point of view. [6]

1173. cadet 曹

This character is written in the order of its elements: *one . . . bend . . . sun.* [11]

1174. encounter 遭

Cadet . . . road. [14]

1175. rowing 漕

Water . . . cadet. [14]

1176. vat

Tree . . . cadet. [15]

1177. Big Dipper

The **Big Dipper** here is of course the constellation of "Ursa Major," of which this kanji is a sort of picture. [4]

* Since we already have a primitive element for a "dipper"—namely, the *ladle*—we shall let this one stand for a *measuring cup*. By the way, it would make a rather large one, since the kanji is also used for a measure of about 18 liters!

1178. fee

料

Measuring cup . . . rice. [10]

1179. department

科

Think here of the faculty or **department** you entered in school, using the elements: *measuring cup . . . wheat.* [9]

1180. map

図

Pent-in . . . Big Dipper. Hint: among the songs which were made part of American folklore from the days of slavery is one called "Follow the Drinking Gourd." It referred to the nighttime travel of runaway slaves (those *pent up*) who had no **maps** other than the stars to guide them, among them the bright and predominant *Big Dipper*, the "Drinking Gourd." [7]

1181. utilize

用

Meat . . . walking stick. Be sure to keep this key-word distinct from

290   REMEMBERING THE KANJI

that for *use* (Frame 990). The stroke-order is exactly as you would expect it from the order of the primitive elements as given. [5]

> * As a primitive element, we shall substitute the image of a *screwdriver,* perhaps the most *utilized* of all tools around the house.

1182. commonplace 庸

Cave . . . rake . . . screwdriver. Do not confuse with *mediocre* (Frame 62) or *usual* (Frame 799). [11]

1183. equip 備

Person . . . flowers . . . cliff . . . screwdriver. In cases like this you can jumble up the primitive into any order that seems best for the composition of a story, provided you feel confident about the relative position that these primitives take to one another in the completed character. [12]

LESSON 32

In this lesson we pick up a few primitives of quantity to complement those we learned in LESSON 7, as well as some others related closely to elements learned earlier.

* salad 艹

The element for *flowers* joins with the long horizontal stroke beneath it to create the picture of a bowl of **salad**. [4]

1184. once upon a time 昔

Salad . . . days. This is the character with which Japanese fairytales commonly begin. [8]

1185. confused   錯

Metal . . . once upon time. [16]

1186. borrow   借

Person . . . once upon a time. [10]

1187. pity   惜

State of mind . . . once upon a time. The sense of the key-word is that of a lost opportunity or bad turn of affairs, as in the phrase, "What a pity!" [11]

1188. set aside   措

Fingers . . . once upon a time. [11]

1189. scatter   散

Salad . . . flesh . . . taskmaster. [12]

1190. twenty   廿

The two *tens* joined at the bottom by a short line is actually the old character for **twenty**, which we might as well learn since we need its primitive form. It is written the same as *salad* except for the shorter final stroke. [4]

---

*   caverns   庐

The primitive for **caverns** is distinguished from that for *cave* by the addition of the *twenty*, suggesting a maze of underground *caves*. [7]

1191. commoner   庶

Caverns . . . oven-fire. [11]

1192. intercept   遮

Commoner . . . road. [14]

1193. seat   席

Caverns . . . towel. [10]

1194. degrees   度

This key-word refers to a gradation of measurement, not to academic diplomas. Its primitives: *caverns . . . crotch.* [9]

1195. transit   渡

Water . . . degrees. [12]

*   haystack   舟

The three *needles* stacked up give us a **haystack** (in which it may be harder to find the hay than the needles). In the rare case that there is nothing underneath this element, as in the following frame, the last three strokes are written virtually the same as *two hands*; that is, the second stroke sweeps down slightly to the left. [5]

十   土   舟

1196. bustle   奔

The hustle and **bustle** of this character is depicted by a *St. Bernard dog* and a *haystack.* [8]

1197. erupt   噴

Mouth . . . haystack . . . clams. [15]

1198. tomb   墳

Soil . . . haystack . . . clams. In order not to confuse this kanji with that
for a *grave* (Frame 231), something like the image of an Egyptian
tomb should be adopted for its special connotations. [15]

1199. aroused   憤

State of mind . . . haystack . . . clams [15]

*   strawman   尭

The two *human legs* added to the *haystack* (with the horizontal
stroke to keep the two parts distinct from one another and avoid a
tangle) give us a **strawman.** [8]

1200. bake   焼

Hearth . . . strawman. Take care to distinguish this kanji carefully
from *cook* (Frame 468) and *burn* (Frame 510) when you compose your
story. [12]

1201. daybreak   暁

Sun . . . strawman. [12]

1202. half   半

Although the writing order is different, one can remember the
appearance of this character by seeing it as a very *small needle*—the
kind used for splitting hairs in **half.** (Again, according to rule, *small*
takes a stroke beneath it in order to be placed over an element which

has no horizontal line at the top.) [5]

丶　丷　丷　丷　半

1203. consort   伴

Person . . . half. [7]

1204. paddy-ridge   畔

Rice-field . . . half. The key-word here refers to the **ridges** that rise up between the sections of a rice **paddy**. [10]

1205. judgment   判

Half . . . sabre. You might recall the famous **judgment** of King Solomon who offered to slice a baby in two with a *sabre* to give *half* to each mother who claimed it as her own. [7]

---

*   quarter   关

This character simply splits the vertical stroke of a *half* in half once again, to get **a quarter**. In so doing, it spreads that stroke to form a sort of enclosure under which its main relative primitive will be placed. It can be used either in its substantive or verbal meaning. [6]

1206. ticket   券

Quarter . . . dagger. [8]

1207. scroll

Quarter . . . snake. The key-word refers to a manuscript rolled up into a **scroll**, not a *hanging scroll* (Frame 407). [9]

1208. sphere 圏

This key-word refers to a realm or orbit, not to a ball. Its elements: *pent up . . . scroll.* [12]

1209. victory 勝

Moon . . . quarter . . . muscle. [12]

1210. wistaria 藤

Flower . . . moon . . . quarter . . . rice grains. [18]

1211. mimeograph 謄

Moon . . . quarter . . . words. [17]

1212. one-sided 片

This kanji is based on the pictograph of a tree with branches going upwards and hanging down, split right down the middle. When that picture's right side is isolated, it becomes the kanji for **one-sided**, in the sense of only one part of a whole. [4]

1213. printing block 版

Although this character also carries the sense of an "edition" of a publication, the elements, *one-sided* and *anti-*, more readily suggest its other meaning of a **printing block.** [8]

1214. of 之

This character is now used chiefly in proper names, and is best learned as the character closest to the hiragana え. [3]

* In order to render its meaning, *of*, less abstract, think of it as *building blocks* with the hiragana written on them, much the same as the A-B-C blocks you played with as a child.

1215. destitution

乏

Drop of . . . building blocks. [4]

1216. turf

芝

Flowers . . . building blocks. [6]

1217. negative

不

While you may play with the primitives of this kanji as you wish (*ceiling . . . person . . . a drop of*), you will probably find that its simplicity and frequency makes it easy to remember just as it is. [4]

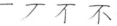

1218. negate

否

Negative . . . mouth. [7]

1219. cupfuls

杯

Tree . . . negative. [8]

LESSON 33

We turn now to the weapons which remain to be examined. To the *sword*, the *dagger*, and the *arrow*, we add three more primitives to complete the list.

1220. dart

矢

When shot high into the *heavens*, the **dart** gets so small it looks like a mere *drop*. Although this character could as well mean "arrow," it has no connection with the primitive of that meaning. Hence the new key-word. [5]

1221. rectify

矯

Dart . . . angel. Compare your stories for *correct* (Frame 379), *revise* (Frame 339), and *reformation* (Frame 528). [17]

1222. tribe

族

Banner . . . dart. [11]

1223. know

知

Dart . . . mouth. [8]

1224. wisdom

智

Know . . . sun. [12]

1225. halberd

矛

The **halberd's** battle-ax head and long shaft are clearly depicted here.

One need only pay attention to the number and order of the strokes. [5].

1226. tender

Halberd . . . tree. [9]

1227. task

Halberd . . . taskmaster . . . muscle. [11]

1228. fog

霧

Weather/rain . . . task. [19]

---

*   spear

This weapon, which has the appearance of the long *sword* but is drawn slightly differently, comes to mean **spear**. Its appearance is a rare event. Among the characters treated in this book, it appears only twice, and both instances can be given here. [2]

1229. squad

班

Spear . . . two balls. [10]

1230. homecoming

Spear . . . broom . . . apron. The character for *lady* (Frame 1151) shares the same right side as this character, though it does not bode for a very happy **homecoming**. [10]

1231. bow

弓

This character pictures the bent wooden **bow**; later we shall learn how to make the *bowstring* that goes with it (Frame 1386). If you stretch this character out and see the indentation on the left as its handle, the pictograph should be clearer. [3]

⼸ ⼘ 弓

1232. pull

引

Bow . . . walking stick. [4]

1233. condolences

弔

A *bow* . . . wrapped around a *walking stick.* [4]

1234. vast

弘

Bow . . . elbow. [5]

1235. strong

強

Vast . . . insect. Note how the elbow is shrunken and elevated to make room for the *insect* beneath. [11]

1236. weak

弱

Two *bows* . . . with *ice* on them. [10]

---

*   dollar sign

弗

Composed of two *canes* run through a *bow,* this character is infrequent as a primitive, and yet easy to remember for what it looks like: the **dollar sign** $. When it is written under another element, the second vertical stroke is abbreviated to a short "tail" as the final stroke, and the first vertical stroke is cut off at the top. [5]

⼘ ⼘ 弓 弗 弗

1237. seethe   沸

Water . . . dollar sign. [8]

1238. expense   費

Dollar sign . . . shells/money. [12]

1239. No.   第

The key-word "No." is the abbreviation for "number," so written to indicate its function as a prefix. Its elements: *bamboo . . . dollar sign.* [11]

1240. younger brother   弟

Horns . . .   dollar signs. [7]

*   snare   弓

The simple **snare** composed of a piece of vine and a bent twig is depicted here as a quasi-abbreviation of the *bow,* to which it is related. [2]

一　弓

1241. adroit   巧

Craft . . . snare. [5]

1242. nickname   号

Mouth . . . snare. [5]

1243. decay

朽

Tree . . . snare. Do not confuse this key-word with *rot* (Frame 1023). [6]

1244. boast

誇

Words . . . St. Bernard dog . . . ceiling . . . snare. [13]

1245. dirty

汚

Water . . . spike . . . snare. Take care: the writing does not follow the order of the primitives exactly. [6]

シ　氵　汚

* slingshot

与

The **slingshot** differs from the *snare* by virtue of the first stroke, which you may take as the strip of rubber you pull back on. [2]

一　与

1246. bestow

与

Slingshot . . . one. Later we shall learn the character for *give* (Frame 1897). But already here we can take care to distinguish this key-word for *impart* (Frame 736) and *grant* (Frame 1052). [3]

1247. copy

写

Crown . . . bestow. [5]

LESSON 34

Although we still have a number of primitives left relating to human activities, we may at this point pick up what remain of those having to do specifically with people and parts of the human body.

1248. somebody

The key-word **somebody** was chosen to convey the double meaning of this kanji: body and person. Its composition is based on the *nose* (which, you will recall, is also the kanji for *oneself*). The extension of the bottom and far right strokes of that element, together with the unusual diagonal stroke, forms the pictograph of **somebody** with a prominent paunch. [7]

1249. shoot

"I **shot** an arrow into the air . . . " begins the poem. But this kanji tells us where it DID land. Its elements: *somebody . . . glued to.* [10]

1250. apologize

Words . . . shoot. [17]

1251. old man

First, do not confuse this character with *venerable old man* (Frame 786), which is far more rarely used. The character for an **old man** begins with an abbreviation of the character for *somebody,* the *nose* having been shortened into a simple criss-cross of lines. But there is another, simpler way to remember it all: The *soil* drawn first indicates that one has come close to the age when "dust to dust" begins to take on a personal meaning; the diagonal *cane* for getting around and the *spoon* for being *spoon*-fed. [6]

土 耂 老

* As a primitive, the meaning is the same, but the final two strokes
are omitted so that they can be replaced with other elements: 耂 .

1252. consider

Old man . . . slingshot. Remember: you already have kanji for
discriminating (Frame 482), *deliberation* (Frame 642), and *think*
(Frame 605). [6]

1253. filial piety

Old man . . . child. [7]

1254. teach

Filial piety . . . taskmaster. [11]

1255. torture

Fingers . . . consider. [9]

1256. someone

Old man . . . sun. This key-word looks to be difficult because of its
proximity to *somebody,* but in fact it is a very common kanji that will
cause you no difficulty at all. At any rate, its meaning should be seen
as the human referent for the abstract noun "something." [8]

 * As a primitive it means a *puppet*-on-a-string.

1257. boil

Puppet . . . oven-fire. [12]

1258. renowned

著

Flowers . . . puppet. [11]

1259. signature

署

Eye . . . puppet. [13]

1260. sultry

暑

The key-word refers to the heat of summer. Its elements: *sun . . . puppet.* [12]

1261. various

諸

Words . . . puppet. Do not confuse with *miscellaneous* (Frame 562). [15]

1262. boar

猪

Pack of wild dogs . . . puppet. [11]

1263. strand

渚

The **strand** referred to here is the stretch of land along a beach or shoreline. Its elements are: *water . . . puppet.* [11]

1264. gamble

賭

Shells/money . . . puppet. [15]

* scissors

This primitive is based on that for *husband.* The two extra strokes represent a pair of **scissors** he is carrying around. [6]

一 ⼝ 立 夹

1265. gorge   峡

Mountain . . . scissors. [9]

1266. cramped   狭

Pack of wild dogs . . . scissors. [9]

1267. sandwiched   挟

Fingers . . . scissors. Do not confuse with the kanji for *pinch* (Frame 657). [9]

*   maestro   自

One should picture a tuxedo-clad **maestro** waving his baton about wildly to go with this primitive meaning. The baton is seen in the *drop* at the top. And the two boxes attached to the long vertical stroke may represent his tux-tails, if you wish. [6]

1268. chase   追

Maestro . . . road. [9]

1269. expert   師

Maestro . . . ceiling . . . towel. [10]

1270. commander   帥

Maestro . . . towel. [9]

1271. bureaucrat 官

By replacing the *maestro's* baton (the drop) with the roof of a *house*, we have his equivalent in the institutional world of big government: the **bureaucrat**. [8]

1272. coffin 棺

Wood . . . bureaucrat. [12]

1273. pipe 管

Bamboo . . . bureaucrat. [14]

1274. father 父

The kindness and hard work of the ideal **father** is seen in this abbreviation of the *taskmaster* which leaves off his rod or whip (the first stroke) and replaces it with the sweat of the **father's** brow (the two *drops* at the top). [4]

1275. mingle 交

Tophat . . . father. [6]

1276. merit 効

Mingle . . . power. Note the distinct connotations which separate **merit** from *achievement* (Frame 863). [8]

1277. contrast 較

Cars . . . mingle. [13]

1278. exam

校

Tree . . . mingle. [10]

1279. leg

足

Mouth . . . mending. Note that the last stroke of *mouth* and the first of *mending* overlap. [7]

* As a primitive on the left, it is amended to 𧾷 ; its meaning remains *leg*, but should be thought of as a *wooden leg* in order to avoid confusion with other similar elements, namely *human legs, animal legs,* and *walking legs.*

1280. stimulate

促

Person . . . leg. [9]

1281. long-distance

距

Wooden leg . . . giant. [12]

1282. path

路

Wooden leg . . . each. [13]

1283. dew

露

Rain . . . path. [21]

1284. hop

跳

Wooden leg . . . portent. [13]

1285. leap

躍

Wooden leg . . . feathers . . . turkey. [21]

1286. tread

践

Wooden leg . . . parade float. [13]

1287. step

踏

The meaning of this character is virtually identical with that of the last frame. Be sure to come up with distinct connotations suggested by phrases in which each is commonly used. *Wooden leg . . . water . . . sun.* [15]

1288. skeleton

骨

This kanji and primitive refers to the *part of the body* composed of the bones and their joints. The top part of the kanji, terminating in the element for *crown*, is a pictograph of a bone-joint. I leave it to you to put the pieces together, so to speak. [10]

1289. slippery

滑

Water . . . skeleton. [13]

1290. marrow

髄

Skeleton . . . possess . . . road. [19]

* jawbone

咼

The meaning for this primitive is taken from the combination of "the joint" above and the *mouth* in the *cowl* below. [9]

宀 咼

1291. calamity	禍
Altar . . . jawbone. [13]	
1292. whirlpool	渦
Water . . . jawbone. [12]	
1293. overdo	過
Jawbone . . . road. [12]	

LESSON 35

The next group of primitives we shall consider has to do with topography and exhausts the list of those remaining in that category.

* pinnacle	ß

This key word has been chosen because of its connotation of "the highest point," thereby suggesting the image of the highest point in a village, that is, a hill or mountain on which sacred or festive events take place. If you have a clear image of the Athenian acropolis, you might use it to express this element for a **pinnacle**. Note that this primitive appears only on the left. On the right, as we shall see later, the same form takes a different meaning. [3]

フ ヲ ß

1294. Heights   阪

This character is used for proper names, much as the English word
"Heights" is. Its primitives: *pinnacle . . . anti-*. [7]

1295. Africa   阿

This kanji, an abbreviation for **Africa**, is now used chiefly for its
sound, "a," not unlike the kanji for *Italy* and the sound "i" as we
learned earlier (Frame 1161). Its elements are: *pinnacles . . . can*. [8]

1296. occasion   際

Pinnacle . . . ritual. [14]

1297. hinder   障

Pinnacle . . . badge. [14]

1298. follow   随

Pinnacle . . . possess . . . road. [12]

1299. obeisance   陪

Pinnacle . . . muzzle. [11]

1300. sunshine   陽

Different from the primitive for *sun* (which figures in the character)
and the kanji for *ray* (Frame 119), the key-word **sunshine** is meant to
convey the meaning of the masculine principle in nature, or "Yang."
(The dark is viewed mythically as the feminine principle; see Frame
1572.) From there it comes to mean *sun* also. The elements are:
pinnacle . . . piggy bank. [12]

1301. exhibit 陳

Pinnacle . . . east. Distinguish well from *display* (Frame 262), *show* (Frame 1086), and *revelation* (Frame 247). [11]

1302. ward off 防

Pinnacle . . . compass. [7]

1303. affixed 附

Pinnacle . . . adhere. [8]

1304. Inst. 院

This key-word, the abbreviation for **"Institution,"** represents the use of that word as a suffix affixed to certain buildings and organizations. Its primitive elements: *pinnacle . . . perfect.* [10]

1305. camp 陣

Pinnacle . . . car. [10]

1306. regiment 隊

Pinnacle . . . animal horns . . . sow. [12]

1307. crash 墜

Regiment . . . ground. [15]

1308. descend 降

Pinnacle . . . walking legs . . . sunglasses (with a lens popped out, see Frame 1036). Distinguish from *fall* Frame 299) and *crash,* which we considered in the previous frame. [10]

1309. storey

階

Pinnacle . . . all. [12]

1310. highness

陛

This key-word indicates a title of address to royalty. Its elements: *pinnacle . . . compare . . . ground.* [10]

1311. neighboring

隣

Pinnacle . . . rice . . . sunglasses. [16]

1312. isolate

隔

Pinnacle . . . ceiling . . . mouth . . . glass canopy . . . human legs . . . spike. Hint: compare the kanji for *dissolve* (Frame 1044). [13]

1313. conceal

隠

Pinnacle . . . vulture . . . broom . . . heart. Hint: compare the elements at the right to the kanji for *calm* (Frame 1147). [14]

1314. degenerate

堕

Pinnacle . . . possess . . . ground. [12]

1315. collapse

陥

Pinnacle . . . bound up . . . olden times. [10]

1316. hole

穴

House . . . eight. [5]

* As a primitive, this kanji uses an alternate form: the primitive for *eight* is replaced with that for *human legs*.

1317. empty   空

Hole . . . craft. [8]

1318. withdraw   控

Fingers . . . empty. [11]

1319. stab   突

Hole . . . St. Bernard dog. [8]

1320. research   究

Hole . . . baseball. [7]

1321. plug up   窒

Hole . . . climax. [11]

1322. stealth   窃

Hole . . . cut. [9]

1323. depression   窪

Hole . . . water . . . ivy. The **depression** referred to here is a sunken place in the ground, rather than in one's spirits. [14]

1324. squeeze   搾

Fingers . . . hole . . . saw. [13]

1325. kiln

窯

Hole . . . sheep . . . oven-fire. [15]

1326. hard up

窮

Hole . . . somebody . . . bow. [15]

*   paper punch

This primitive simply discards the first stroke of that for *hole* to become a **paper punch**. When found at the top of its relative primitive, it undergoes the same change, the *eight* becoming *human legs*. (See Frame 1316.) [4]

1327. grope

探

Fingers . . . paper punch . . . tree. [11]

1328. deep

深

Water . . . paper punch . . . tree. [11]

1329. hill

丘

Since this supposed pictograph of a hill looks like anything but, picture a row of *axes* driven into the ground up to their heads, and see if that doesn't present a more memorable image of **hill**—at least a risker one sliding down! [5]

1330. Point

岳

Think of the key-word as referring to proper names of mountains, but do not confuse with *mountain peak* (Frame 773). The elements are: *hill . . . mountain.* [8]

1331. soldier

兵

Hill . . . animal legs. [7]

1332. seacoast

浜

Water . . . soldier. [10]

LESSON 36

The primitive for *thread* is one of the most common in all the kanji. This means that you are likely to be putting it where it doesn't belong and forgetting to include it where it does. Because of this, it is important to have a vivid image of the element each time it appears. Fortunately for you, nearly all the *thread*-related kanji to be covered in this book will appear in the next 10 pages, so you can learn them all at once.

1333. thread

糸

Remember when your granny used to ask you to bend your arms at the *elbows* and hold them out so that she could use them like a rack to hold a skein of yarn while she rolled it up into a *small* ball? Now can you see the two *elbows* (with the second stroke doubling up) at the top, and the character for *small* below? [6]

1334. weave

織

Thread . . . kazoo. [18]

1335. darning
繕

Thread . . . virtuous. [18]

1336. shrink
縮

Thread . . . inn. [17]

1337. luxuriant
繁

Cleverness . . . thread. [16]

1338. vertical
縦

Thread . . . accompany. [16]

1339. line
線

Thread . . . spring. [15]

1340. tighten
締

Thread . . . sovereign. [15]

1341. fiber
維

Thread . . . turkey. [14]

1342. gauze
羅

Eye . . . fiber. [19]

1343. practice 練

Thread . . . east. [14]

1344. thong 緒

Thread . . . puppet. Although we usually think of a **thong** as coming at the end of a piece of string, this character's meaning allows for it to come at the beginning as well. [14]

1345. continue 続

Thread . . . sell. [13]

1346. picture 絵

Thread . . . meeting. [12]

1347. overall 統

Thread . . . allot. [12]

1348. strangle 絞

Thread . . . mingle. [12]

1349. salary 給

Thread . . . fit. [12]

1350. entwine 絡

Thread . . . each. [12]

1351. tie   結

Thread . . . aerosol can. [12]

1352. end   終

Thread . . . winter. [11]

1353. class   級

Threads . . . outstretched hands. [9]

1354. chronicle   紀

Thread . . . snake. [9]

1355. crimson   紅

Thread . . . craft. [9]

1356. settlement   納

Thread . . . inside. [10]

1357. spinning   紡

For the kanji that means the **spinning** of *thread* and other fibers we
have: *Thread . . . compass.* [10]

1358. distract   紛

Thread . . . part. [10]

1359. introduce 紹

Thread . . . seduce. [11]

1360. sūtra 経

Thread . . . spool. [11]

1361. sire 紳

Thread . . . monkey. [11]

1362. promise 約

It will be helpful to concentrate a moment on the etymology of the word **"promise"** in order to notice its roots in the activity of putting one thing (e.g., one's word of honor) in place of another (e.g., the fulfillment of a task). For as it turns out, this character also means "to abridge, economize and abbreviate"—all activities which involve putting one thing in place of another. With that in mind, we may now work with the elements: *thread . . . ladle.* [9]

1363. dainty 細

Thread . . . brains. [11]

1364. accumulate 累

Threads . . . rice field. Make use of the position of the elements to distinguish this kanji from that of the previous frame. [11]

1365. cord 索

Needle . . . a crown . . . thread. [10]

1366. general   総

This kanji, meaning universal or widespread, is composed of three elements: *thread . . . public . . . heart.* [14]

1367. cotton   綿

Thread . . . white . . . towels. [14]

1368. silk   絹

Thread . . . mouth . . . flesh. [13]

1369. winding   繰

Thread . . . goods . . . tree. [19]

1370. inherit   継

Thread . . . rice . . . fishhook. Compare Frame 1136. [13]

1371. green   緑

Thread . . . broom . . . rice grains. [14]

1372. affinity   縁

Thread . . . broom . . . sow. [15]

1373. netting   網

Thread . . . glass canopy . . . animal horns . . . perish. [14]

1374. tense   紧

Slave . . . crotch . . . thread. [15]

1375. purple   紫

Thread . . . footprint . . . spoon. [12]

1376. truss   縛

Threads . . . acupuncture specialist. [16]

1377. straw rope   繩

Thread . . . eels. [15]

*   cocoon   幺

The two triangular shapes here and their final stroke are intended as a pictograph of a **cocoon**, spun in circles and tied up at the end. It is like the character for *thread*, except that the silkworm's actual product has not yet emerged clearly at the bottom. [3]

1378. infancy   幼

Cocoon . . . muscle. [5]

1379. behind   後

Line . . . cocoon . . . walking legs. [9]

1380. seclude   幽

Two cocoons . . . mountain. Observe how the two *cocoons* are **secluded** from one another and from the outside, within the *mountain*. Also, note that in its printed from the two vertical strokes of the *mountain* are extended upwards; this is so because they serve here as a kind of enclosure. [9]

1381. how many   幾

Two cocoons . . . person . . . fiesta. [12]

* As a primitive, we shall give this shape the meaning of an *abacus*, that is, the bead-instrument used in the orient to calculate *how many*.

1382. mechanism   機

Tree . . . abacus. [16]

1383. mysterious   玄

Tophat . . . cocoon. [5]

1384. livestock   畜

Mysterious . . . rice field. [10]

1385. amass   蓄

Flowers . . . livestock. [13]

1386. bowstring   弦

Bow . . . mysterious. [8]

1387. hug

Fingers . . . mysterious . . . turkey. Note that the *tophat* is extended across both elements, though it belongs only to the *cocoon*. This means that you may either use *mysterious*—as we did here—or take the three elements separately. [16]

1388. nourishing

Water . . . double-*mysterious.* Note the doubling up of the element for *tophat* in the primitive for *mysterious* and assign it a special image, since it will come up in the following frames. [12]

1389. mercy

Double-*mysterious . . . heart.* [13]

1390. magnet

Stone . . . double-*mysterious.* [14]

1391. lineage

The single stroke added to the beginning of the primitive for *thread* gives the image of threads woven into a single cord. Hence the meaning, **lineage.** [7]

  * As a primitive, we shall give this kanji the meaning of *yarn,* as the uniting of many threads into a single strand is most obvious with *yarn.*

1392. person in charge

Person . . . yarn. [9]

1393. grandchild 孫

Child . . . yarn. [10]

1394. suspend 懸

Prefecture . . . yarn . . . heart. [20]

LESSON 37

Earlier we created an image for *seal* (Frame 156). Here we come to a set of primitives based on the shape of a seal and deriving their meanings from the notion of stamping or sealing.

*   stamp 卩

This character is a kind of pictograph of a **stamp** which may best be imagined as a postage stamp to distinguish it from other stamp-like things to come up later. [2]

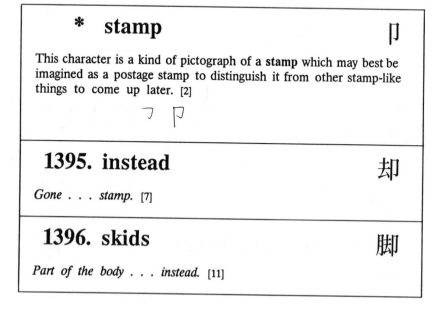

1395. instead 却

Gone . . . stamp. [7]

1396. skids 脚

Part of the body . . . instead. [11]

1397. wholesale 卸

The left primitive is a union of *a horse* and *footprint*. To the right, *the stamp.* [9]

午　茌　卸

1398. honorable 御

Line . . . wholesale. [12]

1399. clothing 服

Flesh . . . stamp . . . crotch. Note how the *stamp* is stretched out here. [8]

1400. fate 命

Fit . . . stamp. The bottom portion of *fit* is squeezed leftwards in order to make room for the *stamp.* [8]

*   chop-seal 卩

The **chop-seal** is the engraved piece of wood or stone used in the Orient to certify documents. Unlike the *stamp,* the top stroke here reaches a good distance to the left of its vertical stroke. When it appears at the top of another primitive, it is abbreviated to ⌐ . [2]

1401. orders 令

Meeting . . . chop-seals. [5]

1402. zero 零

Rain . . . orders. [12]

1403. age

齢

This character is used to express the years of one's **age**. Its elements: *teeth . . . orders.* [17]

1404. cool

冷

Ice . . . orders. [7]

1405. jurisdiction

領

Orders . . . head. [14]

1406. small bell

鈴

Gold . . . orders. [13]

1407. courage

勇

Chop-seal . . . male. [9]

1408. traffic

通

Chop-seal . . . utilize . . . road. Hint: by combining the first two primitives into a single image, you will be able to use that image in a few instances later, one of which comes immediately. [10]

1409. jump

踊

Wooden leg . . . chop-seal . . . utilize. [14]

1410. doubt

疑

Spoon . . . dart . . . chop-seal . . . . . . zoo. [14]

1411. mimic
擬

Fingers . . . doubt. [17]

1412. congeal
凝

Ice . . . doubt. [16]

---

* fingerprint
巳

The primitive for **fingerprint** is like that for *stamp* except that the second stroke bends back towards the right, like an arm. [2]

1413. pattern
範

Bamboo . . . car . . . fingerprint. [15]

1414. crime
犯

Wild dogs . . . fingerprint. [5]

1415. unlucky
厄

Cliff . . . fingerprint. [4]

1416. dangerous
危

Bound up . . . unlucky. [6]

---

* mailbox
夗

Evening . . . fingerprint. [5]

1417. address   宛

House . . . mailbox. [8]

1418. arm   腕

Part of the body . . . address. [12]

1419. garden   苑

Flowers . . . mailbox. [8]

1420. grudge   怨

Mailbox . . . heart [9]

*   receipt   厶

This primitive element is actually the mirror-image of that for *stamp*, but since Japanese does not permit a stroke to go to the left and bottom in one swoop, the visual similarity is not perfectly clear. If you play with the idea with pen and paper, its logic will become obvious. [3]

　　　　　　ノ　　ム　　厶

1421. willow   柳

Tree . . . receipt . . . stamp. [9]

1422. egg   卵

Receipt . . . stamp . . . and *a drop* in each side to represent a little smear of egg-yoke. The third stroke is drawn slightly higher to close the **egg** up tightly and keep the yoke inside. [7]

1423. detain

Receipt . . . dagger . . . rice field. [10]

1424. trade

Receipt . . . dagger . . . shells. Though the meanings are related, do not confuse with *make a deal* (Frame 439) or *wholesale* (Frame 1397). [12]

*   staples

This primitive represents a number of small **staples**, like the kind commonly used in an office and at school. [4]

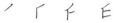

1425. stamp

At last we come to the general character meaning **stamp**. Its elements: *staples . . . stamp.* [6]

1426. entertain 興

Let this character represent a wheel of fortune that has been tampered with. On both sides you see the *staples* separating one number's slot from the next, and between them the character for the *same*—indicating that it has been fixed to repeat the same number. Beneath is the primitive for a *tool*, which refers to the wheel itself. All together, a fitting symbol for **entertainment**, if you happen to be the owner of the wheel. [16]

LESSON 38

The next cluster of kanji has to do with primitives surrounding the activities of eating and drinking.

1427. sign of the bird 酉

Though we shall later encounter the kanji for *bird,* we introduce this one for the tenth sign of the zodiac mainly because of its use as a primitive, though with a different meaning. [7]

* As a primitive, it means *whiskey bottle.* In its pictograph, you can see the loosely corked lid, the bottle and the contents (about one-third full). Think of the Spanish "porrón," a decanter shaped like a long-necked bird.

1428. saké 酒

Water . . . whiskey bottle. [10]

1429. bartending 酌

Whiskey bottle . . . ladle. [10]

1430. fermentation 酵

Whiskey bottle . . . filial piety. [14]

1431. cruel 酷

Whiskey bottle . . . revelation. [14]

1432. repay   酬

Whiskey bottle . . . state. [13]

1433. dairy products   酪

Whiskey bottle . . . each. [13]

1434. vinegar   酢

Whiskey bottle . . . saw. [12]

1435. drunk   酔

Whiskey bottle . . . baseball . . . needle. [11]

1436. distribute   配

Whisky bottle . . . snake. [10]

1437. acid   酸

Whiskey bottle . . . license . . . walking legs. [14]

1438. furthermore   猶

Wild dogs . . . animal horns . . . whiskey bottle. [12]

1439. revered   尊

Animal horns . . . whiskey bottle . . . glue. [12]

1440. beans   豆

This kanji depicts a pot of **beans**, although it looks more like a *table,* which is in fact its meaning as a primitive. [7]

一　口　日　豆

1441. head   頭

Here we meet at last the full kanji on which our primitive is based. The elements: *table . . . head.* [16]

1442. short   短

Dart . . . table. [12]

1443. bountiful   豊

Bend . . . table. Think of a **bountiful** harvest, and you will be not be far from the meaning of this character. [13]

*   drum   壹

The elelment meaning **drum** shows a *samurai* over a *table.* The top stroke of the *table* is missing, or rather doubles-up with the final stroke of the *samurai.* [9]

1444. drum   鼓

The full kanji for the **drum** adds a *branch,* apparently to serve as a drumstick, to the primitive for **drum.** [13]

1445. rejoice   喜

Drum . . . mouth. [12]

1446. timber-trees   樹

Trees . . . drum . . . glue. [16]

1447. dish   皿

The kanji for a dish is a pictograph of a painted or carved bowl. [5]

丨 冂 冚 皿

1448. blood   血

The *drop* in the *dish* is **blood**. It is similar to the *drop* we saw earlier on the *dagger* in the character for *blade* (Frame 84). [6]

1449. basin   盆

Part . . . dish. [9]

1450. alliance   盟

Bright . . . dish. [13]

1451. steal   盗

Next . . . dish. [11]

1452. warm   温

Water . . . sun . . . dish. [12]

1453. oversee   監

Slaves . . . reclining . . . floor/one . . . dish. [15]

1454. overflow 濫

Water . . . oversee. [18]

1455. specimen 鑑

Metal . . . oversee. [23]

1456. fierce 猛

Wild dogs . . . child . . . dish. [11]

1457. boom 盛

Here **boom** refers to something that is popular and prospering. Its
elements: *turn into . . . dish.* [11]

1458. salt 塩

Ground . . . reclining . . . mouth . . . dish. [13]

*   silver 艮

We give this element the meaning of **silver** from the kanji in the
following frame. Both the original pictographic representation and
the primitive elements that make it up are more trouble to hunt out
than they are worth. It is best simply to learn it as is. In doing so, take
careful note of the stroke order, and also the fact that when this
element appears on the left, the penultimate stroke is omitted, giving
us simply 艮 . [6]

ㄱ ㄱ ㅋ 艮 艮 艮

1459. silver 銀

Metal . . . silver. [14]

金 銀

1460. regret   恨

State of mind . . . silver. [9]

1461. root   根

Tree . . . silver. [10]

1462. instant   即

Silver . . . stamp. [7]

1463. baron   爵

Vulture . . . eye . . . silver . . . glue. [17]

1464. node   節

Bamboo . . . instant. [13]

1465. retreat   退

Road . . . silver. [9]

1466. limit   限

Pinnacle . . . silver. [9]

1467. eyeball   眼

Eye . . . silver. [11]

1468. good

良

Drop of . . . silver. [7]

* As a primitive, use the image of a *halo,* the pious symbol of saintly *goodness.* As with *silver,* when drawn on the left, the penultimate stroke is omitted.

1469. melodious

朗

Halo . . . moon. [10]

1470. wandering

浪

Water . . . halo. [10]

1471. daughter

娘

Woman . . . halo. [10]

1472. eat

The obvious elements are *halo* and *umbrella,* and they should do well enough. But you might also try breaking the *halo* down into *drop* and *silver,* which would give you "silverware," an additional meaning that could come in useful later. [9]

* As a primitive, This kanji can mean either *eating* or *food.* As was the case with *silver,* when situated on the left the final two strokes of this element are abbreviated into one.

1473. meal

飯

Food . . . anti-. [12]

1474. drink   飲

Food . . . yawn. [12]

1475. hungry   飢

Food . . . wind. [10]

1476. starve   餓

Food . . . ego. [15]

1477. decorate   飾

Food . . . reclining . . . towel. [13]

1478. Bldg.   館

The abbreviation of **"Building"** suggests that this kanji is used in proper names, as indeed it often is. Keep your connotation distinct from *Inst.* (Frame 1304). Its elements: *food . . . bureaucrat.* [16]

1479. foster   養

Sheep . . . food. The key-word has the sense of promoting the development of something, especially in a psychological or spiritual sense. [13]

1480. sated   飽

Eat . . . wrap. [13]

* waitress   旡

If you draw this character once, you will see that its first three strokes resemble the form for *receipt* (except that the second stroke ends more parallel to the first), with its last stroke stretched to form the first of the two *human legs*. From this we give it its meaning of a **waitress** (who should not be confused with the waiter back in Frame 976). [5]

一 丁 工 午 无

1481. previously   既

Silver . . . waitress. Do not confuse this kanji's key-word with *before* (Frame 248). [10]

1482. outline   概

Roots . . . waitress. Note that the kanji meaning of the two primitives to the right is not used here because we shall later meet a primitive meaning *beforehand* and want to pre-empt any confusion. The same holds true in the following frame. [14]

1483. rue   慨

Regret . . . waitress. [13]

LESSON 39

A number of primitives relating to plant-life remain to be considered, and these we will take up in the next two lessons. In the following pages, as indeed in the rest of the book, we shall meet several elements whose use is quite limited. Nevertheless, it is better to learn them as primitives both in order to acquaint yourself better with the way the Japanese writing system repeats certain combinations of elements, and in order later to facilitate the learning of characters outside the compass of these pages.

1484. even 平

This character is easiest remembered as a pictograph of a water-lily floating on the surface of the water, which gives it its meaning of even. The fourth stroke represents the calm, smooth surface of a pond, and the final stroke the long stem of the plant reaching underwater. [5]

* As a primitive, this kanji can keep its pictographic meaning of a *water-lily*.

1485. call 呼

Mouth . . . water-lily. Note: this is the one time that the "stem" has a barb at the end. Work this fact into your story. [8]

1486. two-mat area 坪

This kanji belongs to an old Japanese system of measurement and indicates an area of about 36 square feet or the space taken up by two *tatami* mats. Its elements: *ground . . . water-lily.* [8]

1487. evaluate 評

Words . . . water-lily. [12]

* sheaf X

The two strokes given here represent a crude drawing of a bundle of stalks bound together into a **sheaf**, which is the meaning we assign it as a primitive. [2]

1488. reap

Sheaf . . . sword. [4]

刈

1489. hope

Sheaf . . . linen. [7]

希

1490. villain

Sheaf . . . shovel. [4]

凶

メ 凶

1491. bosom

Part of the body . . . bound up . . . villain. [10]

胸

1492. detach

離

Top hat . . . villain . . . belt . . . elbow . . . turkey. This is potentially one of the most difficult characters to remember. Tackle it positively and let the image "sink in" by carrying it around with you today and calling it up in your spare moments. [18]

1493. kill

Sheaf . . . tree . . . missile. [10]

殺

*   earthworm

屯

Drop of . . . shovel . . . fishhook. [4]

一 𠃌 𡶂 屯

1494. genuine

純

Thread . . . earthworm. [10]

1495. dull

鈍

Metal . . . earthworm. [12]

1496. spicy

辛

This character pictures food whose taste is so hot and **spicy** that it makes the hairs on your body *stand* up straight as *needles*. [7]

* As a primitive, we shall use this meaning of *spicy*, except when the two extra strokes are added to the bottom, giving it the form of a tree: . Then we take its alternate meaning of a *red pepper* plant. The connection is obvious.

1497. resign

辞

Tongue . . . spicy. [13]

1498. catalpa

梓

Tree . . . spicy. [11]

1499. superintend

宰

House . . . spicy. [10]

---

*   ketchup

Pouring **ketchup** over everything is one way American children learn to cope with eating foods they do not otherwise savor. We can see this depicted in the *mouth* with the *flag* over it (in this case, the star-spangled banner), set along side the element for *spicy* (all of which is

not far removed from the meaning it has when rarely used as a
character on its own: "false"). [13]

1500. wall   壁

Ketchup . . . ground. [16]

1501. evade   避

Ketchup . . . road. [16]

1502. new   新

Red pepper . . . axe. [13]

1503. fuel   薪

Flowers . . . new. [16]

1504. parent   親

Red pepper . . . see. [16]

1505. happiness   幸

Simply by turning the dot at the top of the last primitive into a cross-
form, we move from things bitter and *spicy* to things **happy**. [8]

1506. tenacious   執

Happiness . . . fat man. [11]

1507. report   報

Happiness . . . stamp . . . crotch. Compare Frame 1399. [12]

* cornucopia

Considering the lack of circular lines, this kanji is not an altogether bad pictograph of a **cornucopia**. When drawn at the left of its relative primitive, the first two strokes are written as one. [3]

1508. shout

Mouth . . . cornucopia. [6]

1509. twist

String . . . cornucopia. [9]

1510. income

Cornucopia . . . crotch. Keep distinct from both *earnings* (Frame 893) and *salary* (Frame 1349). [4]

1511. lowly

A drop of . . . brains . . . cornucopia. [9]

1512. tombstone

Rock . . . lowly. [14]

* rice-seedling

As we mentioned back in Frame 234, **rice-seedlings** get an element all their own: *soil* and *man legs* becomes an ideograph of the spikelets of rice bunched together for implanting in the muddy soil of the paddy. [5]

1513. land

The sense of **"land"** carried by this kanji is distinct from *soil* (Frame 150) and *ground* (Frame 515) in that it is meant to represent **land** seen from a distance, that is, **land** as opposed to "water." Its elements: *pinnacle . . . rice-seedlings . . . ground.* [11]

1514. intimate

Eye . . . rice-seedlings . . . ground. [13]

1515. forces

Rice-seedlings . . ground . . . fat man . . . muscle. [13]

1516. heat

Rice-seedlings . . . ground . . . fat man . . . oven-fire. [15]

1517. diamond

Named after a **diamond**-shaped flower (the water **caltrop**), this keyword refers to things shaped like a **diamond**. Its elements: *flower . . . spikelets . . . walking legs.* [11]

1518. mausoleum

Pinnacle . . . rice-seedlings . . . walking legs. [11]

1519. sign of the hog

This character represents the 12th sign of the Chinese zodiac: the **hog**. It is best learned by thinking of an acorn-eating **hog** in connection with the primitive meaning, which follows below. [6]

* The *tophat* represents the external shape of the *acorn:* and the unusual but easily written complex of strokes beneath it (which you might also see as distortions of an *elbow* and *person)* stands for the mysterious secret whereby the *acorn* contains the oak tree in a nutshell.

1520. nucleus

核

Tree . . . acorn. [10]

1521. engrave

刻

Acorn . . . sabre. [8]

1522. above-stated

該

Words . . . acorn. [13]

1523. censure

劾

Acorn . . . muscle. [8]

* resin

朮

This *tree* has become a *pole* (that is, a *tree* with its branches not touching) because most of its branches have been pruned off by a naive but greedy gardener anxious to siphon off its **resin** (the *drop* at the top) as quickly as possible. [5]

1524. mention

述

Resin . . . road. [8]

1525. art

術

Boulevard . . . resin. [11]

* celery   址

This primitive looks very close to that for *salad,* except that an extra horizontal line has been included, reminiscent I should think of the long **celery** sticks in your *salad.* [5]

1526. cold   寒

House . . . celery . . . animal legs . . . ice. [12]

* grass skirt   襄

This unusual looking **grass skirt** is composed of a *tophat* and *scarf,* and *eight celery* sticks. [13]

1527. brew   醸

Whiskey bottle . . . grass skirt. [20]

1528. defer   譲

Words . . . grass skirt. [20]

1529. lot   壌

Ground . . . grass skirt. The **lot** of this key-word refers to a portion of land. [16]

1530. lass   嬢

Woman . . . grass skirt. [16]

LESSON 40

The remainder of plant-related primitives are built up from combinations of vertical and horizontal lines, representing respectively plants and the earth from which they spring. Accordingly it would be a good idea to study the remaining elements of this section at a single sitting, or at least so to review them before passing on to the next grouping.

---

* grow up   圭

As the plant **grows up** it sprouts leaves and a stalk, which are depicted here over a single horizontal stroke for the *soil*. Think of something (its relative primitive) **growing up** in a flash to many times its normal size, much like little Alice in Wonderland who **grew up** so fast she was soon larger than the room in which she was sitting. [4]

一　十　圭　圭

1531. poison   毒

Grow up . . . breasts. [8]

1532. elementary   素

Grow up . . . thread. [10]

1533. barley   麦

Grow up . . . walking legs. [7]

1534. blue   青

Grow up . . . moon. [8]

1535. refined   精

Rice . . . blue. [14]

1536. solicit   請

Words . . . blue. [15]

1537. feelings   情

State of mind . . . blue. Do not confuse with *emotion* (Frame 615). [11]

1538. clear up   晴

Take the key-word in its associations with the weather (unless that tempts you to include the element for *weather,* which doesn't belong here). Its elements: *sun . . . blue.* [12]

1539. pure   清

Water . . . blue. [11]

1540. quiet   静

Blue . . . contend. Do not confuse with *calm* (Frame 1147). [14]

1541. blame   責

Grow up . . . oyster. [11]

1542. exploits   績

Thread . . . blame. [17]

1543. volume

積

This key-word refers to measurement, and should be kept distinct from the kanji for *quantity* (Frame 177)—even though the meaning is nearly equivalent. Its elements: *wheat . . . blame.* [16]

1544. bond

債

Person . . . blame. The key-word here refers to financial debts. [13]

1545. pickling

漬

Water . . . blame. [14]

1546. surface

表

Grow up . . . scarf. This character represents the "outside" of a piece of clothing, just as the kanji for *back* (Frame 399) depicted the "inside" or lining. [8]

1547. bag

俵

Keep this kanji distinct from that for *sack* (Frame 1006). Its elements are: *person . . . surface.* [10]

1548. undefiled

潔

Water . . . grow up . . . dagger . . . thread. Do not confuse with *upright* (Frame 55). [15]

1549. pledge

契

Grow up . . . dagger . . . St. Bernard dog. This character should be kept distinct in its connotation from *vow* (Frame 1133) and *promise* (Frame 1362). [9]

1550. consume 喫

Mouth . . . pledge. [12]

1551. harm 害

House . . . grow up . . . mouth. [10]

1552. control 轄

Car . . . harm. Hint: the image of an auto going "out of **control**" may help keep this key-word distinct from others like it, such as *manipulate* (Frame 801). [17]

1553. proportion 割

Harm . . . sabre. [12]

1554. constitution 憲

The key-word refers to the fundamental guiding principles of a government or other organization. Its elements: *House . . . grow up . . . eyes . . . heart.* [16]

1555. life 生

A single *drop* added to the element for *grow up* gives us the character for **life.** [5]

    * As a primitive, we may think of a microscopic *cell,* that miraculous unit that *grows up* to become a living being.

1556. star 星

Sun . . . cell. [9]

1557. surname

姓

Woman . . . cell. [8]

1558. sex

性

State of mind . . . cell. [8]

1559. animal sacrifice

牲

Cow . . . cell. [9]

1560. products

産

Vase . . . cliff . . . cell. [11]

1561. hump

隆

This character, used for camel-**humps,** suggests also the hunch on the pig's back and hind parts where the best cuts of meat are to be found (and hence the English expression for luxury, "living high off the hog.") The elements we have to work with are: *pinnacle . . . walking legs . . . cell.* [11]

*   bushes

キ

Whatever image you contrived for the character meaning *hedge* (Frame 154), choose something different and clearly distinguishable for this primitive for **bushes.** The element itself differs from that for *grow up* only in the extension of the single vertical stroke beneath the final horizontal stroke and in the order of writing. Though we shall meet only one instance of it in this chapter and one more later on, it is worth noting that when this element appears on the side, the final stroke is sloped somewhat to the left: キ [4]

三   キ

1562. summit

峰

Mountain . . . walking legs . . . bushes. [10]

1563. sew

縫

Thread . . . walking legs . . . bushes . . . road. [16]

1564. worship

拝

Fingers . . . bush . . . suspended from the ceiling. [8]

1565. longevity

寿

Bushes . . . glue. [7]

1566. casting

鋳

Metal . . . longevity. As you probably guessed from the elements, the key-word refers to the **casting** of metals. [15]

* Christmas tree

耒

The addition of the final two strokes to the element for *bushes* gives the sense of a tree that is also a *bush.* Hence, the **Christmas tree.** [6]

丰 耒

1567. enroll

籍

Bamboo . . . Christmas tree . . . once upon a time. [20]

* bonsai

夫

The element for bushes has an extra stroke added (drawn from the point where the second and fourth strokes intersect when it "encloses" something beneath, otherwise from the point where the third and fourth strokes intersect) to give the image of a prop used to hold up a tree that has been bent into a particular form, the way Japanese gardeners often do. From there it is but a short leap to the small **bonsai** plants that imitate this art in miniature. [5]

1568. springtime 春

Bonsai . . . sun. [9]

1569. camellia 椿

Tree . . . springtime. [13]

1570. peaceful 泰

Bonsai . . . rice-grains. [10]

1571. play music 奏

Bonsai . . . heavens. [9]

1572. reality 実

House . . . bonsai. [8]

---

* cornstalk

The element for *bushes* extended the vertical stroke beneath the final horizontal stroke; the **cornstalk** omits that final stroke altogether, leaving only the *stalk* and the leaves bursting forth on all sides. [3]

1573. observance 奉

Bonsai . . . cornstalk. Use a ritualistic, religious meaning. [8]

1574. stipend   俸

Person . . . observance. [10]

1575. rod   棒

Tree . . . observance. [12]

---

*   cabbage   菫

The *flower,* the *mouth,* and the element for *grow up* combine here to
create the primitive for **cabbage**. [10]

艹   苫   菫

1576. discreet   謹

Words . . . cabbage. [17]

1577. diligence   勤

Cabbage . . . muscle. [12]

---

*   scarecrow   莫

By twisting the final two strokes of our *haystack* into a pair of legs,
we get a **scarecrow** with a *cabbage* for a head. [10]

1578. Sino-   漢

Water . . . scarecrow. The key-word has come to refers to things *Chinese
in general,* including the kanji themselves (for which this character is
used). [13]

1579. sigh   嘆

Mouth . . . scarecrow. [13]

1580. difficult   難

Scarecrow . . . turkey. [18]

*   silage   丗

The drawing of this element is difficult to do smoothly, and should be practiced carefully. It is a pictograph of all sorts of plants and grasses thrown together to make **silage**. The vertical stroke will always double up with another primitive element's vertical stroke. [6]

一　二　干　开　丑　丗

1581. splendor   華

Flower . . . silage . . . needle. [10]

1582. droop   垂

A drop of . . . silage . . . walking cane . . . floor. The character is written in the order of its elements. [8]

1583. drowsy   睡

Eyes . . . droop. [13]

1584. spindle   錘

Metal . . . droop. [16]

1585. ride

The simplest way to remember this character is by looking for the *cereal* in it which doubles up with one stroke of *silage*. [9]

1586. surplus

Ride . . . sword. [11]

LESSON 41

Only a few of the primitives relating to time and direction remain. It is to these that we turn our attention in this lesson.

1587. now

The final stroke of this kanji is a rare shape, which we have not met before and will only meet in this character and others that include it as a primitive. We are more accustomed to seeing it straightened out as part of other shapes—for instance, as the second stroke of *mouth*. If you need any help at all with this character, you may picture it as two hands of a clock pointing to what time it is *now*. The element above it, *meeting*, should easily fit into that image. [4]

* We shall use a *clock* as the primitive meaning of this character, in line with the above explanation.

1588. include

Clock . . . mouth. [7]

1589. versify

We have already learned characters for *poem* (Frame 346), *chant* (Frame 21), and *song* (Frame 469), which means that it is important to protect this key-word with an image all its own. Its elements are the same as those above; only the position has changed: *clock . . . mouth.* [7]

1590. wish

Clock . . . heart. [8]

1591. harp

A pair of *jewels . . . clock.* [12]

1592. shade

Just as the *sunshine* (Frame 1300) represents the masculine principle in nature (Yang), the **shade** stands for the feminine principle (Yin). Its elements are: *pinnacle . . . clock . . . rising cloud.* [11]

1593. beforehand

Think of this character as identical to the *halberd* (Frame 1225) except that the final stroke has been omitted. Return to that character and devise some image to take this distinction into account. [4]

1594. preface

Cave . . . beforehand. [7]

1595. deposit

預

Beforehand . . . head. [13]

1596. plains

This character refers to rustic life and rustic fields primarily, and from there gets derived meanings. Its elements: *computer . . . beforehand.* [11]

1597. concurrently 兼

At the top we have *the animal horns* and the single horizontal stroke to give them something to hang onto. Below that, we see one *rake* with two handles. Finally, we see a pair of strokes splitting away from each of the handles, indicating that they are both splitting under the pressure. The composite picture is of someone holding down two jobs **concurrently**, using the same kit of tools to move in two different directions and ending up in a mess. If you take the time to make sense of the character in this way, it becomes, in fact, easy to remember, despite its difficult appearance. [10]

1598. dislike 嫌

Woman . . . concurrently. [13]

1599. sickle 鎌

Metal . . . concurrently. [18]

1600. self-effacing 謙

Words . . . concurrently. [17]

1601. bargain 廉

Cave . . . concurrently. [13]

1602. west

To our way of counting directions, the **west** always comes fourth. So it is convenient to find the character for *four* in this kanji. But since we want only *one* of the *four* directions, the **west** adds the *one* at the top and sucks the *human legs* a bit out of their *mouth* in the process. [6]

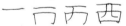

* As a primitive, the meaning of *west* can be expanded to refer to the *Old West* of cowboy-movie fame, just as the character for *east* was expanded into *the East*. Note, however, that in its primitive form the *legs* are straightened out and reach down to the bottom of the *mouth*. Hence, we get the shape 西. With the exception of one kanji, given in the following frame, this element always appears at the top of its relative primitives.

1603. value 価

Person . . . Old West. [8]

1604. need 要

Old West . . . woman. [9]

1605. loins 腰

Part of the body . . . need. [13]

1606. ballot 票

Old West . . . altar. [11]

1607. drift 漂

Water . . . ballot. [14]

1608. signpost   標

Tree . . . ballot. [15]

1609. chestnut   栗

Old West . . . tree. [10]

1610. transition   遷

West . . . St. Bernard dog . . . snake . . . road. [15]

1611. capsize   覆

West . . . restore. [18]

1612. smoke   煙

Hearth . . . Old West . . . ground. [13]

1613. south   南

Belt . . . happiness. Note how the *belt* runs through the middle of *happiness.* [9]

ナ 内 南

1614. camphor tree   楠

Tree . . . south. [13]

1615. offering   献

South . . . dog. [13]

LESSON 42

This next complex of characters is based on the primitive for *gates*. From there we shall go on consider others related to entrances and barriers in general.

1616. gates 門

The pictograph of two swinging **gates** is so clear in this kanji that only its stroke order needs to be memorized. In case you should have any trouble, though, it is helpful to know that it was originally written with two *doors* facing one another; in time the first stroke came to be joined to the others, giving us its present form. The gates usually serve as an enclosure, and are written BEFORE what they enclose. [8]

* As a primitive, we shall continue to give it the meaning of *gates*, but recommend the image of swinging doors (like the kind once common at entrances to saloons) to distinguish it from the primitive for *door*.

1617. question 問

Gates . . . mouth. [11]

1618. review 閲

Gates . . . devil. Keep distinct from the notions of *inspection* (Frame 1093), *revise* (Frame 339), and *perusal* (Frame 855). [15]

1619. clique 閥

Gates . . . fell. [14]

1620. interval   間

Gates . . . sun/day. This **interval** applies to time and space alike, but the latter is better for creating an image. [12]

1621. simplicity   簡

Bamboo . . . interval. [18]

1622. open   開

Gates . . . two hands. [12]

1623. closed   閉

Gates . . . genie. [11]

1624. tower   閣

Gates . . . each. [14]

1625. leisure   閑

Gates . . . tree. [12]

1626. hear   聞

Gates . . . ear. Compare the story you invented for the kanji meaning *listen* (Frame 827). [14]

1627. wet   潤

Water . . . gates . . . king. [15]

1628. column

欄

Tree . . . gates . . . east. [20]

1629. fight

鬪

Gates . . . table . . . glue. Do not confuse with *contend* (Frame 1154). [18]

1630. godown

倉

The single *gate* is used here not in order to represent one *gate,* but many of them, indeed a *meeting of gates.* Add *mouth* (as an entrance here) and you end up with **godown.** That should help keep this character distinct from *storehouse* **(850) and** *warehouse* **(589).** [10]

1631. genesis

創

Godown . . . sabre. [12]

1632. un-

非

This key-word, a negating prefix, is a doodle of a heavy iron pole with bars extending in both directions, to create the picture of a jail cell. From there to the various connotations of "**un-**" is but a short step. [8]

  * As a primitive, we shall draw on the explanation above for the
    meaning of *jail cell.*

1633. haiku

俳

This character is used for the **haiku,** the 17-syllable poem that is widely recognized as one of Japan's most typical arts. Its elements: *person . . . jail cell.* [10]

1634. repudiate   排

Fingers . . . jail cell. [11]

1635. sad   悲

Jail cell . . . heart. [12]

1636. guilt   罪

Eye . . . jail cell. [13]

1637. comrade   輩

Jail cell . . . car. [15]

1638. front door   扉

Door . . . jail cell. [12]

*   key   ユ

This element gets its name and meaning from its pictographic representation of a key. The shape is familiar from the character for *five*. [2]

1639. marquis   侯

Person . . . key . . . dart. Hint: the pun suggested by the pronunciation of the key-word and the primitive for *key* may come in helpful. [9]

1640. climate   候

Marquis . . . walking cane. [10]

* guillotine   夬

This element depicts a large, sharpened *key* coming down on the head of a criminal *St. Bernard.* [4]

1641. decide   決

The etymology of **decide** (de-cidere = cut off) will help here; the elements are: *water . . . guillotine.* [7]

1642. cheerful   快

State of mind . . . guillotine. [7]

* locket   韋

The vertical stroke added to the element for *key* gives us a **locket.** Below that, we find a square container (the *mouth*) and a one-lensed pair of *sunglasses.* The only thing to watch in writing this element is that the final vertical stroke reaches all the way through to touch the *mouth.* [10]

1643. admirable   偉

Person . . . locket. [12]

1644. difference   違

Locket . . . road. [13]

1645. horizontal   緯

Thread . . . locket. [16]

1646. defense   衛

Boulevard . . . locket. Do not confuse with *ward off* (Frame 1302),
protect (Frame 997), *guard* (Frame 186), or *safeguard* (Frame 700). [16]

1647. Korea   韓

As with *Italy* (Frame 1161) and *Africa* (Frame 1295), this character
simply abbreviates the full name of **Korea**. Its elements: *mist . . .
locket.* [18]

LESSON 43

The next group of primitives are only loosely related to one another in the
sense that they all have to do with qualifying material objects in one way
or another.

1648. dry   干

It is best to see this kanji as a pictograph of a revolving circular
clothesline (viewed from the side). Spin it around quickly in your
mind's eye to give it the connotation of to **dry**. [3]

一　二　干

 * The primitive meaning is *clothesline.*

1649. liver   肝

Part of the body . . . clothesline. [7]

1650. publish   刊

Clothesline . . . sabre. [5]

1651. sweat   汗

Water . . . clothesline. [6]

1652. flats   軒

Here is a counter for houses, made up of: *cars . . . clothesline.* [10]

1653. beach   岸

Mountain . . . cliff . . . clothesline. [8]

1654. tree-trunk   幹

Mist . . . umbrella . . . clothesline. The meaning of the kanji extends beyond **tree-trunks** to represent the main stem or line of anything from railway lines to managerial staffs. This should help distinguish it from the stories used earlier for *book* (Frame 211) and *body* (Frame 957), both of which made use of the image of a **"tree-trunk."** [13]

* potato   于

Note how this element differs from *dry* in virtue of the small hook at the end of the third stroke. [3]

1655. potato   芋

Flowers . . . potato. [6]

1656. eaves

宇

House . . . potato. [6]

1657. too much

余

Umbrella . . . potato . . . small. The last stroke of *potato* and the first of *small* coincide in this character. [7]

* Since the phrase *"too much"* is overly abstract, we shall take the image of a *scales* whose indicator spins round and round on the dial because *too much* weight has been set on it. It will help to use this image in learning the kanji itself.

1658. exclude

除

Pinnacle . . . scales. [10]

1659. gradually

徐

Line . . . scales. [10]

1660. confer

叙

Scales . . crotch. The key-word has to do with **conferring** ranks, titles, and awards. It should not be confused with *bestow* (Frame 1246) or *impart* (Frame 736). [9]

1661. route

途

Scales . . . road. [10]

1662. diagonal

斜

Scales . . . measuring cup. [11]

1663. paint

塗

Water . . . scales . . . ground. [13]

1664. bundle

束

In the same way that we saw the *sun* in the *tree* in the kanji for *east*, here we see a square container there in the shape of a *mouth*. [7]

1665. trust

頼

Bundle . . . head. [16]

1666. rapids

瀬

Water . . . bundle . . . head. [19]

1667. imperial order

勅

In order to keep this character distinct from that for an **imperial edict** (Frame 342), we must draw again on a pun. Think of the "order" here as a "mail order" or "an order of pizza" or whatever, made by the Emperor and delivered to the palace. Then it will not be hard to put together *bundle* and *muscle* to form a story about an **imperial order.** [9]

1668. alienate

疎

Zoo . . . bundle. Note that the element for *zoo* is flattened out on the left just as *leg* (Frame 1279) had been. This is the only time in this book we shall meet this form in this book. [12]

1669. quick

速

Bundle . . . road. [10]

1670. organize

Bundle . . . taskmaster . . . correct. [16]

整

---

*   awl

We include this element here because of its visible similarity to the element for *bundle*. To avoid confusion, we construct it differently. out of two ingredients already familiar to us: *fit . . . person*. The stroke order follows the order of the elements exactly, but note how the *person* runs through the *mouth*. [8]

僉

1671. sabre

Awl . . . sabre. [10]

劍

1672. precipitous

Pinnacle . . . awl. [11]

險

1673. examination

Tree . . . awl. [12]

検

1674. frugal

Person . . . awl. [10]

倹

1675. heavy

Thousand . . . computers. Note how the long vertical stroke doubles up to serve both elements. [9]

重

1676. move

動

Heavy . . . muscle. [11]

1677. meritorious deed

Move . . . oven-fire. So as not to confuse this kanji with the general character for *merit* (Frame 1276), you may associate the key-word with military decorations and medals of distinction, both of which it is used for. [15]

1678. work

働

Person . . . move. Do not confuse with *labor* (Frame 860). [13]

1679. species

種

Wheat . . . heavy. [14]

1680. collide

衝

Boulevard . . . heavy. [15]

1681. fragrant

薫

Flowers . . . heavy . . . oven-fire. Do not confuse with *incense* (Frame 911) or *perfume* (Frame 493). [16]

LESSON 44

We may now pick up the remainder of the enclosure primitives, except for those relating to animals, which we shall leave for the conclusion. This lesson should give you a chance to review the principles governing enclosures.

---

* sickness   疒

The enclosure shown in this frame is composed of a *cave* with *ice* outside of it. It is used for a number of kanji related to **sickness**. If you want to picture a *caveman* nursing a hangover with an *ice*-pack, that should provide enough help to remember the shape of this element and its meaning. [5]

1682. ill   病

Sickness . . . third class. [10]

1683. stupid   痴

Know . . . sickness. [13]

1684. pox   痘

Sickness . . . beans. [12]

1685. symptoms   症

Sickness . . . correct. [10]

1686. rapidly   疾

It wil be important to keep this character distinct from *quick* (Frame 1669) and *swift* (Frame 280). Picture a succession of poison *darts* (the sort that inflict *sickness)* flying out **rapid**-fire from a blowgun, so that the phrase "**rapid-fire**" can conjure up the proper image. [10]

1687. diarrhea

痢

Sickness . . . profit. [12]

1688. exhausted

疲

Sickness . . . pelt. [10]

1689. epidemic

疫

Sickness . . . missile. [9]

1690. pain

痛

Sickness . . . chop-seal . . . utilize. [12]

1691. mannerism

癖

Sickness . . . ketchup. [18]

* box

匚

This enclosure, open at the right, represents a **box** lying on its side. When it is not used as an enclosure, its form is cramped to look like this: 匚 . You may distinguish its meaning by picturing it then as a very small **box.** [2]

一 匚

1692. hide

匿

Box . . . young. [10]

一 若 匿

1693. artisan

匠

Box . . . axe. [6]

1694. doctor

医

Box . . . dart. [7]

1695. equal

匹

Box . . . human legs. [4]

1696. ward

区

The **ward** referred to here is a subdivision of a large city. Its elements: *box . . . sheaves.* When used as a primitive element, it may be helpful at times to break it up into these same composite elements. [4]

1697. hinge

枢

Tree . . . ward. [8]

1698. assault

殴

Ward . . . missile. [8]

1699. Europe

欧

Ward . . . yawn. Like the last kanji of LESSON 42, this character is an abbreviation of the name of a geographical region. [8]

1700. repress

抑

Fingers . . . box . . . stamps. [7]

1701. face-up   仰

This character is used both for lying on one's back **face-up,** and for looking up to someone with respect and awe. Its elements: *person . . . box . . . stamps.* [6]

1702. welcome   迎

Box . . . stamps . . . road. [7]

*   teepee   癶

The dots at the top of this tent can be taken to represent the wooden poles protruding outside the canvas walls of a **teepee.** [5]

1703. ascend   登

Teepee . . . table. Do not confuse with to *rise up* (Frame 43). [12]

1704. lucidity   澄

Water . . . ascend. [15]

1705. discharge   発

This key word refers to the **discharging** of guns, trains, people, and even words. The elements: *teepee . . . two . . . human legs.* Contrast the writing with Frame 59. [9]

1706. abolish   廃

Cave . . . discharge. [12]

*   pup tent

The *St. Bernard dog* and its overlapping with the element for *teepee*
are enough to suggest the meaning of this primitive element: a **pup
tent**. The combination of *sun* and *small* at the bottom can mean a
small opening or flap through which the *sun* shines in the morning to
let you know it's time for getting up. [12]

1707. colleague

Person . . . pup tent. Choose some connotation of the key-word that
will keep it distinct for you from *companion* (Frame 19), *friend*
(Frame 704), *consort* (Frame 1203), and *comrade* (Frame 1637). [14]

1708. dormitory

House . . . pup tent. [15]

1709. heal   寮

Sickness . . . pup tent. [17]

LESSON 45

We come now to a class of elements loosely associated with the notion of
shape and form. We then append what remains of elements having to do
with color.

* shape

The three simple strokes of this element actually represent the form or **shape** of the hair of one's beard. But we keep the simple *sense* of *a* **shape,** or its verb "to shape," in order to avoid confusion later when we meet an element for *hair.* When using this element, be sure to visualize yourself **shaping** the thing in question, or better still, twisting it out ot **shape.** [3]

1710. carve

The two primitives here, *circumference* and *shape,* belong naturally to the special connotations which differentiate **carving** from *engraving* (see Frame 1521). [11]

1711. shape

Two hands . . . shape. [7]

1712. shadow

Scenery . . . shape. [15]

1713. cedar

Tree . . . shape. [7]

1714. coloring

Claw . . . tree . . . shape. [11]

1715. patent

Badge . . . shape. The key-word is synonymous with "clear" or "openly expressed." [14]

1716. lad   彥

Vase . . . cliff . . . shape. [9]

立　产　彥

1717. face   顔

Lad . . . head. [18]

1718. ought   須

Shape . . . head. This is the only time that *shape* is placed to the left of
its relative element, the *head.* [12]

1719. swell   膨

Part of the body . . . drum . . . shape. Compare *expand* (Frame 1118). [16]

1720. nonplussed   参

Elbow . . . St. Bernard dog . . . shape. [8]

1721. wretched   惨

A state of mind . . . nonplussed. [11]

1722. discipline   修

Person . . . walking cane . . . taskmaster . . . shape. [10]

1723. rare   珍

Jewel . . . umbrella . . . shape. [9]

1724. check-up

Words . . . umbrella . . . shape. The key-word refers to a medical examination. [12]

1725. sentence

Under the familiar *tophat* we see a criss-cross pattern or design, like that found on woodwork or garments. This should make an ugly enough image to help remember it. It can be associated with **sentence** by thinking of a **sentence** as a grammatical *pattern*. [4]

* The primitive meaning for this character will be *plaid,* the familiar criss-cross pattern frequently used in textiles.

1726. vis-à-vis

Plaid . . . glue. [7]

1727. family crest

Thread . . . plaid. [10]

1728. mosquito

Insect . . . plaid. [10]

* fenceposts

This element means just what it looks like: two **fenceposts**, which enclose whatever comes between them. This is what distinguishes them from merely a pair of *canes* (see Frame 250). [2]

1729. adjusted

Plaid . . . fenceposts . . . two. Do not confuse with *just so* (Frame 388). [8]

1730. dose

Adjust . . . sword. Think of this as a **dose** of medicine. [10]

1731. finish

Water . . . adjust. Do not confuse with *complete* (Frame 97), *end* (Frame 1352), or *perfect* (Frame 187). [11]

1732. purification

Plaid . . . fenceposts . . . altar. This is a "religious" **purification**, which distinguishes it from the simple kanji for *pure* (Frame 1539). [11]

1733. solemn

Rake . . . fenceposts . . . rice. [11]

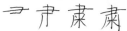

*   sparkler

As the pictograph itself immediately suggests, this element depicts spreading out or scattering from a focal point. To capture this meaning, we choose the image of a **sparkler**. It will often have another primitive put at its center point. [4]

1734. bases

The kanji of this frame refers to the four **bases** that are stationed at the corners of a baseball infield. The elements: *field . . . sparkler . . . ground.* [12]

1735. music 楽

Dove . . . sparkler . . . tree. [13]

1736. medicine 薬

Flowers . . . music. [16]

1737. ratio 率

Mysterious . . . sparkler . . . ten. Do not confuse with *proportion* (Frame 1553). [11]

1738. astringent 渋

Water . . . footprint . . . sparkler. [11]

1739. vicarious 摂

Fingers . . . ear . . . sparkler. Compare *substitute* (Frame 1005). [13]

1740. center 央

The elements depict a *St. Bernard dog* with its head and paws keeping their stick-like form, but with the middle or **center** of its body filled out in a box-like shape. [5]

1741. England 英

Flowers . . . center. Another "country" abbreviation. [8]

1742. reflect 映

Sun . . . center. [9]

1743. red   赤

Ground ... sword ... small. The two strokes of the *sword* take the place
of the middle stroke of *small.* [7]

土 亣 赤 赤

* As a primitive on the left, this kanji keeps the same form. Elsewhere, the first two strokes are abbreviated to a single dot, giving
us 亦 . This latter form will take the meaning of an *apple.*

1744. pardon   赦

Red . . . taskmaster. [11]

1745. unusual   変

Apple . . . walking legs. [9]

1746. tracks   跡

Wooden leg . . . apple. [13]

1747. barbarian   蛮

Apple . . . insects. [12]

1748. romance   恋

Apple . . . heart. [10]

1749. gulf   湾

Water . . . apple . . . bow. [12]

1750. yellow   黄

Salad . . . sprout . . . animal legs. [11]

1751. sideways   横

Tree . . . yellow. [15]

*   mosaic   巴

This element is shaped roughly like the *snake*, but pay attention to
the difference when writing it. [4]

ㄱ ㄲ ㄲ 巴

1752. grasp   把

Fingers . . . mosaic. [7]

1753. color   色

Bound up . . . mosaic. [6]

1754. discontinue   絶

Thread . . . color. [12]

1755. glossy   艶

Bountiful . . . color. [19]

1756. fertilizer   肥

Flesh . . . mosaic. [8]

LESSON 46

A number of containers of various sorts can be gathered together here. Most of them have limited use as primitives, but none of them should cause any particular difficulty.

1757. sweet 甘

This kanji is a pictograph of a small wicker basket. (The extra short stroke in the middle helps keep it distinct from the character for *twenty.*) All one needs to add is some image of **sweet** cakes or breads carried in the basket, and the union of picture and meaning is complete. Take care not to confuse with *candy* (Frame 1122). [5]

  * As a primitive, the pictograph's meaning of a *wicker basket* is used, a small one like the kind used for picnics.

1758. navy blue 紺

Thread . . . wicker basket. [11]

1759. so-and-so 某

The key-word of this character refers to the adjective for an unspecified person or thing. Its elements: *wicker basket . . . tree.* [9]

1760. conspire 謀

Words . . . so-and-so. [16]

1761. mediator   媒

Woman . . . so-and-so. [12]

* bushel basket   其

As the two *legs* at the bottom suggest, this **bushel basket** is a large container, standing on the floor. Its first four strokes indicate that it is made of wicker, much like the small *wicker basket* treated immediately above. To put something inside of the **bushel basket,** the legs at the bottom are attached to the final horizontal stroke and extended to make a kind of enclosure. [8]

甘　其　其

1762. deceit   欺

Bushel basket . . . yawn. [12]

1763. chess piece   棋

Tree . . . bushel basket. [12]

1764. national flag   旗

Banner . . . bushel basket. [14]

1765. period   期

Bushel basket . . . month. As the *month* indicates, this has to do with **periods** of time. By the way, this is the only case in which its relative element appears to the right of the *bushel basket.* [12]

1766. Go   碁

Bushel basket . . . stones. The key-word refers to the Japanese game played with black and white colored *stones* on a lined board. [13]

1767. fundamentals　基

Bushel basket . . . soil. [11]

1768. tremendously　甚

Bushel basket . . . equal. Note how the first stroke of *equal* doubles up with the last stroke of the *bushel basket.* [9]

1769. intuition　勘

Tremendously . . . muscle. [11]

1770. withstand　堪

Soil . . . tremendously. [12]

*　purse　貴

By adding a single stroke at the bottom of the kanji for *in*, we get a quasi-pictograph of a **purse**. [5]

1771. precious　貴

Purse . . . shells. [12]

1772. bequeath　遺

Precious . . . road. [15]

1773. dispatch　遣

This kanji takes away the *maestro's* baton and replaces it with a *purse*. The *road* represents his being **dispatched** on his way as an obvious misfit. You will remember that when he did have his baton, he was being *chased* down the road by his fans. All of which shows what a difference a single stroke can make! [13]

1774. dance   舞

The top two strokes show someone *reclining*, and the next six are a pictograph of an oaken *tub* ribbed with metal strips, like the kind once used for bathing. At the bottom, the *sunglasses* round off the character. [15]

1775. nothingness   無

This character is the Japanese character for the supreme philosophical principle of much oriental thought: **nothingness**. Make use of the oaken *tub* from the previous frame, and add to that the open *fire* at the bottom. [12]

LESSON 47

The several primitives we turn to next are all related to the position and disposition of things. The classification is somewhat arbitrary since we are sweeping up leftover primitives at this stage and no longer have enough for tidy categorization. In addition, from this lesson on, most references to key-words with possibly confusing similarities will be omitted. Try to think of them yourself as you are going through these characters.

---

*   shelf   且

The pictographic representation in the primitive shown here is a small stand with horizontal shelves. Thus we give it the general meaning of a **shelf**. It differs from the kanji and primitive for an *eye* only in its final stroke which extends beyond the two vertical strokes at both ends. Think of it as a **shelf** for special keepsakes or a glass bureau for knick-knacks, keeping it distinct from the kanji we learned in Frame 202. [5]

1776. association   組

Thread . . . shelf. [11]

1777. coarse   粗

Rice . . . shelf. [11]

1778. tariff   租

Wheat . . . shelf. [10]

1779. ancestor   祖

Altar . . . shelf. [9]

1780. thwart   阻

Pinnacle . . . shelf. [8]

1781. investigate   査

Tree . . . shelf. [9]

1782. help   助

Shelf . . . power. The reason why the *shelf* appears on the left here is that the right side is the normal position for *power,* the stronger primitive. Indeed, the only exception in all the kanji is the character for *add* (Frame 867). [7]

1783. best regards 宜

This kanji, a polite way of expressing one's **best regards** to another. Its elements: *house . . . shelf.* [8]

1784. tatami mat 畳

Rice field . . . crown . . . shelf. [12]

1785. row 並

This character represents a slightly stylized duplication of the kanji for *stand.* By lengthening the sixth and seventh strokes, you will see how this is done. [8]

* The primitive meaning remains the same as that of the kanji, but special attention has to be given to the varieties of shape this element can undergo. It is the most difficult one you will meet in this book. When it appears BENEATH its relative primitive, the top two strokes are omitted, and the first horizontal stroke is doubled up with the bottom horizontal stroke of the element above it, wherever possible:  . ATOP its relative primitive, it can keep its kanji shape. When it does not, the top three strokes are removed and all of them are replaced BELOW the primitive's bottom line:  . We shall acknowledge this latter transformation by changing its meaning to "*upside down in a row.*"

1786. universal 普

Row . . . sun. [12]

1787. musical score 譜

Words . . . universal. [19]

1788. damp   湿

Water . . . row . . . sun. [12]

1789. appear   顕

Sun . . . row . . . heads. [18]

1790. slender   繊

Thread . . . Thanksgiving . . . row. [17]

1791. spirits   霊

Rain . . . two . . . row. This character shall refer only to the inhabitants of the "spirit world," and not to moods or temperaments, for which we shall learn another character in Frame 1885. [15]

1792. business   業

In a row upside down . . . not yet. [13]

1793. slap   撲

Fingers . . . husbands . . . upside down in a row. [15]

1794. me   僕

This key-word is yet another synonym for "I," somewhat more familiar in tone. As a rule, it is a word that boys and men use to refer to themselves. Its elements: *person . . . husbands . . . in a row upside down.* [14]

1795. together 共

Salad . . . animal legs. [6]

* The primitive retains the meaning of *together*. Imagine things *strung together* like fish on a line, beads on a thread, or whatever. The main thing is to avoid putting them in a straight row, which would confound this element with the previous one. As we saw with *bushel basket,* this primitive can join its legs to the final horizontal stroke and stretch them to form an enclosure.

1796. submit 供

"Submit" here is a transitive verb, meaning to offer or present. Its elements: *person . . . strung together.* [8]

1797. uncommon 異

Brains . . . together. [11]

1798. wing 翼

Feathers . . . uncommon. [17]

1799. deluge 洪

Water . . . strung together. [9]

1800. harbor 港

Deluge . . . snakes. [12]

1801. outburst 暴

Sun . . . strung together . . . rice-grains. [15]

1802. bomb

爆

Fire . . . outburst. [19]

1803. respect

恭

Strung together . . . valentine. [10]

1804. elect

選

Two *snakes . . . strung together . . . road.* [15]

1805. Mr.

殿

Flags . . . strung together . . . missile. [13]

LESSON 48

The following section is composed of characters whose primitives are
grouped according to shape rather than meaning. Each of them makes use,
in one way or another, of squares and crossing lines. While this might have
brought confusion earlier, we know enough primitives at this stage to
introduce them together without risking any confusion.

1806. well

井

Recalling that there are no circular strokes; and recalling further
that the shape of the square and the square within a square have
already been used, it should be relatively easy to see how this
character can be consider a pictograph of a **well**. [4]

一 二 毛 井

1807. surround 囲

Well . . . pent in. [7]

1808. till 耕

Christmas tree . . . well. [10]

1809. Asia 亜

In this kanji, the abbreviation for **Asia,** you should be able to see the character for *mouth* behind the Roman numeral II. [7]

一 口 冊 亜

1810. bad 悪

Asia . . . heart. [11]

1811. circle 円

This kanji, also used for Yen, is one you are not likely to need to study formally, since you can hardly get around in Japan without it. In any case, the elements are: *glass canopy . . . walking cane . . . one.* [4]

1812. angle 角

Bound up . . . glass canopy . . . walking cane . . . two. If you write the character once, you will see why we avoided using the element for *soil,* which would prompt you to write it in improper order. [7]

* As a primitive, imagine the tool used by drafters and carpenters to draw right-*angles*.

1813. contact   触

Angle . . . insect. [13]

1814. unravel   解

Angle . . . dagger . . . cow. [13]

1815. again   再

Jewel . . . with a belt hung on it. [6]

一 丁 丙 丙 再

* funnel   冓

Celery . . . again. [10]

丑 冓 冓 冓 冓

1816. lecture   講

Words . . . funnel. [17]

1817. subscription   購

Shells . . . funnel. The key-word is meant to suggest magazine-subscriptions and the like. [17]

1818. posture   構

Tree . . . funnel. [14]

1819. gutter

溝

Water . . . funnel. [13]

* scrapbook

冊

Glass canopy . . . flower. It is most rare to see the *flower* come under its relative element. Note how it is straightened out to fill the space available. [5]

1820. argument

論

Words . . . meeting . . . scrapbooks. The **argument** connoted by the keyword is a process of academic reasoning, not a personal quarrel or spat. [15]

1821. ethics

倫

Person . . . meeting . . . scrapbook. [10]

1822. wheel

輪

Car . . . meeting . . . scrapbook. [15]

1823. partial

偏

Person . . . door . . . scrapbook. [11]

1824. everywhere

遍

Door . . . scrapbook . . . a road. [12]

1825. compilation

Thread . . . door . . . scrapbook   [15]

1826. tome

This key-word is a counter for books. It differs from *scrapbook* both in the writing order and in the extension of the second horizontal stroke. [5]

1827. code

We introduce this character here because of its connection to the book-related kanji treated above. It is based on the character for *bend,* whose last stroke is lengthened to coincide with the first stroke of the element for *tool.* [8]

LESSON 49

A few primitives having to do with groupings and classifications of people remain to be learned, and we may bring them all together now.

1828. family name

Pay close attention to the stroke order of the elements when learning to write this character. The elements: a long *drop* . . . *fishhook* . . . another long *drop* (also written right to left) . . . *fishhook.* [4]

1829. paper   紙

Thread . . . family name. [10]

1830. marriage   婚

Woman . . . family name . . . day. [11]

---

* calling card   氏

Family name . . . floor. [5]

1831. lower   低

Person . . . calling card. [7]

1832. resist   抵

Fingers . . . calling card. [8]

1833. bottom   底

Cave . . . calling card. [8]

1834. people   民

In place of the *drop* at the start of the character for *family name*, we have a *mouth*, which you might think of as the "vox populi." [5]

フ コ F F 民

1835. sleep   眠

Eyes . . . people. [10]

*   dog-tag   甫

This primitive refers to all sorts of identification tags, but **dog-tag** has been chosen for its descriptiveness. On the top we see the *arrowhead,* joined to the *screwdriver* below by the lengthened vertical stroke. [7]

一 冂 冃 甫 甫

1836. catch   捕

Fingers . . . dog-tag. [10]

1837. bay   浦

Water . . . dog-tag. [10]

1838. bulrush   蒲

Flowers . . . bay. [13]

1839. shop   舗

Cottage . . . dog-tag. The key-word refers to the noun, not the verb. [15]

1840. supplement   補

Cloak . . . dog-tag. [12]

*   city walls   阝

On the left, and rather more pressed in its form, this element meant the high spot of a village or its *pinnacle.* On the right side, in the form shown here, it means the lowest part of the city, around which its walls rise up as a protection against invaders. Hence we nickname this element: **city walls.** [3]

1841. residence

Calling card . . . city walls. [8]

邸

1842. enclosure

Receive . . . city walls. [11]

郭

1843. county

Old boy . . . city walls. [10]

郡

1844. outskirts

Mingle . . . city walls. [9]

郊

1845. section

Muzzle . . . city walls. [11]

部

1846. metropolis

Puppet . . . city walls. [11]

都

1847. mail

Droop . . . city walls. [11]

郵

1848. home country

Bushes . . . city walls. [7]

邦

1849. home town 郷

Cocoon . . . silver . . . city walls. [11]

1850. echo 響

Home town . . . sound. [20]

1851. son 郎

Halo . . . city walls. [9]

1852. corridor 廊

Son . . . cave. [12]

LESSON 50

In this section we simply present a number of left-over primitives which
were not introduced earlier for want of a proper category or because we
had not enough elements to give sufficient examples of their use.

* drag 厂

Although it is not a pictograph in the strict sense, this primitive
depicts one stroke pulling another along behind it. Note how it
differs from *cliff* and *person* because of this **dragging** effect, further
enhanced by the fact that the first stroke is written right to left.
When this element comes under a different element, the strokes are
drawn apart like this: ⼓ . [2]

1853. shield

盾

Dragging . . . ten eyes. [9]

1854. sequential

循

Line . . . shield. [12]

1855. faction

派

Water . . . drag . . . person . . . rag. In Frame 1048 we said that this latter radical would come up once again, as it does in this and the following two frames. [9]

1856. vein

脈

Part of the body . . . drag . . . person . . . rag. [10]

1857. masses

衆

Blood . . . two drops . . . person . . . rag. [12]

1858. parcel post

逓

Drag . . . cornstalk . . . belt . . . road. [10]

1859. grade

段

The kanji connoting rank or class shows us a new element on the left: the familiar primitive for *staples* with an additional stroke cutting through the vertical stroke. It is easiest in these cases to make a primitive related to what we already know. Hence, we call it a *staple gun*. To the right, *missile.* [9]

′ 丨 千 斤 斤 刍 刍 段 段

1860. forge

鍛

Metal . . . grade. [17]

1861. empress

后

Drag . . . one . . . mouth. [6]

* clothes hanger

コ

Since this element looks like the *hook* set on its head, we shall refer to it as a **clothes hanger**. Used as an enclosure, it begins further left. [1]

1862. phantasm

幻

Cocoon . . . clothes hanger. [4]

1863. director

司

Clothes hanger . . . one . . . mouth. [5]

1864. pay respects

伺

This honorific form of *call on* (Frame 495) is made up of: *person . . . director.* [7]

1865. part of speech

詞

The key-word, **parts of speech,** refers to nouns, verbs, adjective, adverbs, and so on. The elements: *words . . . directors.* [12]

1866. domesticate

飼

Eat . . . director. The sense is of rearing of animals. [12]

1867. heir

Mouth . . . scrapbook . . . director. [13]

嗣

1868. boat

舟

After the *drop* and the *glass canopy*, we come to a combination of three strokes that we met only once before, in the character for *mama* (Frame 101). The pictographic meaning we gave it there has no etymological relationship to this character, but use it if it helps. [6]

′　亻　丿　月　月　舟

1869. liner

舶

The type of *boat* connoted here is a large ocean-going freighter. The main thing is to work with the elements, *boat* and *dove* to make an image distinct from that of the former frame. Don't count on size alone to distinguish the *boat* from the **liner**. [11]

1870. navigate

航

Boat . . . whirlwind. [10]

1871. carrier

般

Boat . . . missile. [10]

1872. tray

盤

Carrier . . . dish. [15]

1873. conveyor

搬

Fingers . . . carrier. [13]

1874. ship

船

Boat . . . gully. [11]

1875. warship

艦

Boat . . . oversee. [21]

1876. rowboat

艇

Boat . . . courts. [13]

1877. melon

瓜

The only thing that distinguishes this from the *claw* is the addition of the *elbow* (drawn with 3 strokes) in the middle. [6]

丶 丿 刀 瓜 瓜 瓜

1878. arc

弧

Bow . . . melon. [9]

1879. orphan

孤

Child . . . melon. [9]

LESSON 51

As we said we would do back in LESSON 28, we now leave the beaten path to gather up those characters left aside because they form exceptions to the rules and patterns we have been learning. The list is not large and has a number of repeating patterns. Aside from the few others we shall interpose in the next section where they belong, and three characters appended at the very end, this will complete our collection of special characters. In my experience, this is the most difficult lesson of the book.

1880. cocoon

Though it's a good thing that the primitive for **cocoon** has been radically abbreviated from this, its full form as a kanji, the story it holds is a charming one. The silkworm (*insect*) eats the leaves of the mulberry bush (the *flowers*), digests them and transforms them into *thread* with which to spin about itself its own coffin (the *hood*). The dividing line that separates the two elements helps the picture of the little worm cutting itself off from contact with the outside world, but as a character stroke, it is a clear exception. [18]

1881. benefit

What we have poised over the *dish* is a pair of *animal horns* attached to a pair of *animal legs* by a single horizontal stroke. [10]

1882. spare time

The element for *day* on the left is logical enough. Next to it we see *staples* being held in *mouth* (one stroke is doubled up), indicating working in one's hobby or handicrafts at home on one's **spare time**. The small *box* at the top right is facing backwards, or more properly "inside out." Finally, we have the *crotch* at the bottom. [13]

1883. spread

At the top we have the *arrowhead* whose vertical line joins it to the *rice field* (or *brains*) below it. Beneath it, the *compass;* and to the right, the *taskmaster.* [15]

1884. come

This odd but common kanji is built up of the character for *not yet* into which a pair of *animal horns* has been inserted. [7]

1885. spirit

The **"spirit"** in this character refers to the changeable moods and airs of one's personality as well as to the more permanent stains of genius or character that distinguish one individual from another. Its elements are: *reclining . . . floor . . . fishhook . . . sheaf.* [6]

1886. vapor

Think of this character as a sibling of that for *spirit*. Simply replace *sheaves* with drops of *water* on the left in order to get **vapor.** [7]

1887. fly

The two *large hooks* have little propellers (the two *drops* repeated on each *hook*) on them for flying. Beneath is the *measuring box*, which serves as the body of this **flying** contraption. The stroke-order will cause some problems, so take care with it. [9]

1888. sink

The technique for **sinking** used in this kanji is unique. Rather than the biblical image of tieing a millstone about the victim's neck, here we see a *crown* tied about one *leg* before the unfortunate party is tossed into the *water.* [7]

氵 氵 沈

1889. wife

妻

Ten . . . rakes . . . woman. [8]

一 ⼹ 尹 ヨ 妻 妻 妻 妻

1890. decline

衰

Let this character stand for the well known *decline* and fall of the Roman Empire. You will have to recall the elements that went into the character for *pathetic* (Frame 401) in order to get the *walking cane* stuck sideways in the *mouth* of your **declining** Roman. [10]

1891. inmost

衷

The *needle* running through the *mouth* at the top is a unique combination. Joined to it at the bottom is the *scarf.* [9]

一 ⼡ 冂 日 吏 声 吏 声 衷

1892. mask

面

Imagine a **mask** with *eyes* peeping out of a *hundred* places from all over your head. (Note the distortion of the latter element.) [9]

一 ⼀ 丆 丏 而 而 面 面

1893. leather

革

After the *flowers* at the top (painted on the **leather** for decoration), we see the element for *car* with the middle stroke left out. Think of the seats having been taken out so that they can be reupholstered with this decorated **leather.** [9]

一 ⼗ 艹 廿 芇 芇 苗 苗 革

1894. shoes

靴

Leather . . . change. [13]

1895. hegemony

覇

Old West . . . leather . . . moon. [19]

1896. voice

声

The *samurai* at the top is familiar enough. The *flag* with the line running through it is not. Try to devise some way to take note of it, and pay attention to the writing. [7]

士 士 声 声 声

1897. give

呉

The complex of strokes in this kanji is rare and difficult, because of the fourth stroke which is unique. The *mouth* and *tool* are already familiar. [7]

口 吕 呉

1898. recreation

娯

Woman . . . give. [10]

1899. mistake

誤

Words . . . give. [14]

1900. steam

蒸

The *flower* at the top, and the *floor* with the *oven-fire* beneath are familiar. The problem is what comes in between. It is formed by the character for *complete* whose vertical stroke doubles up as the first stroke of *water*. [13]

1901. acquiesce   承

The sense of passive acceptance or reception of information is contained in this key-word. The form is based on the middle portion of the former character, with three additional strokes, best thought of as the kanji for *three*. [8]

1902. bin   函

This is the character from which the element for *shovel* derives. Within it comes the element for *snare* with the *sparkler* surrounding it. [9]

1903. poles   極

The **poles** this key-word refers to are the extremities of the earth or the terminals of an electric field. The elements are: *tree . . . snare . . . mouth . . . crotch . . . floor.* [12]

一 十 才 木 朮 朽 朽 柯 柯 極 極 極

LESSON 52

The final grouping of kanji revolves about elements related to animals. It is a rather large group, and will take us all of four lessons to complete. We begin with a few recurring elements related to parts of animal bodies.

1904. tusk 牙

If you play with this primitive's form with pencil and paper, you will
see that it begins with a *box*-like shape, and ends with the final two
strokes of the *halberd,* a convenient combination for the tusk
protruding from the mouth of an animal. [4]

一 匚 チ 牙

1905. bud 芽

Flowers . . . tusk. [7]

1906. wicked 邪

Tusk . . . city walls. [7]

1907. gracious 雅

Tusk . . . an old turkey. [12]

* animal tracks 釆

Having already met the primitive for human *footprints,* we now
introduce that for **animal tracks**. Its elements are simply: *a drop of . . .
rice.* [7]

1908. explanation 釈

Animal tracks . . . shaku hachi. [11]

1909. turn 番

This key-word is chosen for its overlay of several meanings similar to
those of the kanji: *a turn* of duty, a round, a number, and so forth. Its
elements: *animal tracks . . . rice field.* [12]

* As a primitive element, we choose the image of a pair of *dice,* used to decide whose *turn* it is.

1910. hearing

The **hearing** referred to in this character relates to trials in the courts. The elements: *house . . . dice.* [15]

1911. flip

Dice . . . feathers. [18]

1912. clan

Flowers . . . water . . . dice. [18]

1913. fur

This character simply reverses the direction of the final stroke of *hand* to produce **fur.** If you reverse your *hand* and put its palm down, you will have the side on which **fur** grows. [4]

1914. decrease

Christmas tree . . . fur. [10]

1915. tail

Flag . . . fur. [7]

* lock of hair

This element is clearly derived from that for *fur.* By leaving out the second stroke, we get simply a **lock of hair.** [3]

1916. home

House . . . lock of hair. [6]

宅

1917. consign

Words . . . lock of hair. [10]

託

* tail feathers

丂

So as not to confuse this primitive element with the character for *feathers,* think of the extravagant **tail-feather** plumage of the peacock. The form itself is too pictographic to need breaking down further. [5]

1918. do

為

This character rightly belongs to the previous lesson, but we held it until now because of the final element, the *tail feathers.* After the *drop* at the outset, the next three strokes look to be completely novel, but with just a little twist they can be seen as a close relative of the form we took to mean *from.* [9]

1919. falsehood

偽

Person . . . do. [11]

* hairpin

乀

Here we have a quasi-pictograph of the colorful and decorated clips used to bind up long hair. Note the similarity of the bottom portion to that *scarf,* which differs only by an additional stroke. [4]

1920. long   長

Conforming to the story of the previous frame, the *hair* which needs the *hairpin* is **long**. [8]

｜ 厂 F F 三 長 長 長

* The primitive of this kanji has two more shapes in addition to that of the kanji itself. Above its relative primitive, it is abbreviated to the form 镸 and will mean *hair*. Further abbreviated to 镸 , it will mean the long, mangy *mane* of an animal.

1921. lengthen   張

Bow . . . long. [11]

1922. notebook   帳

Towel . . . long. [11]

1923. dilate   脹

Flesh . . . long. [12]

1924. hair of the head   髪

Hair . . . shape. . . . friend. [14]

1925. unfold   展

Flag . . . salad . . . hairpin. [10]

1926. miss   喪

Soil . . . two *mouths . . . hairpin.* Hint: see *spit* (Frame 151). The key-word carries the wide range of meanings readily associated with the English word: error, loss, absence, and so on. [12]

LESSON 53

We turn now to the animals themselves, beginning with the smaller animals. Because we shall meet a fair number of limited-use primitives, this section will supply a larger than normal number of stories in complete or semi-complete form.

---

*   owl

We have already met these three strokes before. When they come under another stroke, they represent a *claw,* and thence a *vulture.* And when placed atop a roof structure, they create a *school house.* The owl has something to do with both: it is a bird of prey, and it has come to be associated in the popular imagination with learning. [3]

1927. nest   巣

Owl . . . fruit. [11]

1928. simple   単

Owl . . . brain . . . needle. The key-word does not connote "easy" or "facile," but rather the opposite of "complex." Note how the stroke order of the last two elements is different from what you might expect just by reading the ingredients. [9]

1929. war 戦

Simple . . . fiesta. [13]

1930. Zen 禅

Altar . . . simple. [13]

1931. bullet 弾

Bow . . . simple. [12]

1932. cherry tree 桜

Tree . . . owl . . . woman. [10]

1933. animal 獣

Owl . . . rice field . . . one . . . mouth . . . chihuahua. [16]

1934. brain 脳

Part of the body . . . owl . . . villain. Unlike most of the primitive elements whose meaning is identical to that of a character, this kanji has no connection with the element for **brains.** [11]

1935. trouble 悩

State of mind . . . owl . . . villain. [10]

1936. stern 厳

Owl . . . cliff . . . daring. [17]

1937. chain

Metal . . . small . . . shells. We have saved this character until now in order to draw attention to the visual difference between the *owl* and *small*. By now your eyes should be so accustomed to these apparently infinitesimal differences that the point is obvious. [18]

1938. raise

Owl . . . tool . . . hand. [10]

1939. reputation

Owl . . . tool . . . speaking. [13]

1940. game-hunting

Pack of wild dogs . . . owl . . . wind . . . cornstalk. [11]

1941. bird

Dove . . . one . . . tail feathers. This is, of course, the character from which we derived the primitive meaning of *dove*. Note the lengthening of the second stroke. [11]

1942. chirp

Mouth . . . bird. [14]

1943. crane

Turkey house . . . bird. The first element only appears on one other occasion, back in Frame 567. [21]

1944. crow

The only thing that distinguishes this character from that for *bird* is the omission of the one stroke that makes it *white*. Which is logical enough, when you consider that there are no **crows** of that color. [10]

1945. vine

Flower . . . bird. [14]

1946. pigeon

Baseball . . . bird. [13]

1947. chicken

Vulture . . . husband . . . bird. [19]

1948. island

The *bird's tail* is tucked under here, because he has come to stop on a *mountain* to rest from his journey across the waters. Thus it comes to mean an **island**. [10]

* migrating ducks

This primitive is simplicity itself. It depicts bird *claws* that are joined to one another (note the *two*) in *friendship*. [9]

1949. warmth

Unlike the character for *warm* weather learned earlier (Frame 1452), this kanji and its key-word can also refer to the **warmth** of human congeniality. Its elements are: *sun . . . migrating ducks.* [13]

1950. beautiful woman   媛

Woman . . . migrating ducks. [12]

1951. abet   援

Fingers . . . migrating ducks. [12]

1952. slacken   緩

Thread . . . migrating ducks. [15]

1953. belong   属

Flag . . . gnats (see Frame 524) *. . . with a belt.* [12]

尸 尸 尾 属 属

1954. entrust   嘱

Mouth . . . belong. [15]

1955. accidentally   偶

The *person* on the left is familiar. As for the right side, we may combine the elements of an *insect* with a *brain* (observe the combination) and a *belt* to get the *Talking Cricket* who served as Pinocchio's conscience. (*The belt* is there because he pulls it off to give unrepentant little Pinocchio a bit of "strap" now and again.) [11]

亻 偶 偶

1956. interview   遇

Talking Cricket . . . road. [12]

1957. foolish

Talking Cricket . . . heart. [13]

1958. corner

Pinnacle . . . Talking Cricket. [12]

* mountain goat

The *animal horns* and *mountain* unite, quite naturally, to give us a **mountain goat**. The extension of the final stroke indicates its tail, which only shows up when it has something under it. In an overhead enclosure, it is to be pictured as standing still, so that its tail droops down and out of sight. [6]

1959. inverted 逆

Mountain goat . . . road. [9]

1960. model 塑

This kanji depicts the art of **modeling** clay or wood into a figure of something else. The elements: *mountain goat . . . moon . . . soil.* [13]

1961. Mount 岡

Here we see a a *mountain goat* "mounted" under a *glass canopy*. In this and the following frame, think of a particular **Mount** you know. [8]

1962. steel

Metal . . . Mount. [16]

1963. hawser

綱

Thread . . . Mount. [14]

1964. sturdy

剛

Mount . . . sword. [10]

1965. tin can

缶

Though the meaning has no reference to animals, the parts do: *horse* with a *mountain* underneath. [6]

1966. pottery

陶

Pinnacle . . . bound up . . . tin can. [11]

* condor

䍃

Vulture . . . king . . . mountain. [9]

ク　厶　凸　䍃

1967. swing

揺

Fingers . . . condor. [12]

1968. Noh chanting

謡

Words . . . condor. [16]

1969. concerning

就

Capital . . . chihuahua with a *human leg* in place of one of its paws. [12]

*   skunk

This primitive represents a **skunk** by combining the *claw* with the first part of the element for a *sow*. Note how the final stroke of *claw* and the first of the *sow* double up. [7]

1970. sociable

Skunk . . . silver . . . heart. [17]

1971. groundbreaking

墾

The **groundbreaking** referred to here is not for the erection of new buildings but for the opening of farmlands. The elements: *skunk . . . silver . . . soil.* [16]

1972. excuse

免

This character is used for **excusing** oneself for a failure of courtesy. The elements are: *bound up . . . sun* (oddly enough, laid on its side) . . . *human legs.* [8]

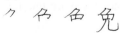

* For the primitive meaning, we shall refer to this character as a *rabbit,* the old form of the character for which is 兎 . [8]

1973. deviate

逸

Rabbits . . . road. [11]

1974. nightfall

晩

Sun . . . rabbit. [12]

1975. exertion

Rabbit . . . muscle. Notice how the last stroke of *rabbit* is stretched out to underlie the element for *muscle.* [10]

1976. elephant

A *rabbit's* head with the body of a *sow* represents an **elephant.** Little wonder that the derived meaning of this kanji is "phenomenon"! [12]

1977. statue

Person . . . elephant. [14]

LESSON 54

Having already gotten as far as the elephant, we may now continue on with the larger animals. Fortunately, this group will cause us much less of a headache than the previous series, since there are fewer new primitives and their use is more frequent.

1978. horse   馬

Let the extra vertical stroke in the *mane* combine with the first vertical stroke to give an image of the **horse's** long neck. The only odd thing is the *tail feathers* at the end, but that should present a good image to remember the character by. The fact that the last stroke of *mane* and the first of *tail feathers* coincide should come as no surprise. [10]

丨 丆 丆 丐 丐 丐 丐 馬 馬 馬 馬 馬

* As a primitive, this character will represent a *team of* **horses** to distinguish it from the single **horse** whose primitive we have used often before.

1979. pony   駒

Team of horses . . . *phrase.* Hint: in American slang, a **"pony"** is also an illicit translation of a studied text, which students who cannot manage the difficult *phrases* of the foreign language they are learning consult and pass on from one generation to the next. [15]

1980. verification   験

Team of horses . . . *awl.* [18]

1981. equestrian   騎

Team of horses . . . *strange.* [18]

1982. stop-over   駐

Team of horses . . . *candlestick.* [15]

1983. drive   駆

Team of horses . . . *ward.* [14]

1984. station   駅

Team of horses . . . *shaku hachi.* [14]

1985. boisterous   騒

Team of horses . . . *crotch* . . . *insect.* [18]

1986. burdensome

Team of horses . . . plump. [14]

1987. wonder

Awe . . . team of horses. [22]

1988. fervent

Bamboo . . . team of horses. [16]

1989. inflation

Meat . . . quarter . . . team of horses. [26]

1990. tiger

虎

The kanji in this frame recalls the famous Bengali fable about the group of magicians (the *magic wand*) who decided to make a **tiger**. It seems that each of them knew how to make one part of the beast, so they pooled their talents and brought all the pieces (*diced* into pieces) together, at which point the fabricated **tiger** promptly ate its makers up (the bodiless *human legs*). Whatever the parable's significance for modern civilization and its arsenals, it should help with this kanji. Oh yes, and that "cliff"-like element: think of it as an abbreviation of the primitive for *zoo* (the first and fourth strokes, actually), in order to fit the **tiger** somewhere into the picture. In fact, the abbreviation is perfectly logical, since the bottom elements usurp the room for the rest of the primitive for *zoo*. [8]

丨　卜　厂　广　卢　卢　虍　虍　虎

* As a primitive element itself, the *human legs* are also swallowed up, but the meaning of **tiger** is kept, and the whole serves as a roof for what comes beneath, giving the **tiger** something else to eat.

1991. captive   虜

Tiger . . . male. [13]

1992. skin   膚

Tiger . . . stomach. [15]

1993. void   虚

Tigers . . . row. [11]

1994. frolic   戲

Void . . . fiesta. [15]

1995. uneasiness   虞

Tiger . . . give. [13]

1996. prudence   慮

Tiger . . . think. [15]

1997. drama   劇

Tiger . . . sow . . . sword. [15]

1998. tyrannize   虐

Tiger . . . one . . . box. [9]

1999. deer 鹿

Drawn on the walls of a complex of *caves* near Niaux in southern France are a number of animal likenesses dating from the Upper Paleolithic period. Among them we find pictures of **deer**. Some of these drawings show men in **deer** masks. By *comparing* their drawings to real **deer**, Stone Age man hoped to acquire power over the animal in the hunt; and by *comparing* himself to the **deer**, to take on that animal's characteristics. But time has "double-*locked*" (the extra pair of vertical strokes through *key*) the real secret of this art-form from us, and we can only surmise such meanings. But more important than the enigmas of anthropology is the way in which *caves*, a double-*lock*, and *comparing* gives us the kanji for **deer**. [11]

广 广 庐 庐 鹿 鹿

* As a primitive, this kanji undergoes an abbreviation similar to the one we just met with the *tiger:* the element for *compare* is dropped and replaced by something else as a relative primitive. Its meaning, however, remains the same. There are a very few cases (see Frame 2002) in which there is no abbreviation. When this happens, we may keep the image suggested by the above explanation: *painting of a* **deer**.

2000. recommend 薦

Flowers . . . deer . . . slingshot . . . tail feathers. Note the doubling up in these last two elements. [16]

2001. jubilation 慶

Deer . . . crown (note the doubling up) *. . . heart . . . walking legs.* You may remember that we met the relative primitives at the bottom here before, namely in the kanji for *melancholy* (Frame 616). [15]

2002. lovely 麗

The *painting of a deer* itself with its form and color is enough to fill the bill for an image of something **lovely**. But to give a bit of contrast, we see two *mediocre* drawings from a later age on two patches of *ceiling* above. (The *drop* in *mediocre* has been lengthened somewhat.) [19]

2003. bear 熊

Elbow . . . meat . . . spoon ATOP *spoon . . . oven-fire*. [14]

2004. ability 能

To relate this kanji to the previous frame, the test of **ability** envisioned here is removing the *bear* from the *oven-fire*. [10]

2005. attitude 態

Ability . . . heart. [14]

LESSON 55

The final grouping of kanji are based on primitives related to fantastical animals and beings. We begin with two animals belonging to the zodiac.

2006. sign of the tiger

House . . . ceiling . . . sprout . . . animal legs. Compare Frame 1750. [11]

2007. performance 演

Water . . . sign of the tiger. [14]

2008. sign of the dragon   辰

Cliff . . . two . . . hairpin. [7]

2009. embarrass   辱

Sign of the dragon . . . glue. [10]

2010. quake   震

Weather . . . sign of the dragon. [15]

2011. shake   振

Fingers . . . sign of the dragon. [10]

2012. with child   娠

Woman . . . sign of the dragon. The key-word is a synonym for *pregnant*, whose character we learned earlier (Frame 507). [10]

2013. lips   唇

Sign of the dragon . . . mouth. [10]

2014. agriculture   農

Bend . . . sign of the dragon. [13]

2015. concentrated   濃

Among other things, the key-word refers to the "thick" consistency of liquids. Its elements: *water . . . agriculture.* [16]

---

* golden calf   关

The story is told of the people of the Exodus that in their disbelief they melted down their valuables to fashion a **golden calf** for an idol. The *animal horns* and *heavens* here represent that god of theirs. [6]

2016. escort   送

Golden calf . . . road. [9]

2017. connection   関

Gates . . . golden calf. [14]

2018. blossom   咲

Mouth . . . golden calf. [9]

2019. ghost   鬼

Drop of . . . brains . . . human legs . . . elbow. [10]

2020. ugly   醜

Whiskey bottle . . . ghost. [17]

2021. soul   魂

Rising cloud of . . . ghosts. [14]

2022. witch   魔

Hemp . . . ghost. [21]

2023. fascination   魅

Ghost . . . not yet. [15]

2024. clod   塊

Soil . . . ghost. [13]

2025. attack   襲

Vase . . . meat . . . slingshot (doubled up with) *snake . . . three . . . clothes.*
The top half of this character is the old form for the kanji in Frame
536. [22]

LESSON 56

This final lesson is intended to complete preparations for learning new
kanji not treated in these pages. A group of 14 such kanji has been
reserved for this purpose and arranged in four groups typifying the kinds
of problems you can run into. Aside from help with unusual stroke order,
no hints will be given.

The first and simplest group will be composed of those whose parts you
will recognize immediately from characters already learned. We list seven
examples, each representing one of the principles governing primitives:

2026. menacing   嚇

2027. majestic plural   朕

2028. atmosphere	雰
2029. item	箇
2030. tempering	錬
2031. abide by	遵
2032. quit	罷

Secondly, you may run into characters that you learned as primitives, but whose meaning is completely unrelated to the primitive meaning we adopted. In taking this into account, do not obliterate the existing primitive meaning.

2033. barracks	屯
2034. moreover	且

In the third place, you will meet kanji using combinations of elements that you can make into a new primitive with its own particular meaning. Recall a previous kanji in which this combination appears and adjust your story to reinforce your new invention.

2035. seaweed	藻
2036. slave	隷

2037. healing

In the fourth and final place, there are shapes that were not covered in this book. You are on your own here, but it may help to consult a kanji dictionary to see whether any of the parts might not be a character with a specific and useful meaning. The second cluster of strokes of the latter of the two examples is a perfect illustration of this.

2038. rust-colored   丹

2039. lagoon   潟

Scattered here and there throughout the foregoing 55 lessons several figures of the Sino-Japanese zodiac were introduced. We conclude this lesson, and the book, with the remaining figures. In all, there are twelve animals, several of which take their writing from other characters quite unrelated in meaning. So far, then, we have learned the following: *rat* (子), *tiger* (寅), *dragon* (辰), *horse* (午), *ram* (未), *monkey* (申), *bird* (酉), *dog* (戌), *hog* (亥). This leaves three for the learning.

2040. sign of the cow   丑

2041. sign of the hare   卯

2042. sign of the snake   巳

INDEXES

INDEX I:

HAND-DRAWN CHARACTERS

The purpose of this Index is to give you an idea of how all the kanji treated in this book should look when drawn in block-form with a regular pen or pencil. Since the printed form of the characters will occasionally obscure the presence of the primitive elements that make them up, you will find it helpful to consult this list regularly as you proceed through the book.

一	二	三	四	五	六	七	八	九	十
1	2	3	4	5	6	7	8	9	10
口	日	月	田	目	古	吾	冒	朋	明
11	12	13	14	15	16	17	18	19	20
唱	晶	品	呂	昌	早	旭	世	胃	旦
21	22	23	24	25	26	27	28	29	30
胆	亘	凹	凸	旧	自	白	百	中	千
31	32	33	34	35	36	37	38	39	40
舌	升	昇	丸	寸	専	博	占	上	下
41	42	43	44	45	46	47	48	49	50
卓	朝	只	貝	貞	員	見	児	元	頁
51	52	53	54	55	56	57	58	59	60
頑	凡	負	万	句	肌	旬	勺	的	首
61	62	63	64	65	66	67	68	69	70
乙	乱	直	具	真	工	左	右	有	賄
71	72	73	74	75	76	77	78	79	80

貢	項	刀	刃	切	召	昭	則	副	別
81	82	83	84	85	86	87	88	89	90
丁	町	可	頂	子	孔	了	女	好	如
91	92	93	94	95	96	97	98	99	100
母	貫	兄	克	小	少	大	多	夕	汐
101	102	103	104	105	106	107	108	109	110
外	名	石	肖	硝	砕	砂	削	光	太
111	112	113	114	115	116	117	118	119	120
器	臭	妙	省	厚	奇	川	州	順	水
121	122	123	124	125	126	127	128	129	130
氷	永	泉	原	願	泳	沼	沖	江	汁
131	132	133	134	135	136	137	138	139	140
潮	源	活	消	況	河	泊	湖	測	土
141	142	143	144	145	146	147	148	149	150
吐	圧	埼	垣	圭	封	涯	寺	時	均
151	152	153	154	155	156	157	158	159	160
火	炎	煩	淡	灯	畑	災	灰	点	照
161	162	163	164	165	166	167	168	169	170
魚	漁	里	黒	墨	鯉	量	厘	埋	同
171	172	173	174	175	176	177	178	179	180
洞	胴	向	尚	字	守	完	宣	宵	安
181	182	183	184	185	186	187	188	189	190
宴	寄	富	貯	木	林	森	桂	柏	枠
191	192	193	194	195	196	197	198	199	200
梢	棚	杏	桐	植	枯	朴	村	相	机
201	202	203	204	205	206	207	208	209	210

本	札	暦	案	燥	未	末	沫	味	妹
211	212	213	214	215	216	217	218	219	220
朱	株	若	草	苦	寛	薄	葉	模	漠
221	222	223	224	225	226	227	228	229	230
墓	暮	膜	苗	兆	桃	眺	犬	状	黙
231	232	233	234	235	236	237	238	239	240
然	荻	狩	猫	牛	特	告	先	洗	介
241	242	243	244	245	246	247	248	249	250
界	茶	合	塔	王	玉	宝	珠	現	狂
251	252	253	254	255	256	257	258	259	260
皇	呈	全	栓	理	主	注	柱	金	銑
261	262	263	264	265	266	267	268	269	270
鉢	銅	釣	針	銘	鎮	道	導	辻	迅
271	272	273	274	275	276	277	278	279	280
造	迫	逃	辺	巡	車	連	軌	輪	前
281	282	283	284	285	286	287	288	289	290
各	格	略	客	額	夏	処	条	落	冗
291	292	293	294	295	296	297	298	299	300
軍	輝	運	冠	夢	坑	高	享	塾	熟
301	302	303	304	305	306	307	308	309	310
亭	京	涼	景	鯨	舎	周	週	士	吉
311	312	313	314	315	316	317	318	319	320
壮	荘	売	学	覚	栄	書	津	牧	攻
321	322	323	324	325	326	327	328	329	330
敗	枚	故	敬	言	警	計	獄	訂	討
331	332	333	334	335	336	337	338	339	340

訓	詔	詰	話	詠	詩	語	読	調	談
341	342	343	344	345	346	347	348	349	350
諾	諭	式	試	弐	域	賊	栽	載	茂
351	352	353	354	355	356	357	358	359	360
成	城	誠	威	滅	減	桟	銭	浅	止
361	362	363	364	365	366	367	368	369	370
歩	渉	頻	肯	企	歴	武	賦	正	証
371	372	373	374	375	376	377	378	379	380
政	定	錠	走	超	赴	越	是	題	堤
381	382	383	384	385	386	387	388	389	390
建	延	誕	礎	婿	衣	裁	装	裏	壊
391	392	393	394	395	396	397	398	399	400
哀	遠	猿	初	布	帆	幅	帽	幕	幌
401	402	403	404	405	406	407	408	409	410
錦	市	姉	肺	帯	滞	刺	制	製	転
411	412	413	414	415	416	417	418	419	420
芸	雨	雲	曇	雷	霜	冬	天	橋	嬌
421	422	423	424	425	426	427	428	429	430
立	泣	章	競	帝	童	瞳	鐘	商	嫡
431	432	433	434	435	436	437	438	439	440
適	滴	敵	七	北	背	比	昆	皆	混
441	442	443	444	445	446	447	448	449	450
渇	謁	褐	喝	旨	脂	壱	毎	敏	梅
451	452	453	454	455	456	457	458	459	460
海	乞	乾	腹	複	欠	吹	炊	歌	軟
461	462	463	464	465	466	467	468	469	470

次	茨	資	姿	諮	賠	培	剖	音	暗
471	472	473	474	475	476	477	478	479	480
韻	識	鏡	境	亡	盲	妄	荒	望	方
481	482	483	484	485	486	487	488	489	490
妨	坊	芳	肪	訪	放	激	脱	説	鋭
491	492	493	494	495	496	497	498	499	500
曽	増	贈	東	棟	凍	妊	廷	染	燃
501	502	503	504	505	506	507	508	509	510
賓	歳	県	栃	地	池	虫	蛍	蛇	虹
511	512	513	514	515	516	517	518	519	520
蝶	独	蚕	風	己	起	妃	改	記	包
521	522	523	524	525	526	527	528	529	530
胞	砲	泡	亀	電	竜	滝	豚	逐	遂
531	532	533	534	535	536	537	538	539	540
家	嫁	豪	腸	場	湯	羊	美	洋	詳
541	542	543	544	545	546	547	548	549	550
鮮	達	羨	差	着	唯	焦	礁	集	准
551	552	553	554	555	556	557	558	559	560
進	雑	雌	準	奮	奪	確	午	許	歓
561	562	563	564	565	566	567	568	569	570
権	観	羽	習	翌	曜	濯	日	困	固
571	572	573	574	575	576	577	578	579	580
国	団	因	姻	園	回	壇	店	庫	庭
581	582	583	584	585	586	587	588	589	590
庁	床	麻	磨	心	忘	忍	認	忌	志
591	592	593	594	595	596	597	598	599	600

誌 601	忠 602	串 603	患 604	思 605	恩 606	応 607	意 608	想 609	息 610
憩 611	恵 612	恐 613	惑 614	感 615	憂 616	寡 617	忙 618	悦 619	恒 620
悼 621	悟 622	怖 623	慌 624	悔 625	憎 626	慣 627	愉 628	惰 629	慎 630
憾 631	憶 632	慕 633	添 634	必 635	泌 636	手 637	看 638	摩 639	我 640
義 641	議 642	犠 643	抹 644	抱 645	搭 646	抄 647	抗 648	批 649	招 650
拓 651	拍 652	打 653	拘 654	捨 655	拐 656	摘 657	挑 658	指 659	持 660
括 661	揮 662	推 663	揚 664	提 665	損 666	拾 667	担 668	拠 669	描 670
操 671	接 672	掲 673	掛 674	研 675	戒 676	械 677	鼻 678	刑 679	型 680
才 681	財 682	材 683	存 684	在 685	乃 686	携 687	及 688	吸 689	扱 690
大 691	史 692	吏 693	更 694	硬 695	又 696	双 697	桑 698	隻 699	護 700
獲 701	奴 702	怒 703	友 704	抜 705	投 706	没 707	設 708	撃 709	殻 710
支 711	技 712	枝 713	肢 714	茎 715	怪 716	軽 717	叔 718	督 719	寂 720
淑 721	反 722	坂 723	板 724	返 725	販 726	爪 727	妥 728	乳 729	浮 730

将	奨	採	菜	受	授	愛	払	広	拡
731	732	733	734	735	736	737	738	739	740
鉱	弁	雄	台	怠	治	始	胎	窓	去
741	742	743	744	745	746	747	748	749	750
法	会	至	室	到	致	互	棄	育	撤
751	752	753	754	755	756	757	758	759	760
充	銃	硫	流	允	唆	出	山	拙	岩
761	762	763	764	765	766	767	768	769	770
炭	岐	峠	崩	密	蜜	嵐	崎	入	込
771	772	773	774	775	776	777	778	779	780
分	貧	領	公	松	翁	訟	谷	浴	容
781	782	783	784	785	786	787	788	789	790
溶	欲	裕	鉛	沿	賞	党	堂	常	裳
791	792	793	794	795	796	797	798	799	800
掌	皮	波	婆	披	破	被	残	殉	殊
801	802	803	804	805	806	807	808	809	810
殖	列	裂	烈	死	葬	瞬	耳	取	趣
811	812	813	814	815	816	817	818	819	820
最	撮	恥	職	聖	敢	聴	懐	慢	漫
821	822	823	824	825	826	827	828	829	830
買	置	罰	寧	濁	環	還	夫	扶	渓
831	832	833	834	835	836	837	838	839	840
規	替	賛	潜	失	鉄	迭	臣	姫	蔵
841	842	843	844	845	846	847	848	849	850
臓	賢	堅	臨	覧	巨	拒	力	男	労
851	852	853	854	855	856	857	858	859	860

慕	劣	功	勧	努	励	加	賀	架	脇
861	862	863	864	865	866	867	868	869	870
脅	協	行	律	復	得	従	徒	待	往
871	872	873	874	875	876	877	878	879	880
征	径	彼	役	徳	徹	徴	懲	微	街
881	882	883	884	885	886	887	888	889	890
衡	稿	稼	程	税	稚	和	移	秒	秋
891	892	893	894	895	896	897	898	899	900
愁	私	秩	秘	称	利	梨	穫	穂	稲
901	902	903	904	905	906	907	908	909	910
香	季	委	秀	透	誘	穀	菌	米	粉
911	912	913	914	915	916	917	918	919	920
粘	粒	粧	迷	粋	糧	菊	奥	数	楼
921	922	923	924	925	926	927	928	929	930
類	漆	様	求	球	救	竹	笑	笠	笹
931	932	933	934	935	936	937	938	939	940
筋	箱	筆	筒	等	算	答	策	簿	築
941	942	943	944	945	946	947	948	949	950
人	佐	但	住	位	仲	体	悠	件	仕
951	952	953	954	955	956	957	958	959	960
他	伏	伝	仏	休	仮	伯	俗	信	佳
961	962	963	964	965	966	967	968	969	970
依	例	個	健	側	侍	停	値	倣	倒
971	972	973	974	975	976	977	978	979	980
偵	僧	億	儀	償	仙	催	仁	侮	使
981	982	983	984	985	986	987	988	989	990

便	倍	優	伐	宿	傷	保	褒	傑	付
991	992	993	994	995	996	997	998	999	1000
符	府	任	賃	代	袋	貸	化	花	貨
1001	1002	1003	1004	1005	1006	1007	1008	1009	1010
傾	何	荷	俊	傍	久	畝	囚	内	丙
1011	1012	1013	1014	1015	1016	1017	1018	1019	1020
柄	肉	腐	座	卒	傘	夂	以	似	併
1021	1022	1023	1024	1025	1026	1027	1028	1029	1030
瓦	瓶	宮	営	善	年	夜	液	塚	幣
1031	1032	1033	1034	1035	1036	1037	1038	1039	1040
弊	喚	換	融	施	旋	遊	旅	勿	物
1041	1042	1043	1044	1045	1046	1047	1048	1049	1050
易	賜	尿	尼	泥	塀	履	屋	握	屈
1051	1052	1053	1054	1055	1056	1057	1058	1059	1060
掘	堀	居	据	層	局	遅	漏	刷	尺
1061	1062	1063	1064	1065	1066	1067	1068	1069	1070
尽	沢	訳	択	昼	戸	肩	房	扇	炉
1071	1072	1073	1074	1075	1076	1077	1078	1079	1080
戻	涙	雇	顧	啓	示	礼	祥	祝	福
1081	1082	1083	1084	1085	1086	1087	1088	1089	1090
祉	社	視	奈	尉	慰	款	禁	襟	宗
1091	1092	1093	1094	1095	1096	1097	1098	1099	1100
崇	祭	察	擦	由	抽	油	袖	宙	届
1101	1102	1103	1104	1105	1106	1107	1108	1109	1110
笛	軸	甲	押	岬	挿	申	伸	神	捜
1111	1112	1113	1114	1115	1116	1117	1118	1119	1120

果	菓	課	裸	斤	析	所	祈	近	折
1121	1122	1123	1124	1125	1126	1127	1128	1129	1130
哲	逝	誓	暫	漸	断	質	斥	訴	昨
1131	1132	1133	1134	1135	1136	1137	1138	1139	1140
詐	作	雪	録	尋	急	穏	侵	浸	寝
1141	1142	1143	1144	1145	1146	1147	1148	1149	1150
婦	掃	当	争	浄	事	唐	糖	康	逮
1151	1152	1153	1154	1155	1156	1157	1158	1159	1160
伊	君	群	耐	需	儒	端	両	満	画
1161	1162	1163	1164	1165	1166	1167	1168	1169	1170
歯	曲	曹	遭	漕	槽	斗	料	科	図
1171	1172	1173	1174	1175	1176	1177	1178	1179	1180
用	庸	備	昔	錯	借	惜	措	散	廿
1181	1182	1183	1184	1185	1186	1187	1188	1189	1190
庶	遮	席	度	渡	奔	噴	墳	憤	焼
1191	1192	1193	1194	1195	1196	1197	1198	1199	1200
暁	半	伴	畔	判	券	巻	圏	勝	藤
1201	1202	1203	1204	1205	1206	1207	1208	1209	1210
膳	片	版	之	乏	芝	不	否	杯	矢
1211	1212	1213	1214	1215	1216	1217	1218	1219	1220
矯	族	知	智	矛	柔	務	霧	班	帰
1221	1222	1223	1224	1225	1226	1227	1228	1229	1230
弓	引	弔	弘	強	弱	沸	費	第	弟
1231	1232	1233	1234	1235	1236	1237	1238	1239	1240
巧	号	朽	誇	汚	与	写	身	射	謝
1241	1242	1243	1244	1245	1246	1247	1248	1249	1250

老	考	孝	教	拷	者	煮	著	署	暑
1251	1252	1253	1254	1255	1256	1257	1258	1259	1260
諸	猪	渚	賭	峽	狹	挾	追	師	帥
1261	1262	1263	1264	1265	1266	1267	1268	1269	1270
官	棺	管	父	交	効	較	校	足	促
1271	1272	1273	1274	1275	1276	1277	1278	1279	1280
距	路	露	跳	躍	践	踏	骨	滑	髓
1281	1282	1283	1284	1285	1286	1287	1288	1289	1290
禍	渦	過	阪	阿	際	障	隨	陪	陽
1291	1292	1293	1294	1295	1296	1297	1298	1299	1300
陳	防	附	院	陣	隊	墜	降	階	陛
1301	1302	1303	1304	1305	1306	1307	1308	1309	1310
隣	隔	隱	墮	陷	穴	空	控	突	究
1311	1312	1313	1314	1315	1316	1317	1318	1319	1320
室	窃	窪	搾	窯	窮	探	深	立	岳
1321	1322	1323	1324	1325	1326	1327	1328	1329	1330
兵	浜	糸	織	繕	縮	繁	縦	線	締
1331	1332	1333	1334	1335	1336	1337	1338	1339	1340
維	羅	練	緒	統	絵	統	絞	給	絡
1341	1342	1343	1344	1345	1346	1347	1348	1349	1350
結	終	級	紀	紅	納	紡	紛	紹	経
1351	1352	1353	1354	1355	1356	1357	1358	1359	1360
紳	約	細	累	索	総	綿	絹	繰	継
1361	1362	1363	1364	1365	1366	1367	1368	1369	1370
緑	縁	網	緊	紫	縛	縄	幼	後	幽
1371	1372	1373	1374	1375	1376	1377	1378	1379	1380

幾	機	玄	畜	蓄	弦	擁	滋	慈	磁
1381	1382	1383	1384	1385	1386	1387	1388	1389	1390
系	係	孫	懸	却	脚	卸	御	服	命
1391	1392	1393	1394	1395	1396	1397	1398	1399	1400
令	零	齢	冷	領	鈴	勇	通	踊	疑
1401	1402	1403	1404	1405	1406	1407	1408	1409	1410
擬	凝	範	犯	厄	危	宛	腕	苑	怨
1411	1412	1413	1414	1415	1416	1417	1418	1419	1420
柳	卯	留	貿	印	興	酉	酒	酌	酵
1421	1422	1423	1424	1425	1426	1427	1428	1429	1430
酷	酬	酪	酢	酔	配	酸	猶	尊	豆
1431	1432	1433	1434	1435	1436	1437	1438	1439	1440
頭	短	豊	鼓	喜	樹	皿	血	盆	盟
1441	1442	1443	1444	1445	1446	1447	1448	1449	1450
盗	温	監	濫	鑑	猛	盛	塩	銀	恨
1451	1452	1453	1454	1455	1456	1457	1458	1459	1460
根	即	爵	節	退	限	眼	良	朗	浪
1461	1462	1463	1464	1465	1466	1467	1468	1469	1470
娘	食	飯	飲	飢	餓	飾	館	養	鉋
1471	1472	1473	1474	1475	1476	1477	1478	1479	1480
既	概	慨	平	呼	坪	評	刈	希	凶
1481	1482	1483	1484	1485	1486	1487	1488	1489	1490
胸	離	殺	純	鈍	辛	辞	梓	宰	壁
1491	1492	1493	1494	1495	1496	1497	1498	1499	1500
避	新	薪	親	幸	執	報	叫	糾	収
1501	1502	1503	1504	1505	1506	1507	1508	1509	1510

卑	碑	陸	睦	勢	熱	菱	陵	亥	核
1511	1512	1513	1514	1515	1516	1517	1518	1519	1520
刻	該	劾	述	術	寒	釀	讓	壞	孃
1521	1522	1523	1524	1525	1526	1527	1528	1529	1530
毒	素	麦	青	精	請	情	晴	清	静
1531	1532	1533	1534	1535	1536	1537	1538	1539	1540
責	績	積	債	漬	表	俵	潔	契	喫
1541	1542	1543	1544	1545	1546	1547	1548	1549	1550
害	轄	割	憲	生	星	姓	性	牲	産
1551	1552	1553	1554	1555	1556	1557	1558	1559	1560
隆	峰	縫	拝	寿	鋳	籍	春	椿	泰
1561	1562	1563	1564	1565	1566	1567	1568	1569	1570
奏	実	奉	俸	棒	謹	勤	漢	嘆	難
1571	1572	1573	1574	1575	1576	1577	1578	1579	1580
華	垂	睡	錘	乗	剰	今	含	吟	念
1581	1582	1583	1584	1585	1586	1587	1588	1589	1590
琴	陰	予	序	預	野	兼	嫌	鎌	謙
1591	1592	1593	1594	1595	1596	1597	1598	1599	1600
廉	西	価	要	腰	票	漂	標	栗	遷
1601	1602	1603	1604	1605	1606	1607	1608	1609	1610
覆	煙	南	楠	献	門	問	閲	閥	間
1611	1612	1613	1614	1615	1616	1617	1618	1619	1620
簡	開	閉	閣	閑	聞	潤	欄	闘	倉
1621	1622	1623	1624	1625	1626	1627	1628	1629	1630
創	非	俳	排	悲	罪	輩	扉	侯	候
1631	1632	1633	1634	1635	1636	1637	1638	1639	1640

決	快	偉	違	緯	衛	韓	干	肝	刊
1641	1642	1643	1644	1645	1646	1647	1648	1649	1650
汗	軒	岸	幹	芋	宇	余	除	徐	叙
1651	1652	1653	1654	1655	1656	1657	1658	1659	1660
途	斜	塗	束	頼	瀬	勅	疎	速	整
1661	1662	1663	1664	1665	1666	1667	1668	1669	1670
剣	険	検	倹	重	動	勲	働	種	衝
1671	1672	1673	1674	1675	1676	1677	1678	1679	1680
薫	病	痴	痘	症	疾	痢	疲	疫	痛
1681	1682	1683	1684	1685	1686	1687	1688	1689	1690
癖	匿	匠	医	匹	区	枢	殴	欧	柳
1691	1692	1693	1694	1695	1696	1697	1698	1699	1700
仰	迎	登	澄	発	廃	僚	寮	療	彫
1701	1702	1703	1704	1705	1706	1707	1708	1709	1710
形	影	杉	彩	彰	彦	顔	須	膨	参
1711	1712	1713	1714	1715	1716	1717	1718	1719	1720
惨	修	珍	診	文	対	紋	蚊	斉	剤
1721	1722	1723	1724	1725	1726	1727	1728	1729	1730
済	斎	粛	塁	楽	薬	率	渋	摂	央
1731	1732	1733	1734	1735	1736	1737	1738	1739	1740
英	映	赤	赦	変	跡	蛮	恋	湾	黄
1741	1742	1743	1744	1745	1746	1747	1748	1749	1750
横	把	色	絶	艶	肥	甘	紺	某	謀
1751	1752	1753	1754	1755	1756	1757	1758	1759	1760
媒	欺	棋	旗	期	碁	基	甚	勘	堪
1761	1762	1763	1764	1765	1766	1767	1768	1769	1770

貴	遺	遣	舞	無	組	粗	租	祖	阻
1771	1772	1773	1774	1775	1776	1777	1778	1779	1780
査	助	宜	畳	並	普	譜	湿	顕	繊
1781	1782	1783	1784	1785	1786	1787	1788	1789	1790
霊	業	撲	僕	共	供	異	翼	洪	港
1791	1792	1793	1794	1795	1796	1797	1798	1799	1800
暴	爆	恭	選	殿	井	囲	耕	亜	悪
1801	1802	1803	1804	1805	1806	1807	1808	1809	1810
円	角	触	解	再	講	購	構	溝	論
1811	1812	1813	1814	1815	1816	1817	1818	1819	1820
倫	輪	偏	遍	編	冊	典	氏	紙	婚
1821	1822	1823	1824	1825	1826	1827	1828	1829	1830
低	抵	底	民	眠	捕	浦	蒲	舗	補
1831	1832	1833	1834	1835	1836	1837	1838	1839	1840
邸	郭	郡	郊	部	都	郵	邦	郷	響
1841	1842	1843	1844	1845	1846	1847	1848	1849	1850
郎	廊	盾	循	派	脈	衆	遁	段	鍛
1851	1852	1853	1854	1855	1856	1857	1858	1859	1860
右	幻	司	伺	詞	飼	嗣	舟	舶	航
1861	1862	1863	1864	1865	1866	1867	1868	1869	1870
般	盤	搬	船	艦	艇	瓜	弧	孤	繭
1871	1872	1873	1874	1875	1876	1877	1878	1879	1880
益	暇	敷	来	気	汽	飛	沈	妻	衰
1881	1882	1883	1884	1885	1886	1887	1888	1889	1890
袁	面	革	靴	覇	声	呉	娯	誤	蒸
1891	1892	1893	1894	1895	1896	1897	1898	1899	1900

承	函	極	牙	芽	邪	雅	釈	番	審
1901	1902	1903	1904	1905	1906	1907	1908	1909	1910
翻	藩	毛	耗	尾	宅	託	為	偽	長
1911	1912	1913	1914	1915	1916	1917	1918	1919	1920
張	帳	脹	髪	展	喪	巣	単	戦	禅
1921	1922	1923	1924	1925	1926	1927	1928	1929	1930
弾	桜	獣	脳	悩	厳	鎖	挙	誉	猟
1931	1932	1933	1934	1935	1936	1937	1938	1939	1940
鳥	鳴	鶴	烏	蔦	鳩	鶏	島	暖	媛
1941	1942	1943	1944	1945	1946	1947	1948	1949	1950
援	緩	属	嘱	偶	遇	愚	隅	逆	塑
1951	1952	1953	1954	1955	1956	1957	1958	1959	1960
岡	鋼	網	剛	缶	陶	揺	謡	就	懇
1961	1962	1963	1964	1965	1966	1967	1968	1969	1970
墾	免	逸	晩	勉	象	像	馬	駒	験
1971	1972	1973	1974	1975	1976	1977	1978	1979	1980
騎	駐	駆	駅	騒	駄	驚	篤	騰	虎
1981	1982	1983	1984	1985	1986	1987	1988	1989	1990
虜	膚	虚	戯	虞	慮	劇	虐	鹿	薦
1991	1992	1993	1994	1995	1996	1997	1998	1999	2000
慶	麗	熊	能	態	寅	演	辰	辱	震
2001	2002	2003	2004	2005	2006	2007	2008	2009	2010
振	娠	唇	農	濃	送	関	咲	鬼	醜
2011	2012	2013	2014	2015	2016	2017	2018	2019	2020
魂	魔	魅	塊	襲	嚇	朕	零	箇	錬
2021	2022	2023	2024	2025	2026	2027	2028	2029	2030

遵　罷　屯　且　藻　隷　癒　丹　潟　丑
2031　2032　2033　2034　2035　2036　2037　2038　2039　2040

卯　巳
2041　2042

INDEX II:

PRIMITIVE ELEMENTS

The primitive elements listed in this Index do not include those treated separately as kanji. If you do not find a particular element, consult the kanji indexes. As with the previous Index, all the elements are hand-drawn here and arranged according to their number of strokes. The numbers refer to the page on which the primitive is treated.

1	´	丨	ㄴ	㇄	ㄱ	2	卜	八	儿
	26	26	42	264	403		31	33	34

几	ク	ク	ˇ	ナ	ナ	刂	厂	冂	入
34	34	34	35	44	44	46	54	77	102

冂	乂	ム	亻	凵	刂	丂	丩	乂	丩
152	212	220	253	287	298	300	301	339	343

工	ㄷ	川	3	六	⺌	川	巛	氵	宀
364	373	379		43	54	61	61	61	79

艹	ㄐ	犭	厶	辶	夂	弋	又	巾	也
90	97	98	102	114	117	134	145	149	179

194	196	197	205	210	221	241	268	283	309
321	328	343	353	361	377	398	411	414	**4**
51	71	82	100	122	128	135	135	147	152
155	173	197	209	214	218	223	231	262	268
273	284	284	286	290	303	314	329	347	351
351	365	380	383	412	**5**	19	122	127	137
143	146	147	151	151	183	185	216	228	244
248	282	292	299	299	312	327	334	337	343
345	351	355	369	372	375	386	395	397	412
413	432	**6**	124	128	128	136	139	147	186
219	241	250	264	267	286	294	304	305	334
336	351	355	359	382	387	419	424	429	**7**
171	184	188	218	233	291	307	398	410	413

INDEX III:

THE KANJI

The following list contains all the kanji treated in this book, arranged according to number of strokes and "strong" primitive elements, and marked with their respective frame number. By the time you are mid-way through this book, you should be familiar enough with counting strokes to use this Index confidently.

欠	466	外	111	皿	1447	兆	235	州	128
予	1593	央	1740	目	15	先	248	巡	285
双	697	失	845	矛	1225	光	119	帆	406
允	765	奴	702	矢	1220	全	263	年	1036
		写	1247	石	113	両	1168	式	353
5		尼	1054	示	1086	共	1795	忙	618
		左	77	礼	1087	再	1815	成	361
		巧	1241	穴	1316	刑	679	扱	690
且	2034	巨	856	立	431	列	812	旨	455
世	28	市	412	台	744	劣	862	早	26
丘	1329	布	405	旧	35	匠	1693	旬	67
丙	1020	平	1484	処	297	印	1425	曲	1172
主	266	幼	1378	号	1242	危	1416	会	752
仕	960	広	739	弁	742	叫	1508	有	79
他	961	庁	591	辻	279	各	291	朱	221
付	1000	弘	1234	込	780	合	253	朴	207
仙	986	必	635	辺	284	吉	320	朽	1243
代	1005	打	653	瓦	1031	圭	155	机	210
令	1401	払	738	丑	2040	同	180	次	471
以	1028	斥	1138	卯	2041	名	112	死	815
只	53	旦	30	凸	34	后	1861	毎	458
兄	103	未	216	凹	33	吏	693	気	1885
冊	1826	末	217			吐	151	汗	1651
冬	427	本	211			向	183	汚	1245
出	767	札	212	**6**		吸	689	江	139
刊	1650	正	379			回	586	汐	110
功	863	母	101	旭	27	因	583	池	516
加	867	民	1834	亘	32	団	582	灯	165
包	530	氷	131	亥	1519	在	685	灰	168
北	445	永	132	交	1275	地	515	芝	1216
半	1202	汁	140	瓜	1877	壮	321	争	1154
占	48	犯	1414	仰	1701	多	108	当	1153
去	750	玄	1383	仲	956	好	99	尽	38
古	16	玉	256	件	959	如	100	百	1071
句	65	甘	1757	任	1003	妃	527	竹	937
召	86	生	1555	企	375	妄	487	米	919
可	93	用	1181	伏	962	字	185	糸	1333
史	692	田	14	伐	994	存	684	缶	1965
右	78	由	1105	休	965	宅	1916	羊	547
司	1863	甲	1113	仮	966	宇	1656	羽	573
囚	1018	申	1117	伝	963	守	186	老	1251
四	4	白	37	伊	1161	安	190	考	1252
圧	152	皮	802	充	761	寺	158	耳	818

肉	1022	別	90	廷	508	男	859	**8**
肌	66	利	906	弟	1240	町	92		
自	36	助	1782	形	1711	社	1092	乳	729
至	753	努	865	役	884	秀	914	事	1156
舌	41	労	860	忌	599	私	902	享	308
舟	1868	励	866	忍	597	究	1320	京	312
色	1753	却	1395	志	600	系	1391	佳	970
芋	1655	卵	1422	忘	596	声	1896	使	990
虫	517	即	1462	決	1641	肖	114	例	972
血	1448	君	1162	快	1642	肝	1649	侍	976
行	873	吟	1589	応	607	臣	848	供	1796
衣	396	否	1218	我	640	良	1468	依	971
西	1602	含	1588	戒	676	花	1009	侮	989
弐	355	呈	262	戻	1081	芳	493	併	1030
迅	280	呉	1897	扶	839	芸	421	価	1603
		吹	467	批	649	見	57	免	1972
7		串	603	技	712	角	1812	具	74
		呂	24	抄	647	言	335	典	1827
乱	72	告	247	把	1752	谷	788	函	1902
亜	1809	吾	17	抑	1700	豆	1440	岡	1961
伯	967	困	579	投	706	貝	54	到	755
伴	1203	囲	1807	抗	648	売	323	制	418
伸	1118	図	1180	折	1130	赤	1743	刷	1069
伺	1864	坂	723	抜	705	走	384	券	1206
似	1029	均	160	択	1074	足	1279	刺	417
但	953	坊	492	改	528	身	1248	刻	1521
位	955	坑	306	攻	330	車	286	効	1276
体	957	壱	457	更	694	辛	1496	劾	1523
低	1831	寿	1565	杏	203	辰	2008	卒	1025
住	954	妊	507	杉	1713	迎	1702	卓	51
佐	952	妙	123	材	683	近	1129	協	872
何	1012	妥	728	村	208	返	725	参	1720
作	1142	妨	491	束	1664	邦	1848	叔	718
来	1884	孝	1253	条	298	医	1694	取	819
克	104	完	187	求	934	酉	1427	受	735
児	58	対	1726	汽	1886	里	173	周	317
兵	1331	尾	1915	沈	1888	防	1302	味	219
冷	1404	尿	1053	没	707	阪	1294	呼	1485
初	404	局	1066	沖	138	余	1657	命	1400
判	1205	岐	772	沢	1072	麦	1533	和	897
		希	1489	災	167			固	580
		床	592	状	239			国	581
		序	1594	狂	260			坪	1486

怠	745	津	328	肺	414	夷	1891	宮	1033
急	1146	洪	1799	胃	29	卸	1397	宰	1499
恒	620	活	143	背	446			害	1551
恨	1460	派	1855	胎	748	**10**		宴	191
悔	625	海	461	胞	531			宵	189
怨	1420	浄	1155	胆	31	烏	1944	家	541
括	661	浅	369	臭	122	修	1722	容	790
拷	1255	炭	771	茨	472	俳	1633	射	1249
拾	667	為	1918	茶	252	俵	1547	将	731
持	660	牲	1559	草	224	倉	1630	展	1925
指	659	狩	243	荒	488	俸	1574	峰	1562
挑	658	狭	1266	荘	322	値	978	島	1948
挟	1267	独	522	虹	520	個	973	差	554
政	381	珍	1723	虐	1998	倍	992	師	1269
故	333	甚	1768	要	1604	倒	980	席	1193
叙	1660	界	251	訂	339	候	1640	帯	415
施	1045	畑	166	計	337	借	1186	座	1024
星	1556	疫	1689	変	1745	倣	979	庫	589
映	1742	発	1705	貞	55	倫	1821	庭	590
春	1568	皆	449	負	63	倹	1674	弱	1236
昨	1140	皇	261	赴	386	兼	1597	徐	1659
昭	87	盆	1449	軌	288	准	560	徒	878
是	388	盾	1853	軍	301	凍	506	従	877
昼	1075	省	124	迷	924	剖	478	恐	613
県	513	看	638	追	1268	剛	1964	恥	823
枯	206	砂	117	退	1465	剤	1730	恩	606
架	869	研	675	送	2016	剣	1671	恭	1803
柏	199	砕	116	逃	283	勉	1975	息	610
柄	1021	祖	1779	逆	1959	匿	1692	悦	619
栃	514	祝	1089	郊	1844	原	134	悟	622
染	509	神	1119	郎	1851	員	56	恵	612
柔	1226	秋	900	重	1675	哲	1131	悩	1935
査	1781	科	1179	限	1466	唆	766	恋	1748
某	1759	秒	899	面	1892	唇	2013	扇	1079
柱	268	窃	1322	革	1893	唐	1157	振	2011
柳	1421	彦	1716	頁	60	埋	179	挿	1116
相	209	糾	1509	音	479	夏	296	捕	1836
栄	326	紀	1354	風	524	姫	849	搜	1120
段	1859	約	1362	飛	1887	娘	1471	挙	1938
泉	133	紅	1355	食	1472	娯	1898	敏	459
洋	549	級	1353	首	70	娠	2012	料	1178
洗	249	美	548	香	911	孫	1393	旅	1048
洞	181	耐	1164	点	169			既	1481

欲	792	笹	940	責	1541	傘	1026	御	1398
穀	710	粒	922	赦	1744	備	1183	循	1854
渉	372	粗	1777	軟	470	割	1553	悲	1635
涯	157	粘	921	転	420	創	1631	惑	614
液	1038	累	1364	逮	1160	勝	1209	惰	629
涼	313	細	1363	週	318	募	861	愉	628
淑	721	紳	1361	進	561	勤	1577	慌	624
淡	164	紹	1359	逸	1973	博	47	扉	1638
深	1328	紺	1758	部	1845	善	1035	掌	801
混	450	終	1352	郭	1842	喚	1042	提	665
清	1539	組	1776	郵	1847	喜	1445	揚	664
添	634	経	1360	都	1846	喪	1926	搭	646
渇	451	翌	575	郷	1849	喫	1550	替	842
渓	840	習	574	酔	1435	圏	1208	握	1059
渚	1263	粛	1733	曹	1173	堅	853	援	1951
渋	1738	脚	1396	釈	1908	堤	390	揮	662
済	1731	脱	498	野	1596	堪	1770	揺	1967
綿	1456	脳	1934	釣	273	報	1507	敢	826
猪	1262	舶	1869	閉	1623	場	545	散	1189
猫	244	船	1874	陪	1299	堕	1314	敬	334
猟	1940	菊	927	陰	1592	塔	254	晩	1974
率	1737	菱	1517	隆	1561	塚	1039	普	1786
現	259	菌	918	陳	1301	塀	1056	景	314
球	935	菓	1122	陵	1518	塁	1734	晴	1538
理	265	菜	734	陶	1966	奥	928	智	1224
瓶	1032	著	1258	陸	1513	婿	395	晶	22
産	1560	虚	1993	険	1672	媒	1761	暑	1260
略	293	蛇	519	雪	1143	媛	1950	暁	1201
異	1797	蛍	518	頂	94	富	193	換	1043
盛	1457	術	1525	魚	171	寒	1526	最	821
盗	1451	袋	1006	鳥	1941	蜜	776	朝	52
眺	237	規	841	鹿	1999	尊	1439	期	1765
眼	1467	視	1093	麻	593	尋	1145	棋	1763
票	1606	訟	787	黄	1750	就	1969	棒	1575
祭	1102	訪	495	黒	174	属	1953	棟	505
移	898	設	708	斎	1732	嵐	777	森	197
窒	1321	許	569	亀	534	帽	408	棺	1272
窓	749	訳	1073			幅	407	植	205
章	433	豚	538			幾	1381	棚	202
笛	1111	貧	782	**12**		廊	1852	極	1903
符	1001	貨	1010			廃	1706	検	1673
第	1239	販	726	偉	1643	弾	1931	欺	1762
笠	939	貫	102	傍	1015	復	875	款	1097

腰	1605	鉢	271	憎	626	聞	1626	鳴	1942
腸	544	鉄	846	摘	657	腐	1023	鼻	678
腹	464	鉱	741	旗	1764	膜	233	雌	563
艇	1876	隔	1312	暮	232	蔦	1945		
蒲	1838	零	1402	暦	213	製	419	**15**	
蒸	1900	雷	425	構	1818	複	465		
蓄	1385	電	535	概	1482	誌	601	儀	984
虜	1991	靴	1894	模	229	認	598	億	983
虞	1995	預	1595	様	933	誓	1133	劇	1997
裏	399	頑	61	歌	469	誘	916	勲	1677
裸	1124	頌	783	歴	376	語	347	器	121
褐	453	飼	1866	滴	442	誤	1899	噴	1197
解	1814	飽	1480	漁	172	説	499	嘱	1954
触	1813	飾	1477	漂	1607	読	348	嬌	430
試	354	塩	1458	漆	932	豪	543	墜	1307
詩	346	鼓	1444	漏	1068	踊	1409	墳	1198
詰	343	鳩	1946	演	2007	適	441	審	1910
話	344			漫	830	遭	1174	寮	1708
該	1522			潰	1545	遮	1192	導	278
詳	550	**14**		漸	1135	酵	1430	履	1057
誇	1244			漕	1175	酷	1431	幣	1040
誠	363	像	1977	熊	2003	酸	1437	弊	1041
誉	1939	僕	1794	獄	338	銀	1459	影	1712
豊	1443	僚	1707	疑	1410	銃	762	徹	886
賃	1004	塾	309	碑	1512	銅	272	慮	1996
賄	80	境	484	磁	1390	銑	270	慰	1096
資	473	増	502	種	1679	銘	275	慶	2001
賊	357	墨	175	稲	910	銭	368	憂	616
跡	1746	奪	566	穀	917	閣	1624	憤	1199
路	1282	嫡	440	端	1167	閥	1619	戯	1994
跳	1284	察	1103	箇	2029	関	2017	摩	639
践	1286	寡	617	算	946	際	1296	撤	760
較	1277	寧	834	管	1273	障	1297	撮	822
載	359	窪	1323	精	1535	隠	1313	撲	1793
辞	1497	層	1065	緑	1371	雑	562	撃	709
農	2014	裳	800	維	1341	需	1165	敵	443
違	1644	彰	1715	綱	1963	静	1540	敷	1883
遠	402	微	887	網	1373	領	1405	暫	1134
遣	1773	徳	885	綿	1367	駄	1986	暴	1801
酬	1432	態	2005	緒	1344	駆	1983	槽	1176
酪	1433	慕	633	練	1343	駅	1984	標	1608
鈴	1406	慢	829	総	1366	髪	1924	横	1751
鉛	794	慣	627	罰	833	魂	2021		

類	931	爆	1802	髄	1290	譲	1528	鶴	1943
顕	1789	簿	949	鯨	315	醸	1527	魔	2022
翻	1911	繰	1369	鶏	1947	鐘	438		
騎	1981	羅	1342	艶	1755	響	1850		
騒	1985	臓	851	麗	2002	騰	1989		
験	1980	藻	2035			懸	1394		
鯉	176	覇	1895					驚	1987
闘	1629	識	482					襲	2025
		譜	1787						
		警	336	欄	1628				
		鏡	483	競	434	艦	1875		
		霧	1228	籍	1567	躍	1285	鑑	1455
瀬	1666	韻	481	議	642	露	1283		
		顧	135	護	700	顧	1084		

19

20

21

22

23

INDEX IV:

KEY-WORDS
AND PRIMITIVE MEANINGS

This final Index offers a cumulative list of all the key-words and primitive meanings used throughout the book. Key-words are listed with their respective kanji and frame number. Primitive meanings are listed in italics and are followed only by the number of the page on which they are introduced.

B

F

G

H

I

J

K

L

ladle	勺	68	*line*			*241*
lady	婦	1151	lineage	系	1391
lagoon	潟	2039	linen	布	405
laid waste	荒	488	liner	舶	1869
lake	湖	148	lips	唇	2013
lament	悼	621	listen	聴	827
lamp	灯	165	little	小	105
land	陸	1513	livelihood	暮	232
lap		*125*	lively	活	143
large	大	107	liver	肝	1649
lass	嬢	1530	livestock	畜	1384
laugh	笑	938	load	載	359
laundry	濯	577	location	場	545
lazy	惰	629	lock	錠	383
lead (metal)	鉛	794	*lock of hair*			*411*
leader	将	731	*locket*			*365*
leaf	葉	228	logic	理	265
leak	漏	1068	loins	腰	1605
lean	傾	1011	loneliness	寂	720
leap	躍	1285	long	長	1920
learn	習	574	long-distance	距	1281
leather	革	1893	long time	久	1016
lecture	講	1816	longevity	寿	1565
left	左	77	longing	欲	792
leg	足	1279	look back	顧	1084
legitimate wife	嫡	440	look to	臨	854
leisure	閑	1625	loose	漫	830
lend	貸	1007	lord	主	266
length	丈	691	lose	失	845
lengthen	張	1921	lot	壌	1529
level	均	160	love	愛	737
levy	賦	378	lovely	麗	2002
license	允	765	lower	低	1831
lidded crock		*124*	lowly	卑	1511
lie	詐	1141	loyalty	忠	602
lie down	寝	1150	lucidity	澄	1704
life	生	1555	lumber	材	683
lightly	軽	717	lunatic	狂	260
lightning-bug	蛍	518	lungs	肺	414
likeness	如	100	luxuriant	繁	1337
limb	肢	714			
limit	限	1466			
line	線	1339			

M

P

Q

R

summit	峰 1562	task	務 1227
sunflower	*23*	*taskmaster*	*128*
sunglasses	*233,265*	tassel	房 1078
sunshine	陽 1300	tatami mat	畳 1784
superfluous	冗 300	tax	税 895
superintend	宰 1499	tea	茶 252
supplement	補 1840	teach	教 1254
suppose	存 684	*team of horses*	*423*
surface	表 1546	tears	涙 1082
surname	姓 1557	technique	芸 421
surpass	越 387	*teenager*	*53*
surplus	剰 1586	*teepee*	*375*
surround	囲 1807	tempering	錬 2030
suspend	懸 1394	temporarily	暫 1134
suspicious	怪 716	tempt	唆 766
sūtra	経 1360	ten	十 10
swamp	沢 1072	tenacious	執 1506
sweat	汗 1651	tender	柔 1226
sweep	掃 1152	tenderness	優 993
sweet	甘 1757	tense	緊 1374
swell	膨 1719	ten thousand	万 64
swift	迅 280	test	試 354
swiftly	疾 1686	texture	肌 66
swim	泳 136	*Thanksgiving*	*136*
swing	揺 1967	the following	翌 575
sword	刀 83	thick	厚 125
symptoms	症 1685	thin	淡 164
system	制 418	thing	物 1050
		think	思 605
		third class	丙 1020
T		thirst	渇 451
		thong	緒 1344
T'ang	唐 1157	thorn	刺 417
tag	札 212	thousand	千 40
tail	尾 1915	thread	糸 1333
tail feathers	*412*	threaten	脅 871
tailor	裁 397	three	三 3
take	取 819	throw	投 706
take along	連 287	thunder	雷 425
tale	話 344	thwart	阻 1780
Talking Cricket	*418*	ticket	券 1206
tall	高 307	tide	潮 141
tariff	租 1778	tie	結 1351

V

W

Y

Z

| Zen | 禅 1930 |
| zero | 零 1402 |

zoo		146
I (one)	壱	457
II (two)	弐	355

ACKNOWLEDGEMENTS

It only remains for me to express my gratitude to those who helped this book through its Second and Third Editions.

Sasabe Midori 佐々部 緑, who set the bulk of the text into computer and prepared the pages for the printing of the Second Edition, also supervised the layout of the present edition. Without her help and meticulous attention, the task would have taken a great deal more time to complete.

Furuhashi Mine 古橋実根 penned the characters in the text and Indexes. Not only was she more than generous with her time, but patiently put up with the considerable strain of bending her skills as a calligrapher to the unusual demands of this book.

Finally, I wish to acknowledge the Japan Publications Trading Company for their assistance in distributing the book in its Second Edition and for arranging the printing and distribution of this Third Edition.